Revolutionary Diplomacy

The Revolutionary Age

Francis D. Cogliano, Christa Breault Dierksheide,
Eliga H. Gould, and Patrick Griffin, Editors

Revolutionary Diplomacy

Spanish Connections and the
Birth of the United States

THOMAS E. CHÁVEZ

University of Virginia Press
Charlottesville and London

The University of Virginia Press is situated on the traditional lands of the Monacan Nation, and the Commonwealth of Virginia was and is home to many other Indigenous people. We pay our respect to all of them, past and present. We also honor the enslaved African and African American people who built the University of Virginia, and we recognize their descendants. We commit to fostering voices from these communities through our publications and to deepening our collective understanding of their histories and contributions.

University of Virginia Press
© 2025 by the Rector and Visitors of the University of Virginia
All rights reserved
Printed in the United States of America on acid-free paper

First published 2025

9 8 7 6 5 4 3 2 1

ISBN 978-0-8139-5289-5 (hardback)
ISBN 978-0-8139-5290-1 (paperback)
ISBN 978-0-8139-5291-8 (ebook)

Library of Congress Cataloging-in-Publication Data is available for this title.

Cover art: "Ô qu'el d'Estain," 1779 (French Political Cartoon Collection, Library of Congress; LCCN 2004676883). The leopard represents England under attack by the American serpent, Spanish lion, and French rooster.
Cover design: David Drummond

*Dedicated to
Allen C. Sprowl
More of a brother than an uncle*

Contents

	Foreword by Karl Schaffenburg	ix
	Acknowledgments	xi
	Introduction	1
1	On the Stage of Human Affairs	7
2	To Cultivate the Good Will	23
3	Intrigue and Contact	31
4	An Unofficial Alliance	43
5	An Interlude of Hope and Persistence	60
6	Saratoga and a Diplomatic Gambit	74
7	A Declaration of War and a New Focus	85
8	Corsairs and Intrigue	95
9	Betrayal and the Making of Peace	112
	Epilogue	125
	Notes	133
	Bibliography	159
	Index	165

Foreword

Growing up in Texas and Mexico endowed me with a fascination of history. My Mexican grandparents were amused by my frequent forays to "*las piramides*"—otherwise known as Teotihuacán, and the National Museum of Anthropology and History in Mexico City. Moving to Philadelphia in the year 2000 introduced me to a new aspect in my research and career: early US history. I quickly realized that I, like many Americans, had a lot to learn. Nevertheless, I enjoyed the journey along the way, and I came to better appreciate and understand the founding and history of the United States, especially vis-à-vis the American Revolution's most indispensable person, Benjamin Franklin.

Surprisingly to me, my knowledge of the Hispanic world and the founding of the United States converged in Philadelphia. Hidden in plain sight throughout my Philadelphia sojourns are the echoes of Spain, her colonies, and their peoples. Juan de Miralles, Spain's first envoy to the United States, and his successors Francisco Rendón, Josef de Jáudenes y Nebot, and Carlos María Martínez, Marqués de Yrujo, all lived in revolutionary Philadelphia, very close to the headquarters of the founding of the United States—buildings we now refer to as Independence Hall and Congress Hall. To this day, it boggles the mind that so many Spaniards and Latinos, not to mention US citizens, are unaware that our founding fathers could not have succeeded during the American Revolution without the immense military and financial support of Spain and her colonies.

Perhaps part of the reason for this lies in the way we teach American history or in the particular agendas of some past historians. Franklin himself reminded us of this problem when he wrote in *Poor Richard*, "Historians relate not so much what is done, as what they would have believed" (1739).

Nevertheless, some historians in recent years, particularly Thomas Chávez, have been eroding the edifice of historical indifference to the role of Spain and Latinos in our nation's founding. There are other reasons for a lack of awareness or understanding over the years regarding Spain's role, but Dr. Chávez reveals these reasons brilliantly throughout his research, both in the current volume and in his seminal work *Spain and the Independence of the United States: An Intrinsic Gift* (2002).

Almost accidentally, I discovered the above-mentioned work at a bookstore in Albuquerque in 2006. Reading this book opened my eyes. Here were answers to nagging questions: How and why did we win? Where did the money come from? Yes, France helped us—we were all taught that in grade school. But, upon conducting further research on the period, it just did not make sense to me that France, having recently lost her empire to Britain in the Seven Years' War and heavily in debt, was strong enough economically or militarily to tip the balance in America's favor. As it turns out, she was not.

Without Spain's direct support of the United States and France through the Bourbon "*pacte de famille*," there would be no American independence, at least not in this war. Without Miralles's support of Congress in Philadelphia, Bernardo de Gálvez's military brilliance in the Gulf of Mexico, and his father Matias's triumphs in Central America; without the taxes paid by Spanish subjects from California to Louisiana and the weapons and ammunition provided by Spain to the Continental Army at Saratoga in 1777 and elsewhere throughout the war, the entire effort fails. Without Cuban money and Mexican silver pesos, Americans lose the war. Without a very diverse group of American citizens, indigenous peoples, free Blacks, enslaved African Americans, and Spanish subjects fighting shoulder-to-shoulder under the Spanish flag throughout the South and the Gulf of Mexico, there would be no American independence. Finally, without the diplomatic efforts of Franklin and his colleagues in Paris, neither France nor Spain and her colonies join the American cause.

What motivated America's diplomats? What were the challenges and who, among some of Franklin's closest colleagues, intrigued behind his back and why? Based in large part on new research, this book will answer those questions and stimulate not only further research, but likely a reevaluation of the course of American history. When we consider *all of those* who made American independence possible, perhaps we will also reevaluate what it means to be "American" and why Spaniards referred to Franklin as "the father of his country."

Karl Schaffenburg
Independence National Historical Park
Philadelphia, Pennsylvania

Acknowledgments

As always, I must acknowledge and thank the Fulbright organization. That Fulbright Research Fellowship many years ago has been the lynchpin for four previous publications and now this one. Had I not had the opportunity to spend quality time in Spain's archives, the vector of my historical curiosity would have taken a different direction. Instead, I was thrown into an investigative process that I did not foresee. That fellowship was enhanced by a subsequent grant from the Foreign Ministry of Spanish Government, which provided funds for me to spend three months in a one-room apartment in Seville, where I began writing about the subject of Spain's role in the independence of the United States. At that time, I could not avoid encountering Benjamin Franklin, and the idea that was to become this book was born.

Throughout this process, the interest shown by the Daughters of the American Revolution and the Granaderos y Damas de Gálvez constantly inspired and supported me. Moreover, on more than one occasion, they became my sounding board.

Rob and Patricia Kurz of the Kurz Foundation, along with Kevin and Leonor Daniels, organized financial support for the Franklin Project that resulted in this book. I will always be grateful to R. C. "Doc" Weaver for his constant enthusiasm, humor, and encouragement as well as for his introduction to me of Carl Van Doren's indispensable biography of Franklin. Ambassador Edward L. Romero, a friend and confidant, in some ways was an inspiration for this book. He was the United States ambassador to Spain from April 1998 until May 2001. My friend Marcia Glenn meticulously edited the manuscript before it was submitted. Her contribution has been invaluable. Every author needs a good editor like her.

Familial encouragement is invaluable. The goal of making my parents proud has always been an inspiration. My mother, Marilyn Sprowl Chávez, and my father, Judge Antonio E. Chávez, always encouraged me and, before their passing, reviewed my manuscripts. I hope that I have done the same for my daughters Nicolasa Marie and Christel Angélica. Christel died flying a C-130 for the United States Air Force. Her sister has made a career as a historian working in museums as well as serving as New Mexico's deputy state historian.

Above all, credit for this book must go to Dr. Celia López-Chávez, an excellent historian who, as mentioned, had the original idea for this book. Moreover, she reviewed pages and made helpful suggestions.

Nor should I ignore the historians who have preceded me, for I, like every historian, have benefited from their research and books. Our historical knowledge will always ride on the shoulders of those who came before us, even as we try to improve upon it. Special appreciation must go to another historian, Dr. Larrie D. Ferreiro, who recommended that I submit this manuscript to the University of Virginia Press.

Finally, I have an uncle, who, because of our close respective ages, is more like a brother. He has read each of my previous books as they were published. His constant support has given me great satisfaction and is enough said, except that with this work's dedication, this book will always be his.

Introduction

History, we are told, is an investigative process that must start somewhere. In the case of this book, it begins with Benjamin Franklin, one of the most popular "founding fathers" of the United States.

By the time I graduated from high school, I had read one of his numerous biographies as well as his unfinished autobiography. Obviously, in my youthful mind, it seemed there was nothing new that could be learned about him.

On the three-hundredth anniversary of his birthday in 2006, a number of new books were published about him. Some of them were written by Pulitzer Prize winners or, at the very least, authors popular enough to guarantee healthy sales. Three of these stood out, not for any new information they provided but for the quality of their writing and points of view.[1] They are cited many times in this study. None, however, surpassed Carl Van Doren's classic and Pulitzer Prize–winning 1938 biography of Franklin for its detail and its impeccable research.[2] Over eighty years later, his book remains an excellent resource. Nevertheless, all of Franklin's biographies only touch on Spain, if they mention it at all.

After reading some of these books, I came upon the idea of researching the role of Spain in the independence of the United States. This led to a series of grants, including a Fulbright Research Fellowship, a subsidy from Spain's Dirección General de Relaciones Culturales y Científicas in its Foreign Ministry, and a private grant from Judge Henry Bigbee of Santa Fe. These grants enabled me to carry out intensive research in the archives of Spain and thereafter in the archives and published papers of the United States; this research ultimately resulted in a book entitled *Spain and the Independence of the United States: An Intrinsic Gift* (2002), which was subsequently published in Spain under the title *España y la independencia de Estados Unidos* (2006, 2016).

My research in Spain's archives uncovered a number of documents that could be attributed to Franklin, even though he never went to Spain. He spent time in England, Scotland, Ireland, and France, and he also travelled to Holland, but he never set foot anywhere on the Iberian Peninsula.

Encountering documents in the Spanish archives that dealt with Franklin was something of a surprise, and it raised questions. Precisely what was Franklin's connection to Spain? How did it happen? And, given Spain's key role in the outcome of the Revolutionary War, what connection did Franklin, as the major colonial diplomat in Europe, have with Spain's involvement in that war? Moreover, what is the story of the rebelling colonies' first diplomatic attempt with Spain? Did these things even matter?

Some of these questions became clear as I wrote *Spain and the Independence of the United States.* Still, the overwhelming silence in American historiography regarding Spain's role in the birth of the United States has remained. US historians of the founding fathers either overlooked that role, could not read Spanish and therefore did not have access to Spain's archives, or, if they did, they concentrated on other subjects, such as, for example, early Spanish exploration of the Americas and the history of the Spanish borderlands. US attitudes formed by the siege at the Alamo, the US-Mexican War, the Spanish American War, and the dictatorship of Franco confirmed viewpoints shaped by an English heritage of the Protestant Reformation from the sixteenth century. Spain was the major proponent of the Catholic Church and the Counter-Reformation that stood in opposition to the new Protestant movement. That Spain played a key role in the success of the American Revolution could easily be—and was, in fact—overlooked.

Until relatively recently, almost nothing in English literature dealt with Spain's contribution to the War of Independence. Some books treat the subject as part of local history. Jonathon Dull wrote two important books about the French navy and France's diplomacy during the war in which he acknowledged that Spain had exerted a significant influence. Some literature has emphasized a more general theme of Spain's role. Prime examples are this author's *Spain and the Independence of the United States,* Larrie D. Ferreiro's *Brothers at Arms* (2016), as well as the anthologies *Spain and the American Revolution: New Approaches and Perspectives* (2020, 2022) and *European Friends of the American Revolution* (2023). Ferreiro and the editors of the anthologies each wrote detailed accounts as to why Spain has been overlooked.[3]

But there was more. That thought became the impetus for my "Benjamin Franklin in the Archives of Spain" project, which lasted six years. Carried out under the auspices of the Latin American and Iberian Institute of the University of New Mexico, the project spawned three books. The first of these is a limited-edition essay published in a handcrafted book entitled *Doctor Franklin and Spain: The Unknown History.* The next two books are compilations of Franklin documents found in the archives of Spain. In 2019, the Instituto Franklin of the Universidad de Alcalá de Henares in Spain produced a Spanish edition entitled *La diplomacia de la independencia: Documentos de Benjamin Franklin en España*. In 2024, the American Philosophical Society published an expanded English edition that includes transcriptions of the original Spanish and French documents. It is entitled *The Diplomacy of Independence: Benjamin Franklin Documents in the Archives of Spain*. Naturally, research for that project led me to the invaluable multivolume compilation of Franklin's papers published by the Yale University Press, which has more recently been made available online.[4]

The goal of locating Franklin documents in Spain was to make information more obviously available and accessible to historians. Hopefully, those documents will be a source of inspiration for new research and publications that will possibly generate more inquiries about Spain's connection to early United States history.

Since I worried about getting the collection published, my historian wife, Dr. Celia López-Chávez, asked why I did not write a book myself based on the documents, or, at the very least, write an overview that itself would be a first.

Thus began the research and compilation of this book. Of course, any good history is not based on any one source but instead on all available sources. And so it is in this case as well. As I researched and wrote, the book morphed into something different and more expansive than the story of Benjamin Franklin and Spain: it became a story of the first American diplomatic efforts with the Hispanic world.

Research began with the various archives of Spain in which documents exist that are pertinent to the diplomacy between the rebelling colonies and Spain: Archivo General de Indias (AGI), Archivo Histórico Nacional (AHN), Archivo General de Simancas (AGS), Archivo General del Palacio Real (AGP), Biblioteca Nacional (BN), Archivo de la Real Academia de la Historia (RAH), Archivo Zárate-Cólogan, which is located in el Archivo Histórico Provincial de Santa Cruz en Tenerife (AHPTF/AZC), and in the private Archivo Privado de la Familia Gasset. Then came a return, so to speak, to the archives and published papers in the United States, including the National Archives, the Library of Congress, and the American Philosophical Society, as well as the published papers of the Continental Congress, Benjamin Franklin, George Washington, John Jay, and other founding fathers.

History is an evolutionary discipline. It builds upon itself. Previous research and histories become the basis for new research and books. And history has always revised itself. In a sense, all historians are revisionists. And so it is with this book as well. Specifically, this book is a natural progression of my previous books. Every person and every resource mentioned in the forewords of my previous efforts can take credit for this latest endeavor.

I hope that my work will continue to be surpassed by future volumes, which will be built, at least partially, upon the information provided here. Rather than being considered as dated histories, they will become part of the process leading to an advanced understanding. This book is not the definitive study on this particular subject. Rather, it is a launching point for new information and offers hints of myriad lines for future research. New and revealing publications about early American diplomacy, piracy, Spain, the birth of the United States, international relations, and so on, are left to the creative minds of future historians and their histories.

The story related here is especially poignant in the United States because this country and its society must come to grips with the reality of its history rather than its myths. The United States was born out of a world war and with the aid and participation of many peoples and countries. The success of the revolution was the result of an inclusive environment. If nothing else, the early contacts with Spain clearly hint at the role of Spain and, in reality, of its American colonies of Nueva España (Mexico), Cuba, Guatemala (which at the time included all of today's Central American countries), Venezuela, and others.

All of this adds up to an expanded and much richer history of the revolution that resulted in the independence of the United States. Words written in one of my earlier publications are apropos here: "Today, three centuries after the birth of Benjamin Franklin, there is more to learn about this influential and interesting man." More importantly, his life is a catalyst, and it has been used here as such. There is more to learn about the diplomacy with Spain in which he was involved. From his contact with the son of Spain's King Carlos III until his initiation into Spain's Real Academia de la Historia, we are reminded that, unlike my assumption as a high school graduate over a half a century ago, there remains much more to be learned.

What is provided here is one part of a whole. Franklin's trip to France in the late fall of 1776 and his delays in route to Paris are well known and have been written about in his many biographies. But the Spanish reaction to his arrival on the Continent and their anxiety to hear from Congress through him have been overlooked. Nor has anyone exclusively studied the early American relationship with Spain and Spaniards. Recent diplomatic historians, however, have touched on Franklin's efforts with Spain's ambassador while in Paris and on John Jay's failed mission to Madrid.

The importance of this moment in history should be reconsidered, given the issue of France's plan to prepare for war, which was shared with Spain in draft form by its ambassador. Against the backdrop of French and Spanish cooperation, as well as Spain's plan to help the American cause on its own, these issues persisted for the duration of the American Revolution. Indeed, both issues played heavily into the American Commission's very mission to Paris. Nor can we avoid the fact that the American commissioners, at times, contradicted their own words while criticizing Spain's involvement in the war, seemingly unaware of Spain's aid that had been given and loaned in various forms.

1

On the Stage of Human Affairs

On a winter's day in January 1774, a preoccupied Benjamin Franklin could not have expected the person who was calling at his door. To call Franklin "preoccupied" would be an understatement. He had been in London for eleven years and had come to realize that his efforts to reconcile his native colonies and Great Britain had become futile. Just a few days before, he had been called before England's Privy Council to be questioned, scolded, and ridiculed in the ominous hall known as the Cockpit, a place where cockfights had been held during the reign of Henry VIII over two centuries earlier. At best, he was accused of dishonesty and betrayal. Rather than discuss the status of Gov. Thomas Hutchinson of Massachusetts, as was the announced topic, the tone turned critical of Franklin, who, when asked to defend himself, invoked the need of counsel and a period of three weeks to prepare a defense.[1]

A year earlier, Franklin had come across letters written by Governor Hutchinson. Feeling that they would shed clear light on the bad intentions of the British government, he secretly shared them with some compatriots in the Massachusetts legislature, an action that thereby assured the expected controversy. Many theories abounded as to how and by whom the letters had been revealed, creating a mystery. Franklin's involvement in the matter remained a secret until he publicly admitted to the deed to prevent two men from engaging in a second duel after one had accused the other of being the culprit. While he was not a perfect man and was by no means convinced that he had acted rationally in releasing those letters, Franklin could not sit idly by and allow another man to die for the sake of his anonymity.

The letters were damning to Hutchinson. They resulted in colonial petitions for his removal from office and acted as an incentive to the movement for independence, which was an idea that Franklin had only recently started to entertain. As a result, the British government—from the king to the Parliament—considered him to be a troublemaker. His brief moment before the Privy Council left no doubt that he was in serious disfavor, and he knew that his next scheduled appearance before it would not bode well.

Now he stood in his doorway at 7 Craven Street, face-to-face with a man who introduced himself as Francisco Escarano, secretary and chargé d'affaires of the Spanish embassy in London.[2] If that were not odd enough, the ensuing conversation proved to be even more so. Escarano explained that he was in search of a glass armonica, an instrument that Franklin reputedly invented or redesigned.[3] The instrument consisted of a series of glass bowls that were pitched to different notes; they sat on a spindle within a clavichord casing and were played with wet fingers.

The Spanish envoy explained that he had already asked Mademoiselle Marianne Davis, an admirer of Franklin's who had gained a reputation for giving concerts throughout Europe with the instrument. She informed Escarano that she had two glass armonicas, one in London and the other in Italy, but told him that she would not give up either.[4]

Thus, Escarano asked "Doctor Franklin" if he by chance had a glass armonica that he would sell. He explained that he wanted the instrument for his sister. Apparently not expressing surprise or annoyance, Franklin replied that he had two glass armonicas, one in Philadelphia and another with him in London. He said that he would happily give up the latter if it were in perfect condition, but unfortunately, it needed repair. It had four or five broken bowls, and its repair would be very difficult. The expense to have it fixed could be prohibitive, perhaps amounting to as much as fifty pounds sterling. Franklin suggested a man "who, in another time, had the hobby of working with instruments."

Escarano unsuccessfully tried to convince Franklin to sell his broken armonica. Left with no option, Escarano determined to visit the repairman, whom he referred to as "the artisan." Not finding him at home, the persistent Escarano returned to the artisan's dwelling the following day, where he succeeded in meeting him. Upon hearing what the Spanish envoy wanted, the artisan begrudgingly showed him his own glass armonica. Escarano immediately made him an offer, but the artisan replied that he would not sell it under any circumstance or for any amount. Nor would he make a similar one. A dejected but undeterred Escarano returned to his office to write a report to his superiors in Madrid, in which he described Franklin as "the Philosophe, who is the best person in the world."[5] Moreover, he said that he would not give up and that he planned to visit Franklin again.

Meanwhile, news of the so-called Boston Tea Party reached London. Many members of the British government concluded that the Hutchinson letters had played a role in causing this event, which Franklin abhorred for its violence. He described the action as one of "violent injustice on our part" that had permanently squandered any opportunity to turn public opinion in favor of the colonies by means of peaceful processes.[6] He had no doubt that public opinion in Britain had turned against him, which made his upcoming date before the Privy Council even more problematic.

Franklin returned to the Cockpit on January 29 to appear before the Lord President, who sat on a raised dais under a draped canopy. Presiding over thirty-four eminent members of the church and government arrayed on either side of him, he was represented by the sharp-tongued, mean-spirited solicitor general Alexander Wedderburn. The floor of the large hall and the gallery that encircled it were filled to capacity as anticipation ran high.

After the formality of introductory remarks, Franklin's counsel, who had a weak voice resulting from a previous lung disease, tried to speak, but Wedderburn leapt to his feet, cut him off, and began an almost hour-long harangue attacking Franklin. In a profanity-laced tirade, he condemned Franklin as a wily, secretive, dispassionate, and incendiary traitor to the crown. Wedderburn roared that Franklin's use of the Hutchinson letters had been a heinous crime. The people witnessing Wedderburn hooted, hollered, and laughed, thus encouraging him to continue.

Through it all Franklin, formally dressed in a blue "full-dress suit of spotted Manchester velvet," stood silent and stoic. He appeared, as one witness said, "as if his features had been made of wood." His face not betraying the slightest emotion, Franklin refused to grace Wedderburn's tirade with any reaction or response. Having nothing more to do, the Privy Council rejected the petition by Massachusetts to remove Hutchinson and then adjourned.[7]

The next day, a letter informed Franklin that the British government had terminated him from his position as American postmaster, thereby making him a political outcast in London. He also feared the possibility of arrest; so, taking a trunk of his papers, he moved to a friend's house in Chelsea for a few days until he felt that the climate was safe enough for him to return to his Craven Street residence and resume receiving guests.[8]

Now, three days after encountering the Privy Council's abuse, one of Franklin's first guests, if not the first, was the Spaniard Escarano, who was standing at his door again.[9] Franklin patiently listened to Escarano's story about the artisan. Perhaps sensing the seriousness of his situation, Franklin told Escarano that since he was preparing to return to America, he would give Escarano his broken instrument. The envoy could not believe his good fortune and felt that seeing "the honorable, good man that [Franklin] is," he could not keep Franklin from the truth. So he told Franklin that he sought the glass armonica not for his sister but for don Gabriel de Borbón, the third son of Spain's King Carlos III.

The *Infante*, as he was called, was twenty-two years old. He had spent his youth with the royal family in Naples, where his father ruled as King Carlos VI of Naples before ascending to the throne as Carlos III of Spain. The precocious don Gabriel was a willing product of the enlightenment. He studied literature, Latin, music, art, and science. He played the clavichord and published his own translations of ancient Latin. He was a favorite of his father, and his interest in Franklin and the glass armonica could not be more natural.

Franklin must have been both bemused and surprised as Escarano continued to say that the *Infante* "would be pleased" to receive Franklin's armonica. Impressed with this new information and despite the political pressures mounting against him, Franklin volunteered to take on the task of getting the instrument repaired. Franklin felt that such an important person should receive it in good repair, but he warned that the repairs would take at least a month.[10] An ebullient Escarano wrote to report the good news. In a note at the end of his letter, he wrote that the glass armonica was being repaired and would be delivered in three weeks.[11] He must have received an update, either from Franklin or from the artisan. Interestingly, the Spanish diplomat did not mention Franklin's commonly known troubles with the British government but rather emphasized Franklin's generosity, a gesture that had occurred almost immediately after one of the most trying moments of his life.

In a subsequent meeting a few weeks later, on February 17, Franklin told Escarano that the glass armonica would be delivered within a week. Escarano then asked Franklin how to play the instrument. Franklin replied that in one of his translated and printed works in French, Escarano would find a letter he had sent to the celebrated Padre Giambattista Beccaria of Turin, a person with whom he had corresponded while perfecting the instrument. The letter contained instructions for playing it. Moreover, if the published instructions were not clear enough, he would write clearer instructions and send them to the diplomat.

Once again, Escarano wrote to his superiors without mentioning the controversy swirling around Franklin, instead expressing his appreciation for the man: "Your Excellency can see that Dr. Franklin could not have acted more graciously, and we should be grateful to him."[12] A few weeks later, in a subsequent letter, he did note that Parliament was beginning "to deal with the difficult issue of the American colonies."[13]

The delay took a little longer than expected, for it was not until March 10, 1774, that Franklin would deliver the repaired glass armonica, along with a copy of the French book that contained the instructions. Probably due to Franklin's influence, the price for fixing the instrument came in at considerably less than the original estimate. The cost to the Spanish government for the repairs amounted to 17 pounds, 17 shillings. Escarano and his superiors were extremely pleased. The former made it a point to personally thank Franklin.[14] Surely, he was one of the many people that Franklin counted in his favor during such a trying time.

Mail and transportation tended to be slow, even when the shipments were destined for a king's son. Escarano had to wait for one of two ships to depart for the Spanish ports of Bilbao or San Sebastian. Both were expected to sail within a month. On one or the other he could transport the armonica back to Spain's northern coast and from there overland to Madrid. The last portion of the journey, through mountainous terrain and rough roads, would be very slow. He lamented that it would take as long as two months "before His Highness has the armonica there."[15]

Escarano arranged for the instrument and two books to be sent "with utmost care" and wrapped in oilcloth "so that they will not get wet."[16] Having paid the costs, Escarano sent a request for reimbursement. The expense for the repairs, the packing, and the customs amounted to twenty pounds sterling. In addition to the repairs, he paid one pound, five shillings for packing and eighteen shillings for "transportation and customs."[17]

Eight days after receiving the armonica, Escarano happily reported that the ship that would be transporting it had been selected and was ready to embark. Escarano's ebullience, however, quickly faded, because fifteen days later and into the next month, the ship had not yet left port. Although he was worried about the delay, Escarano was happy to hear that, in gratitude, the *Infante* was sending his recently published book to Franklin. Whether he shared that information with Franklin is unknown.[18]

Despite his situation, Franklin lingered in London. At first, he defended himself in the press; when Parliament passed the Intolerable Acts to punish the colonies, and Boston in particular, he felt obligated to stay. The two sides were moving toward war—something that he had worked for years to avoid.

Upon hearing news that the colonies would hold a continental convention in Philadelphia in September, Franklin decided to wait to see what resolutions the congress would pass. He urged his American compatriots to be resolute and stay united.

Although Franklin had to endure bad press and governmental condemnation, some people in London knew him better. Fellow scientist and travel companion John Pringle observed about his friend "that as long as there was any prospect (at least in his eyes) of accommodation, he labored to bring it about; and that if his advice had been taken, all the mischief would have been prevented and England and her colonies had been again on the best terms possible."[19]

Franklin was surprised to be secretly approached and asked to help find a peaceful solution; however, his influential contacts failed to move Parliament. Now, Franklin had no reason to remain in England. Another friend, the intellectual Edmund Burke, summed it up: "A great empire and little minds go ill together."[20] He spent his last days in England with his friends Burke and Joseph Priestly, and in March 1775, he sailed for home.

After a relatively uneventful voyage, he arrived in May to great fanfare in Philadelphia. While he was at sea, the battles at Lexington and Concord had taken place. Open rebellion had broken out, and a second Continental Congress was being organized in Philadelphia.

At the time, Spain was already aware of Franklin's exploits. As early as September 1767, Franklin's name had appeared in Madrid's newspapers. By 1773, the *Gaceta de Madrid* reported that Doctor Franklin clearly declared that his fellow Americans would not agree to the acts of England's Parliament without having representation. A few months later, both the *Gaceta* and *El Mercurio* reported on both the movement for independence and the Boston Tea Party. From that beginning in the Spanish press, Franklin was primarily associated with the revolution that would result in the birth of the United States. As Spanish historian Miguel Ángel Ochoa Brun wrote, in the eyes of Spain, Franklin was the "principal actor" in the movement toward independence.[21]

Nor did the Spanish lose direct interest in Franklin or the startling events in the British American colonies. Upon Franklin's departure from England, Escarano reported that the news from the colonies was bad, despite the British government's insistence that all was well. Lord Suffolk, the secretary of state, must have "a reason to publicize that affairs of America are going well [when the situation] is patently contrary." Newly passed legislation would inflame American emotions "to a point of desperation." Then, for the first time, he connected Franklin to the crises by writing, "The Ministry [Suffolk] has with great sorrow seen the celebrated Doctor Franklin leave here. Resentful as he was against this government . . . it is likely that he will be doing a good deal of harm in that Province, where they look on him as the Father of the Homeland." Escarano surmised that only a change of government could save the situation; otherwise, "the differences with the Colonies" would not "be mended."[22] Then, in June 1775, the Prince of Masserano, who had been convalescing from gout, returned to his position as Spain's ambassador to Great Britain.[23] He sent a detailed report of the hostilities that had broken out in the colonies, adding that the Continental Congress wanted to issue a "manifesto begging for the protection of foreign powers," which would indicate that "there will be no reconciliation with the government of Great Britain." He noted that two letters from Philadelphia reported the arrival "of the famous Doctor Franklin, who has been received in a manner little short of triumphant."[24] In a subsequent report, he related the news that the Continental Congress had named Franklin postmaster, the position that the British government had taken away from him.[25]

Appreciation for Franklin's gesture with the armonica extended to don Gabriel. In 1772, the prince had translated into Spanish and privately published a limited edition of Cayo Salustio Crispo's *La conjuración de Calatina y la Guerra de Jugurta*, a history in Latin that was originally published in the first century BC. The prince wanted to send Franklin a copy as a thank-you gift. In addition, he was anxious to hear about Franklin's reaction to his work. But the task of getting the book to Franklin proved to be even more circuitous than getting the glass armonica to Spain, since the book was sent through the Spanish embassy in London.[26]

Almost a month after Franklin arrived in Philadelphia, the Prince of Masserano invited Jonathon Williams Jr. to his London residence. The ambassador entrusted Williams with the *Infante's* book, which had just arrived. He also shared the news that Franklin's gift of the glass armonica had arrived in Madrid in good repair. Masserano wanted to make sure that Franklin received the *Infante's* gift in return, along with the knowledge that His Excellency was very pleased with the glass armonica.

Williams, in turn, sent the book and accompanying letters to Franklin under the care of a Captain Miller.[27] After an uneventful, quick voyage across the Atlantic, Miller arrived in Philadelphia with the package in the middle of August, and the book was finally delivered.[28]

At that time, the Second Continental Congress was proceeding at full speed. The representatives had just passed the "Olive Branch Petition," an appeal to King George III that was a last, futile effort at reconciliation.

Franklin voted for it with little, if any, confidence that it would succeed. Work with the Congress and his duties as chair of Pennsylvania's "Defense Committee" more than occupied his time. He worked daily from six a.m. to four p.m., after which he conceivably rested before spending time with his reunited family, with whom he was trying to reconcile.

Franklin all but declared his position for independence on July 21, 1775, when he introduced his Articles of Confederation plan for the new American government. His idea was both a call for independence and for colonial reunification. In effect, these Articles were his declaration in support of war.

While the Articles and his arguments for war did not receive approval from the Congress, Franklin could not help but be preoccupied when he received the prince's gift. Printed in the newly invented Bodoni Old Face type that Franklin admired, he noted that it was "beautifully and magnificently" printed and typographically superior to the best printing in Paris. Franklin wrote this with some knowledge, for he had stayed abreast of developments in printing his entire life, and he would later write a letter praising Giambattista Bodoni's essay on type as "one of the most beautiful that Art has hitherto produced." Bodoni was the royal typographer for the Spanish court, and the book had been produced on Bodoni's press.[29]

Soon after Franklin received the book, Congress bestowed upon him another assignment—that of preparing a system of paper currency. He then accepted the assignment to travel to Cambridge, Massachusetts, to meet with George Washington to discuss maintaining financial support for the Continental Army. He departed overland in October.

Finally, on December 12, 1775, a little over a month short of his seventieth birthday, Franklin found time to pick up his quill and scratch out a telling letter to don Gabriel. If the Spanish government, a potential ally, had any doubts about the activities of the Continental Congress or what he personally believed, Franklin hoped to leave no doubt. Perhaps because of the letter's importance, he made three copies.[30]

He began by thanking "His Highness" for the "much esteemed present . . . of your excellent version of Salust." In lieu of sending another book in return, Franklin used the opportunity to send the prince a copy of "the late Proceedings of our American Congress." He used that opening to suggest that Spain's "wise Politicians may contemplate the first efforts of a rising state" that will likely "soon . . . act a Part of some Importance on the Stage of Human Affairs, and furnish Materials for a future Salust." He then proposed that Spain and the American colonies had a common interest in being close allies and that "a good foundation" already existed in the colonies because of a "well-informed popular opinion entertained here of Spanish Integrity and Honour." He continued that his advanced age probably would prevent him from seeing the "Event of This great Contest" that he could foresee.[31]

As prophetic as this letter seems, it is more understandable if we consider the possibility that Franklin had an idea that he would be dealing with Spain as a diplomat. Later, when he was in Europe and writing about his grand reception in France, he conveyed a less diplomatic view of Spain. "The Spaniards are by common opinion supposed to be cruel, the English proud, the Scotch insolent, the Dutch avaricious, etc., but I think the French have no national vice."[32] Nevertheless, while he was corresponding with friends in France, Franklin was preparing for what he was sure to come.[33]

Spain was very much aware of the events taking place in the colonies. The same letters that reported on Franklin also reported that colonial forces had surrounded the British Army in Boston and demanded that the British vacate the city. The British commander, Gen. Thomas Gage, was reluctant to do so, but the move seemed imminent. The American force at Boston was far superior to that of the occupiers, and Gage's wife was sent packing. The American capture of Fort Ticonderoga and the reinforcement of the "castles" at Crownpoint and Kingsborough were important new stories. The reports even noted which armed British ships had set sail for the colonies.[34]

As early as 1770, shortly after the end of the Seven Years' War (1756–63), Spain consciously collected any information it could glean about British movements and strategy. The reason for this was two-fold. First, the Marquis of Grimaldi, Spain's minister of state, feared a British surprise attack on one of Spain's American ports. Second, the progress of the colonial rebellion lessened the chances of such an attack and presented an opportunity for Spain to take advantage of the situation. Historian Light Townsend Cummins concludes that as early as 1776, as the Spanish came to realize that the revolt had evolved into a full-blown revolution, the court began to view the "rebels as a serious force worthy of support."[35]

Congress needed financial aid to help pay for the war. Its first priority was to approach France, a country that the Americans correctly assumed would be the most open to their overtures. Taking into account France's bitterness over losing the Seven Years' War to Great Britain, Congress realized that the French government would be more receptive, simply because France had lost all of its major American colonies and would be more focused on helping the American cause.

Spain, on the other hand, had expansive American holdings and sought to be more cautious. In 1761, Carlos III had entered into the last of three alliances between the Bourbon kings of Spain and France. The first of these agreements ended the War of Spanish Succession that brought the house of Bourbon, of which Carlos was a part, to the throne of Spain. The three agreements of cooperation were supposed to take care not to untie the two thrones. However, what became known as the Third Bourbon Family Compact drew Spain into the Seven Years' War as a late ally to France. As a result, Spain had gained Louisiana and lost east and west Florida. Great Britain had become aggressive, setting up illegal colonies in Spanish Central America. In conjunction with its ally Portugal—whose minister of state, Sebastiao José de Carvalho Mello, Marquis of Pombal, ran the government—Great Britain had started to set up settlements along the Brazilian coast as far south as the Río de la Plata, opposite Buenos Aires.

The Continental Congress remained aware of Spain's concerns. The Committee of Secret Correspondence, formed on November 29, 1775, within weeks of Franklin penning his letter to don Gabriel, immediately sent George Gibson and a contingent of colonial soldiers down the Ohio and Mississippi Rivers to solicit aid from Spanish New Orleans. On his arrival, Gibson presented Luis de Unzaga y Amézaga, Spain's governor of Louisiana, with a letter asking two questions: Would the King of Spain desire "the acquisition of the town and harbor of Pensacola"? And would he "receive possession" of the town and port from the Americans?[36]

A second letter from Washington's subordinate Gen. Charles Lee (unrelated to diplomat Arthur Lee, one of Franklin's fellow commissioners to France), detailed the Americans' desire to circumvent the British seaborn blockade with a systematic trade route through New Orleans and up the Mississippi and Ohio Rivers. Lee also spelled out the rebels' intent to attack Pensacola. Gibson asked the governor for supplies and specifically for gunpowder.[37]

At the same time, Franklin demonstrated his understanding of Spain's position. He wrote to his son William Temple Franklin, "Should Spain be disinclined to our cause from an apprehension of danger to her South American domain, cannot France be prevailed on at our request and assurances not to disturb theirs to guarantee to that Crown her Territories there against any molestation from us?"[38]

Many things would occur before Franklin had his next known contact with representatives of Spain. Thomas Paine's essay titled *Common Sense* galvanized the independence movement. He succeeded in turning attention onto the king of England, claiming that he enabled Parliament in its acts against the colonies. He questioned the logic of an island ruling a continent.[39] While arguing that "nothing can settle our affairs so expeditiously as an open and determined declaration for independence," he cautioned that it would be foolish to think that France and Spain "will give us any kind of assistance" for anything less. If not for independence, "those powers would be sufferers by the consequences." He further anticipated a significant part of what would become the colonies' foreign policy when he recommended that a memorial be sent to those courts expressing "our peaceable disposition toward them, and of our desire of entering into trade with them."[40] The fifty-one-page pamphlet resonated in the colonies.

In 1775 and early 1776, the Colonial Army's ground struggle did not match congressional enthusiasm. Washington needed more support, and Benedict Arnold commanded a besieged and trapped force in Canada. Arnold turned to Congress for relief. Once again, Congress asked Franklin to lead a delegation north to Montreal to meet with Arnold. Apparently unable to decline such assignments, Franklin began his overland journey northward in March 1776. The trip was brutal. Freezing weather and primitive nighttime conditions left Franklin near death, or so he felt. Nor did the futility of the trip lighten his feelings, for he returned after concluding that the Canadian effort would fail, and he recommended that the American army withdraw. He wrote to Arnold, "If money cannot be had to support your army here with honour, so as to be respected instead of hated by the people, we repeat it as our firm and unanimous opinion that it is better immediately to withdraw it."[41] The disappointment and hardship of that journey left Franklin bedridden and exhausted, suffering from both boils and severe gout.

Despite the apparent setbacks on the military side, Congress would not be deterred as it prepared for a declaration of independence. Virginia's Richard Henry Lee, one of Arthur Lee's brothers, made a motion on June 7. "These united colonies are, and of right ought to be free and independent states." He added, "It is expedient forthwith to take the most effectual measures for forming foreign Alliances."[42] His motion passed on July 2 and resulted in the removal and arrest of the royal governors, including Franklin's estranged son William, who was a staunch loyalist and the governor of New Jersey. The political statement also resulted in the appointment of a committee to draft a declaration that would explain the decision for independence.

Still sick and bedridden, Franklin was named to the committee. Thomas Jefferson was chosen to write the initial draft, after which he incorporated some changes from John Adams. Then he delivered it to Franklin, who made some minor but key changes. The Continental Congress voted for independence on July 2 and then convened as a committee of the whole to consider Jefferson's declaration. After some revisions, the Declaration of Independence was passed on July 4, and its official signing took place on August 2, 1776.

The work of forming a new government on both the national and state levels became the priority. Pennsylvania named Franklin as chair of its constitutional convention. As if he were not overworked enough, the ailing and aged Franklin was burdened with another assignment that would take him to Staten Island, New York.

Admiral Richard Howe, who had been appointed commander of all British forces in America, arrived with the authority to try to negotiate a reconciliation. As one of Franklin's secret backers in London, Howe sent a letter to his "worthy friend."[43] This resulted in Franklin being named head of a delegation that would go to meet with Howe. Franklin, John Adams, and Edward Rutledge of South Carolina traveled north and made it clear to the disappointed admiral that his efforts had come too late. News of this event, as well as of Franklin's mission to Quebec, arrived in London, where Masserano dutifully reported it to the Spanish minister of state, Jerónimo Grimaldi.[44]

Upon Franklin's return from Staten Island, the Committee of Secret Correspondence choose him to join Silas Deane and Thomas Jefferson on a mission to France to secure aid and treaties from France and Spain. Jefferson declined to go out of concern for his wife's health. Arthur Lee replaced him. Congress knew that without achieving these goals, the colonial movement toward independence could not prevail.[45]

The committee had sent Deane to Paris a few months earlier, and Lee was in London, where he had taken Franklin's place. Still suffering from his maladies and seventy years old, Franklin remarkably needed only a couple of weeks to prepare for his departure. He conferred with Robert Morris, another member of the Committee of Secret Correspondence, who also was managing Congress's finances. Franklin learned that France would not formally enter into war but, nonetheless, would be sending a gift of 200,000 schillings worth of arms and ammunition. Morris explained that the shipment would go to a port in the West Indies, where he could arrange for the transfer of the supplies to the colonies. Franklin would manage the arrangement from Europe.[46]

Franklin also arranged to take his two grandsons with him, for he felt this was a life-changing opportunity for Temple Franklin, who was around seventeen years old, and Benny Bache, who was seven years old. Just before they departed on the cramped American war ship *Reprisal* on October 27,

Figure 1. Silas Deane, an American commissioner recalled as a result of Lee's accusations; 1781 engraving by B. L. Prevost in Paris. (Library of Congress)

1776, Franklin received the good news that France had agreed to secretly send aid through a fake-front company.[47]

Apparently, what he did not know was that the governments of Spain and France had already set up the company in May. Both countries agreed to contribute an initial one million *livres* (about 500,000 *pesos fuertes,* or over $15 million in today's currency) worth of munitions and supplies.[48] The company, Roderique (Rodríquez) Hortalez et Cie was put under the charge of the opportunist Pierre-Augustin Caron de Beaumarchais, who had just authored *The Barber of Seville* and was about to write *The Marriage of Figaro*. Franklin had to have known that Spain was covertly supplying the colonies, since Gibson's gambit had paid off. In New Orleans, Unzaga sent enough munitions to save Forts Pitt and Willing from defeat. In addition, coinciding with Franklin's arrival in France, a royal order had been issued from Madrid that instructed all responsible officials, including the governors in Havana and Louisiana, to supply the "Americanos" with whatever gunpowder and muskets (*fusiles*) were available. They were to ship the munitions on free merchant ships.[49]

Spain initially dealt with Great Britain on two fronts—sending covert aid to the colonies and, most importantly, taking military action to stop British expansion in South America while also serving notice to Portugal, a British ally. Knowing that Great Britain could not risk going to war or acknowledge its illegal operations, Spain sent to South America an armada

Figure 2. Arthur Lee, an American commissioner jealous of Franklin and Deane. (*Lambs Biographical Dictionary of the United States,* vol. 5)

of seven ships of the line, eight frigates, four smaller ships, and many transports carrying fourteen infantry battalions and four cavalry squads. The force would successfully attack and destroy Portuguese and British establishments and smuggling operations. They took what is today Uruguay from the Portuguese and secured the Río de la Plata and the city of Buenos Aires. Described by one observer as "one of the best organized and best provisioned enterprises" ever prepared in Spain, the fleet left the port of Cádiz on November 13, 1776, exactly when Franklin was suffering a hard sea voyage to France.[50] At the same time, another fleet sailed up the Tajo River and anchored, with its guns trained on Lisbon, Portugal's capital. A very stark and obvious point had been made.[51]

Spain had its own reasons for supporting the North American colonies. Along with France, Spain suffered the loss of the recent Seven Years' War. Late in the war, King Carlos III had honored the Bourbon Family Compact and had finally committed his unprepared country. Now, he and his advisors considered the results of that war as well as what would be needed to succeed in the case of a much-anticipated future confrontation with Great Britain. The British had taken some of Spain's territory and moved into other parts of its vast American empire. A weakened Spain was in

Figure 3. Carlos III, king of Spain; oil on canvas, painting by Antono Rafael Mengs. (Prado Museum, Madrid. Accession number P02200)

no position to openly confront the victorious Great Britain, and the latter flexed its commercial and military muscle with impunity. In addition, France, the ultimate loser in the recent war, was in no position to help. Except for a few holdings in the Caribbean, France had lost its New World possessions. This left Spain and Great Britain as the two major competitors for American territory and trade.

Spain had a clear incentive, which was to recoup all that it had lost as part of the settlement that ended the Seven Years' War. The 1763 Treaty of Paris resulted in Spanish losses in Florida, the West Indies, and along the Mississippi, as well as giving tacit permission to allow British trade and woodcutting operations in Central America, which was then called "Goatemala." This last concession led to extensive smuggling to the financial detriment of Spain's settlements in the region.[52]

Those British subjects who also expected a renewed conflict had begun to intentionally subvert Spain's Indian alliances. This, along with new British settlements that had been situated opposite Spanish settlements along the Mississippi River at Baton Rouge, Manchac, and Natchez, heightened Spain's anxiety. They saw the area of Louisiana as a buffer protecting expansion into its prize colony, the Viceroyalty of New Spain, or Mexico. Spain also saw that Louisiana and Florida were now held by Great Britain and were key to its desire to control the West Indies trade. From Spain's point of view, the unexpected colonial rebellion had become an opportunity. With Great Britain thus occupied and, over time, weakened, Spain had time to prepare itself for an eventual war.[53] When Spain ultimately decided to enter the conflict with an open declaration of war against Great Britain, it also openly stated its conditions. The Spanish Crown wanted to expel the British from Central America and the Mississippi River and regain West Florida, the Bahamas, Gibraltar, and the Mediterranean island of Menorca, and to take Jamaica, as well.[54]

Whether Franklin knew of Spain's desires is not known, although his subsequent negotiations and colonial correspondence indicate that the American colonies were aware of Spain's desire for trade and for obtaining Pensacola.

At the time, Franklin was otherwise distracted, as he was trying to survive a winter crossing of the North Atlantic. The *Reprisal* made a quick, thirty-day crossing, even capturing two British merchantmen en route; however, during the voyage, the ship pitched violently, robbing Franklin of sleep and rest. The food was terrible. Finding the chicken too tough for his teeth, Franklin had to rely on salted beef. His boils and rashes returned. As he put it, the voyage "almost demolished me."[55]

With his two British prizes, Capt. Lambert Wickes diverted the *Reprisal* to Quiberon Bay off the coast of Brittany. He intended to sail on to Nantes, but unfavorable winds delayed him.[56] Rather than remain on board any longer than necessary, Franklin rented a fishing boat that ferried him and his grandsons to the small village of Auray on the southern coast of the Breton Peninsula. From there he contracted carriages to convey him and the boys to Nantes, where he arrived on December 7 and was feted with a grand dinner. After an eight-day respite in the house of a partner of Penet, a commissioned merchant who was busy with shipments from Nantes to the colonies, he suffered another "miserable" ride to Versailles, where he arrived on December 20, 1776.[57] He entered Paris the next day. Unbeknownst to him, the Spanish ambassador anxiously waited to meet him.

2

To Cultivate the Good Will

Pedro Pablo Abarca de Bolea, Count of Aranda, was a person who could throw a temper tantrum that was sometimes real and at other times feigned.[1] As Spain's ambassador to France, Aranda's reputation for a no-nonsense approach and confrontational attitude preceded him. So, too, did his intelligence and pedigree. Above all he was loyal to Spain and its king, Carlos III. Simultaneously a liability and an asset, Aranda was appointed by the king and his advisors to the crucial post in Paris, which advantageously got him out of Madrid.

The fifty-eight-year-old aristocratic count, a highly decorated and wounded combat veteran with a long diplomatic career, was about to pen one of his direct missives to the Count of Vergennes, minister of state to Louis the XVI.[2] Regarding Aranda, Vergennes observed that he had "never seen anything like this ambassador."[3]

For more than a few years, Aranda had maintained the position that the rebellion in America gave Spain and France an opportunity to gain revenge upon Great Britain. For his own patriotic reasons, he had argued with his superiors that the colonies should be supported and that Spain and its ally France should prepare for war sooner rather than later. Back in Madrid, his superiors, led by the minister of state the Marquis of Grimaldi, disagreed with his aggressive position. They championed caution, but by the time Franklin had been assigned to France, they had moved closer to Aranda's position.[4]

Aranda knew that the American statesman and scholar Benjamin Franklin had arrived in Paris in late December 1776, three weeks after his arrival in France. He had already reported as much to Madrid. As early as June 28 of that year, he had received a letter from Jacques Barbeu-DuBourg, a French scientist and writer who worked as a secret agent for the colonies.[5] Invited to have a personal conversation, DuBourg went to Aranda's residence. The colonial agent explained that he was authorized to speak as an informant of Franklin's, and he asked that Spain match Frances's recent aid to the colonies. DuBourg was apparently unaware that the Spanish support

Figure 4. Pedro Pablo Abarca de Bolea, the Count of Aranda, Spain's ambassador to France, who dealt with the American commissioners; oil on canvas, painting by Ramon Bayeu. (Museo de Huesca, Huesca)

already being sent and was being laundered through the dummy company run by Beaumarchais, nor that half of France's aid had come from Spain. He argued that the arms sent thus far had all been made in France, and it would be less obvious if Spanish armaments could be added. He was unaware that Spanish money had purchased many of the French weapons; in hindsight, this may have been a good policy to avoid revealing the Spanish-French alliance to Britain.

That same month, DuBourg reported that the colonies, "in general," were in agreement about "throwing off the yoke of the English" and were about to declare their independence. He noted that the colonial naval force would be impressive because the colonies had a natural disposition to "navigation." Aranda listened but made no commitments.[6]

DuBourg and Aranda apparently kept in touch. On December 14, the latter reported that DuBourg had informed him of Franklin's arrival in the port of Nantes, correctly adding that he had arrived "in a well-armed frigate that seized two English vessels while in transit." With Franklin on his way to Paris, Aranda met with Vergennes and told him that it would be "natural" for Franklin to come to Paris as a "fully empowered" representative of the newly declared independent Congress. He added that knowledge of Franklin's mission might alarm the English. Vergennes advised that they should wait for Franklin's arrival.[7]

The Spanish ambassador was already in favor of aiding the colonies. He believed that in the future, the colonies would become a powerful nation with a rapidly increasing population composed primarily of European immigrants. He believed that the rebellion would open a new horizon in the history of the Americas and that Spain had a vested interest in that history. He felt that Spain could not be indifferent to this historical development.[8]

After the colonial declaration of independence, Aranda wanted to see what proposals Franklin would bring to him from Congress.[9] In irritation, he paced about in his elegant residence, which had become legendary for its wine cellar and polished silver place settings. When he once again asked Vergennes about Franklin, he felt that the minister had given him an inadequate reply. "Ambiguous" was how he described it.[10] That the French had not informed him of or even mentioned Franklin's presence seemed to be a betrayal of their countries' respective friendship and, even more so, of their formal alliance, the Third Bourbon Family Compact.

He set about getting the powerful French minister's attention. First, he reminded Vergennes that he knew of the famous American's arrival because the agent DuBourg, "in muted conversation," had told him exactly when and where Franklin had arrived. It had been almost three weeks since his arrival at the "Bay of Quiberon." Aranda also suspected that Vergennes had talked with Franklin about the reasons for the latter's presence in this kingdom. Vergennes answered only in vague terms in response to Aranda's questions.[11]

According to Vergennes, Franklin had not yet arrived in Paris, but Aranda was not so sure about this. The French could have him sequestered in the royal palace at Versailles some twelve miles outside the city. Aranda suspected French duplicity, and he was beyond wondering why. The urgency of the matter dictated that Aranda forego writing a letter; instead, he would personally confront Vergennes.

A recent diplomatic packet from Madrid gave Aranda the perfect *entrée* for a meeting with Vergennes. He had received instructions to convey to Vergennes the status of Spain's relationship with the Portuguese queen, who was Carlos III's niece, and also to introduce the idea that Spain wanted to aid the rebelling North American colonies on its own, instead of continuing the cooperative effort that the two countries had undertaken up to this point.

Thus, early Sunday morning, December 22, 1776, Aranda rode out to Versailles to meet with Vergennes. After dealing at some length with the Portuguese matter, Aranda used the news that Spain intended to directly aid the colonies to delve into "the matter of Franklin." In his usual confrontational manner, Aranda told Vergennes that time was of the essence, and indeed, had been lost, if the only reason for Franklin's presence in France was to avoid the disturbances in America. He added that perhaps Franklin had come with a commission and therefore was on an official mission. Vergennes became uneasy and had to admit that he knew the answer.[12] Aranda had his opening.

He stated that as an ambassador, he had no choice but to request a "clearly stated" response. Spain had a right to know Franklin's whereabouts and status based on both its previous aid and its desire to send future aid to the rebelling American colonies. In accordance with his instructions, he informed Vergennes that in addition to what had been done jointly, Spain was contemplating sending aid by a means different from that of the current concerted effort with the French court.

Up to this point, the two countries had coordinated their efforts to send covert aid to the rebelling colonies, mostly through Roderique Hortalez et Cie. Now Spain wanted to expand its support but send it unilaterally. Because of this, Aranda directly stated that his king "should not be kept in ignorance of anything that came to France's knowledge, nor should the proper news be detained from him for the success of his plans."[13]

Thus confronted and put on the defensive, Vergennes admitted that Franklin had arrived in Paris the day before and had met with Silas Deane, another American. Vergennes added that he did not want to see them yet, for he wanted to wait until they had settled in.[14]

Vergennes and Aranda would soon find out that the Continental Congress had appointed Franklin, Deane, and Arthur Lee to a Committee of Secret Correspondence and that the three men were sent to Paris to negotiate aid and treaties from friendly European countries.

Aranda left his meeting with Vergennes partially satisfied, but he remained suspicious. A day later Aranda received news that Franklin had been in Paris "some days" before the date he had been told. To him, it seemed most likely that the American's arrival had been kept secret. As Aranda later reported to Madrid, this latest news "did not fail but to increase the suspicions that I already harbored."[15]

The next day Aranda voiced his suspicions to Vergennes. Vergennes denied it all. Franklin had not come to Paris earlier in order to be hidden, neither in the city nor in Versailles. Vergennes did admit that he had communicated with Silas Deane through an intermediary. Actually, Deane had arrived in Paris in July and knew about, or even claimed to have helped arrange, the aid being sent by the Roderique Hortalez company. Vergennes had requested that neither Deane nor Franklin speak with anyone about their purpose—and especially to avoid DuBourg and Beaumarchais.

Vergennes apparently did not know that DuBourg was an American agent. Beaumarchais, on the other hand, was well known to him as one of his own agents, but one that was not to be completely trusted. Beaumarchais had been sent to London only to return to give an exaggerated account of England's sad state, postulating that with a slight turn of events, even the king could lose his head. He warned that Spain and France must be ready to profit from England's bad luck.[16] Vergennes also knew that both Beaumarchais and DuBourg had been confidantes, if not business partners, with Deane.

Then Vergennes shared with Aranda his request that the Americans put Franklin's commission in writing, including what proposals he would make. He had granted them some time to fulfill the task. Aranda thought that the delay in waiting for the written commission and proposals was unnecessary. In his opinion, a "consummate man like Franklin" had plenty of time, during his voyage or before, to have laid out his commission and proposals. Surely he had instructions from which he had formed the "first proposals." Plenty of time had already passed since his arrival in France. He did not need more time, which, from the Spaniard's point of view, was a perplexing delay.[17]

Vergennes then changed the subject and took Aranda into his confidence to share a draft of a plan that he was preparing in anticipation of an armed conflict with England. Aranda bowed in acknowledgement and let Vergennes read his draft. Aranda felt that sharing the draft was a ruse to win back his trust. The Spanish ambassador left the meeting deeply suspicious.

A somewhat frustrated Aranda felt that another meeting would not be useless, because Vergennes would give him "some token explanation about Franklin." Instead, he decided to put his concerns in writing. With quill in hand, he dashed out a hurried, but detailed letter to the minister. On December 28, almost a week after their first meeting in Versailles, Aranda sent Vergennes the short missive.[18]

The letter drew an immediate reaction. Vergennes could hardly ignore Aranda's matter-of-fact statement that his next report back to Madrid would not receive a favorable reaction without some definitive information about Franklin.

Figure 5. Charles Gravier, the Count of Vergennes, minister of state and new foreign minister of France, as well as King Louis XVI's most trusted advisor; oil on canvas, painting by Antoine François Callet. (Palace of Versailles. Accession number MV3979)

Vergennes penned a reply the same day and admitted that he had met with "Dr. F. . . . and his colleagues" that morning. He added that nothing of substance had come from the brief meeting. Franklin talked about trade, but he did not want to go into detail about the conflict or about further requests, rather preferring to put those details in writing. Vergennes then added that Franklin "seems to be an intelligent individual, but very wary." Franklin promised to present a written summary of the colonial position. The French minister reported that he had made clear to the Americans that France and Spain were working together in "perfect unity." As requested, Franklin agreed that he would not speak directly with anyone else except Aranda.

Vergennes made the small excuse of writing a reply in lieu of a direct meeting because he learned that Aranda had decided not to meet on the next day, December 29, as originally planned. Vergennes felt it best to write and schedule a meeting for the following Tuesday.[19]

Before Vergennes' letter was delivered, that evening Aranda received a letter written in English from Franklin, Deane, and Lee. Specifically, they wrote that they had been sent to Paris "to cultivate the good will of the courts of Spain and France." They would like to pay their respects to

Aranda personally and let him see their proposals "tomorrow or whatever day would be convenient."[20] Aranda told the carrier that he could not reply immediately. He was waiting for a reply from Vergennes that arrived soon thereafter. He was pleased that his letter to Vergennes had worked.[21]

Now Aranda was free to work directly with Franklin and the American Commission, and he did not hesitate. He sent a message informing Franklin that he would meet with him the day after next at seven p.m., to avoid suspicion. Franklin, Deane, and Lee arrived at Aranda's residence at the appointed time. Aranda invited them into his sumptuous home without informing the rest of his family. Thus, Franklin and his colleagues had their first official meeting with a representative of the Spanish government in the final days of 1776.

After introductions were made, Franklin confirmed Vergennes's last message to Aranda. He had a memorial about trade and commerce and shared that Vergennes had stressed the unity between France and Spain.[22] Franklin would give Aranda a copy of the memorial so that he could forward it to Madrid. Franklin then thanked Spain for granting asylum to American ships in its ports, specifically mentioning that they appreciated the good treatment their countrymen had received in "the Catholic King's domains."[23]

Aranda patiently listened to these opening statements. He assured Franklin that both the memorial and America's gratitude would be conveyed to the Spanish court. But he wanted more definitive information. He asked if Franklin had come with the "full powers from the Congress for everything?" Franklin affirmed that he had. Was the memorial written by him in transit or put together by Congress? Franklin replied that Congress had written it.[24]

Then Aranda became blatant. Given the situation in which the North American colonies found themselves, he was surprised that the memorial did not ask for anything more than "good correspondence." He continued that he would have thought they would seek aid rather than "treating about good relationships." He asked: What value were good relations when "thus far they were not peaceable possessors of their freedom?" Should not their freedom be the priority?

No doubt reeling from such a direct onslaught, Franklin answered that he would explain his position in more detail with a second memorial.

Aranda continued to press for more information. He received assurances from Franklin that the rebellion was serious and that he did not have to worry about the Americans' determination. Franklin rather cleverly changed the subject by asking if American corsairs would be welcomed in

Spanish ports not only for food and shelter but also for the opportunity to sell their spoils there. Aranda answered that the first part of the question had been answered affirmatively earlier in the meeting. As to the second part, he would have to confer with his superiors.

Aranda later reported to Grimaldi that he had done everything possible to learn if Franklin had undertaken discussions with Vergennes or one of his ministers before he had presented them with the memorial. Either because of a language difficulty "or due to some hesitation," however, he never got a direct answer. Aranda also added that "Franklin speaks very little French, Deane much less, and Lee nothing." Nevertheless, they did their best to understand each other.[25]

At Aranda's insistence, Franklin had to reiterate that his powers as granted by Congress were ample enough to deal with everything "that might be treated." With that, plans were made for second encounter and the meeting ended. The young "United Provinces of America," as the commissioners' letter to Aranda had stated, had officially made contact with Spain.[26] Franklin reported to Congress that the "Conde de Aranda appears to have a good disposition toward us."[27] Franklin and Aranda were men of their time who represented different worlds. Their contact eventually would bear fruit enough to assure the independence of the new American country.

Unknown to Franklin, Aranda's report to Grimaldi, dated January 4, 1777, also included an appraisal of the plan for war presented to him by Vergennes as well as the American memorial. Like his country, Aranda himself wanted to aid the colonies.[28] Perhaps because of the convergence of Franklin's arrival and that report, Aranda wrote in a subsequent letter:

> Spain has many possessions to guard in America and cannot ignore them either now, at this moment, or in what lies ahead. One should not doubt that England shall go after Spain at all times through those parts, and with many options will direct herself to the most exposed; in the face of which, what would be the radical remedy to avoid these risks if not to take England down that she can never rise again?[29]

Whether the American Commission knew it or not, they had a champion in Aranda.

 3

Intrigue and Contact

In 1777, Paris was the second-largest city in Europe, with a population that ranged somewhat over six hundred thousand people. The splendor of its public buildings and recently completed structures like the Teâtre de l'Orleans and the medical school on the Left Bank was awe-inspiring. Despite the new buildings and the magnificence of nearby Versailles, Paris's high-rises, which often rose to six stories, lost their luster because of the thick black soot that covered them; moreover, many of its churches had fallen into disrepair due to the financial problems of the Catholic Church.

Nor could one ignore the constant stench that hovered in the narrow, crowded streets. Street vendors, shoppers, people looking for work, beggars, and the sick crammed the thoroughfares. The sick remained a problem despite a plethora of overcrowded jails and church-run hospitals. New construction, which was underway everywhere, impeded passage with stacks of lumber and stone, scaffolds and pulleys, and large piles of rubble. Sounds of hammering and shouting echoed in thin corridors and resonated off buildings. The butcher shops generally slaughtered animals on-site, frequently allowing the resulting blood to run into the streets, where it mixed with human and animal waste that the throngs walked in or rode through. The putridness eventually found its way into the utterly polluted Seine River, where it was not uncommon to see decomposed human body parts that had been washed into the water from old riverside graveyards.

People resorted to drinking wine to augment the water worthy of drinking that came from wells. Hard-crusted bread dipped in wine was a main staple, and it was government regulated. Meat, usually pork, supplemented the wine and bread. Adding to the noise and filth was the occasional pig hidden and hoarded by recently arrived poor immigrants from the countryside as an insurance policy against hard times—the forerunner of the piggy bank.

Anchored on the Seine River, Paris's neighborhoods, or districts as they were called, divided the city based on class. The nobles and wealthy tended to avoid the city's center. The Saint-Germain-des-Prés neighborhood housed the small Jewish community, including some Sephardim from

Figure 6. Louis XVI receiving the American commissioners to France, Benjamin Franklin, Arthur Lee, and Silas Deane. The caption in German reads, "Dr. Franklin, as envoy of the American ?? State, receives his first audience in France at Versailles." (Library of Congress)

Spain. The salons and prostitutes were concentrated in the Palais-Royal district. Nonetheless, no part of Paris sufficed for the royal court. Some eighty years earlier, beginning with the reign of Louis XIV, the kings and their entourages had moved twelve miles away to the Versailles palace and grounds. Naturally, the influential and wealthy followed suit, moving out of town toward Versailles along the beautiful Bois de Boulong, a walled forest and royal hunting grounds elevated above the Seine River. The wealthy suburban communities of Passy and Auteuil were built on small rises next to the forest.

Benjamin Franklin may have been acclimated to a city like Paris, for he had spent many years in London, then Europe's largest city. He may not have noticed the city's negative aspects, for he was welcomed as a hero. Throngs of visitors sought his attention at the Hôtel d'Hambourg, where he spent his first months. He was more popular in France than he was in America.

Franklin, however, was nevertheless more than pleased to leave the city and accept residence in a wealthy Passy estate with large gardens. There he could bathe three times a week, relax in the gardens, and receive visitors at his leisure. He was closer to Versailles, where most of his and his colleagues' work would take them. A personal advantage was the relative proximity to the Palais-Royal salons. He could avoid the center of the city and still partake in the frivolity and opulence that had become famous among the Parisian elite. All in all, the new environment revived his health.

Initially, Franklin had little time to become acquainted with or enjoy Paris. Franklin, Deane, and Lee represented a country that did not yet exist. Added to that difficulty was the daunting task of seeking aid and alliances from monarchies to enable their aspiring country to sever its ties *from* a monarchy.

In rapid succession, the three commissioners met with France's minister of state and Spain's ambassador to France. The initial meetings served as a means of introduction.

Vergennes was almost complacent, while Aranda was confrontational. Both men quickly reminded the Americans that a declaration of independence did not mean that independence had been accomplished. If they did not yet represent a country, how could there be an alliance? Aranda's direct attitude contrasted with Franklin's celebrated deceptions and wordplay.

Franklin and his colleagues did not have ready answers for the Spanish diplomat. Franklin could only offer the weak excuse that they would provide a memorial that was not yet completed, along with some official papers that he had from the Continental Congress.[1] One can only imagine the impressions and subsequent conversations among the three American commissioners after they left Aranda's sumptuous residence; Abigail Adams could subsequently not resist an exaggerated observation that the Spanish ambassador had seventy-five servants.[2]

One thing was made clear to the Americans—the Bourbon Compact was in place. Both Vergennes and Aranda confirmed to the commissioners that France and Spain were working in harmony—at least, in as much as he and the other American ministers were concerned.[3] Franklin also realized that he should prepare for his next meeting with Aranda and that he had better do so quickly.

Nevertheless, Franklin, Deane, and Lee knew that both Spain and France had already sent aid to the colonies. Acting on a request from Luis de Unzaga, the governor of Louisiana, the Spanish government had sent a shipment out of the port of Bilbao that was destined for New Orleans, to then be transferred to the colonies. No doubt placed under the auspices of Diego de Gardoqui, a man with whom the commissioners would become acquainted, the shipment was augmented with supplies and gunpowder from Havana and Mexico, all of which arrived in New Orleans in May 1777.[4] The shipment included three hundred 16-caliber muskets; ten thousand pounds of gunpowder; cloth that was dyed red, white, and blue; quinine; and more. The commissioners also learned that further aid would be forthcoming. This confirmed Spain's willingness to open its ports to American ships, although France remained hesitant to follow suit, in part because of Dunkirk, a French port that England had already destroyed twice during the eighteenth century. Moreover, per treaty, Dunkirk had been given special status as a demilitarized port, with a British commissioner stationed there.[5]

Franklin promised to compose and deliver a memorial that would clarify the colonies' proposals; however, this effort was delayed when Silas Deane contracted malaria. Upon hearing this, Aranda provided the commissioners with quinine from his personal stock to help cure Deane of the disease.[6]

Unbeknownst to the American commissioners, Aranda had met with Vergennes, who told him that it seemed that Franklin's only goal was a treaty of friendship and trade, the offer of which had been presented to him in writing. Aranda noted that Franklin was guarded, intelligent, and wary and that he "avoided relying on his memory," preferring to put his thoughts in writing.[7]

Vergennes then forwarded two documents to Aranda. One was a colonial proposal for a treaty of friendship and trade. The other was a French plan for war that Vergennes had prepared. He had shared an earlier draft of this with Aranda a few days before, but this time, Vergennes provided Aranda with the finished product that had been approved by his king. Vergennes asked that Aranda share it with his king.[8]

Aranda prepared for his next meeting with the colonial representatives. He wrote, "It seemed to me that it would be very helpful to avail myself of [the services of] the Count of Lacy ... who knows the English language, so that he should make clear to Franklin and Lee the meaning of the points that should be addressed." Lacy, a native of Ireland, was the Spanish ambassador assigned to Saint Petersburg, Russia. At the time, he was temporarily residing in Aranda's house.[9]

Aranda was anxious to see Franklin's written statement, and after a few days, he invited the American commissioners to his residence for a second meeting. On Saturday, January 4, 1777, Franklin and Lee left the ailing Deane in bed and met with Aranda. When questioned by Aranda, Franklin had to admit that even though there would be no significant differences between the memorial being given to Vergennes and the one intended for Aranda, the latter copy was not yet ready because he "only needed to compare it" to the original copy.[10] Franklin excused the delay "because Mr. Deane had been somewhat indisposed."[11]

Upon hearing that the expected report was not ready, Aranda pressed for more information. When asked if the report being prepared for Spain differed from the one given to Vergennes, Franklin answered that it was "identical." Aranda then wanted to know how the report could be identical to the French one, since the existing Spanish "dominions" varied from those in France and required "some necessary difference." To this, Franklin parried the observation by stating that the Congress had authorized him "to treat with each of the two Courts to their interests."[12]

At this point Aranda again pointed out the reality of the Americans' position: "How it is that, without yet finding themselves assured of their independence, nor being recognized as yet by these Powers, the colonies came proposing treaties when everyone believed that Dr. Franklin's arrival was more immediately directed at requesting aid until they secured their separation."[13] This time, Franklin was prepared. He forthrightly stated that such a treaty would demonstrate to them who their friends were. This implied his confidence that the revolution would succeed, which meant that those who became allies would subsequently benefit. Franklin knew that both Spain and France wanted to divert the colonial trade in their direction. He continued to exert his confidence in the revolution by telling the Spanish ambassador that they preferred not to deal with the "matter of need, all the more so since" the colonial situation "was not such that would immediately require direct assistance." In other words, Franklin's priority was an alliance, after which they could talk about aid.

Aranda then asked if they had already received aid from France, at the same time inquiring if the *Amphitrate,* a ship carrying supplies to the rebels, had embarked, or if two other shipments had left? Here, Franklin demonstrated his astuteness. He answered no to the first question and continued to note that the only aid that the colonies had received had come from a company. This was a clear reference to the Roderique et Hortalez. He added that the company had furnished merchandise, arms, and munitions; and he noted that the rebelling forces had also benefited from the "services of foreign officers" who had been sent to the colonies. He continued that although France had not sent any monetary aid, it at least had not opposed the rebellious colonies, thus allowing them "the freedom" to pursue their independence. Franklin knew that the company was a front to send aid to the colonies. He cleverly did not let on that he knew this, but instead chose to tell Aranda only that he knew about the company. Whether he understood that the company was a joint Spanish and French endeavor is unclear.

The *Amphitrite* made a successful voyage to Philadelphia, where it arrived in early May 1777. The Americans were happy to receive its cargo of 216 bronze cannons, 12,825 bombs with fuses, 30,000 rifles with bayonets, 20,000 uniforms, 27 mortars, and 4,000 tents, among other supplies. It was the first shipment arranged by Beaumarchais through the bogus Roderigue et Hortalez company, which was financed equally by Spain and France.

For some unknown reason, none of the American recipients seemed to know that Spain had helped to finance the shipment. Historian Reyes Calderón Cuadrado notes that the papers of the Continental Congress, as well as those of George Washington, referenced the ship and reported that it had come from France, but they made no mention of Spain's financing of at least half the shipment. One reason for the confusion might be that Spanish money had been used to purchase French arms that were then delivered to America.[14] This omission led to a misapprehension that has persisted for almost 250 years: that France had provided abundant aid and that Spain had given almost none. Calderón Cuadrado proposes that this misconception arose from the manner that each country arranged the aid. While France had used public channels, Spain took advantage of its private channels made up of a network of established businessmen from both Spain and North America. As a result, the Spanish financial figures are dispersed and hidden, not necessarily found in convenient public archives but rather in the records of historical societies and museums and in private archives, most of which are in the United States.[15]

Franklin, however, could not ignore Aranda's reference to the shipments and the *Amphitrite*. He acknowledged that he thought the ship had set sail but that the two subsequent shipments had been suspended. The answer seemed to placate Aranda, who followed up with a less aggressive question. He wanted to know what the Americans' most urgent need was. Franklin succinctly responded that the rebels needed bronze cannons and warships.

Here, Franklin went into detail about the state and potential of the colonial and British navies. With its loss of American sailors, the British navy had become depleted and overburdened. Franklin proffered the generality that the British fleet had lost a third of its manpower to the rebelling colonies. He explained that if the rebellion were properly supported, Britain would need to dedicate another third of its fleet to counter the Americans. Significantly, from Aranda's point of view, this calculus meant that only another third of Britain's navy would be left to counter any other enemy, such as the combined fleets of Spain and France.[16] Franklin had given Aranda something to consider.

The discussion then gravitated to how Spain should be approached. Franklin volunteered to send either Deane or Lee to Madrid to deal directly with the Spanish court. Aranda demurred. He explained that although the distance from Paris to Madrid was great and having to use the mail system was inconvenient, it was otherwise to the Americans' advantage to confine their negotiations to him in Paris. He claimed that Spain would want to consult with France about any proposal that the American commissioners might make. Left unsaid here was everyone's understanding that mail was opened with regularity and that spies were everywhere—including, as it turned out, Franklin's own private secretary, Edward Bancroft.[17]

Aranda concluded that for the reasons detailed above, namely distance and the mail situation, it would be the better course "to put forth the explanations here," because they could then be sent to Madrid after the French court had rendered its "opinion." According to Aranda, Franklin and Lee readily agreed, making "many demonstrations of respect toward the Catholic King," while claiming that their principal purpose was that of convincing him and everyone that "they earnestly hoped for his protection."[18]

A placated Aranda then asked Franklin and Lee if they had any further questions of him. Franklin inquired about six shipments the colonies had sent to the Spanish port of Cádiz under the auspices of a British firm, Buick and Company. That company, he continued, had withheld its payments for the shipments. Congress needed the proceeds, because it had allotted money to make necessary purchases in France. Franklin asked what recourse could be taken. After some discussion, Aranda concluded that the solution would be to present a specific case, including pertinent evidence of the company's debt. With the necessary power of attorney before a proper tribunal, and with the support from the authorities involved, Aranda concluded, "justice could be done without delay."[19]

The implication of this exchange was that the complaint would be brought before a tribunal in Spain, where the shipment had been received. Also clear in this discussion was that Spain, as a neutral country, could be used to mediate the business of two belligerents, in this case the rebelling American colonies and Great Britain. Moreover, the colonies knew that the proceeds from the business would be used to purchase goods in France. In other words, the rebelling colonials were doing business with a British company to support the rebellion. Spain's neutrality was a key component in this somewhat covert transaction.

Whether Franklin knew it or not, Aranda, for his own chauvinistic reasons, favored the American rebellion. The count felt that Spain should not pick at England and hope for independence for her North American colonies but should strike now "to destroy England forever." He argued that after the success of the revolution, about which he apparently had no doubts, the new nation would be more peaceful than England and with Spain's aid would become a good trade partner.[20] He followed up his meeting with Franklin and Lee to inform Vergennes of what had been said. While attending a regular conference of ambassadors on January 7, 1777, Aranda and Vergennes compared notes. Aranda even accepted Vergennes's offer to translate the as yet undelivered memorial promised by Franklin. On the following day, Wednesday, January 8, Franklin and Lee personally delivered the documents to Aranda.

Two days later Aranda went to Versailles to meet with Vergennes. The French minister told him that Franklin had delivered a request for French warships but that the response could only be one of secret aid. Warships, which had also been mentioned to Aranda, were out of the question. Both Spain and France were busy building up their own navies in anticipation of the pending conflict. Vergennes noted to Aranda that France had already granted 2 million livres, which, by sleight of hand, a little luck, and a favorable business community, the Americans could convert into 6 million. Then Vergennes shared the knowledge that the *Amphitrite* had returned to port because of bad weather. It would set out again, and two other supply ships in Le Havre would also set sail; however, this time greater care would be taken to ensure secrecy.[21]

On January 13, 1777, a few days after his meeting with the Americans in Versailles, Aranda sat down to pen two remarkable letters or reports for his minister of state and for his king. He probably used the intervening days to gather his notes and his thoughts, because the letters went into detail about what had happened and laid out the justifications for what should happen. The first letter contained thirty-three pages in addition to copies of the documents that had passed between him, the Americans, and Vergennes. The second letter was even longer, at thirty-eight pages.

The first letter detailed Aranda's suspicions and his actions taken during Franklin's delay and arrival in Paris. He reported the disappointing result of the first meeting and his conversations with Vergennes, including the status of the *Amphitrite*. He devoted the last third of the letter with what could only be described as a diatribe in reaction to France's memorial anticipating the possibility of war.

He essentially scoffed at France's ideas about its land forces and navy relative to a possible invasion of Ireland or England. Success would require Spain's help, but he warned of the veracity of France's intentions regarding Spain: "The French Court is chagrined to appear indolent, while at the same time it looks toward preparing itself for when it is set upon. It is trying to dissuade Spain from the indifference it accuses her of and likewise, not communicating this to her in order to keep Spain in such a state as to take advantage of her for its own purposes and urgent needs."[22] Aranda, obviously, did not completely trust the French.

The remainder of the letter laid out his thinking as to why now was the time to act. Given Great Britain's problems with its colonies and its resulting economic and political burdens at home, he wrote, there could be no better time to confront the island empire. He added that Spain, not France, should take the lead, thus securing itself from any allied trickery: "If both powers, taking advantage of England's embarrassment, truly move to take her on, Spain, on an equal footing, has the right independently to secure its own interest from the shadow of France." Aside from defeating a longtime adversary, Aranda believed that the action was needed to protect Spain's American empire, both now and in the future, with the bonus of having the former British colonies as their newly won friends. And that could happen only if Spain, along with France, supported the rebelling colonies in their struggle for independence.[23]

Then Aranda composed the second letter.[24] Although dated the same day as the first letter, this longer missive contained more detail and clarified elements of the first letter. Aranda must have thought either that he had not been clear or, possibly, that his arguments had not been strong enough in the first composition. With what must have been an ink-stained hand, he penned his thoughts, which vacillated from solid reason and knowledge to total misconceptions. The letter reflected his well-deserved reputation: it was confrontational—"I am going to explain to the king the present posture of his Monarchy, and that of his future interests"—and informative, adding to the Spanish court's knowledge as he correctly detailed the geography of North America.

After sharing the litany of his attempts to meet with Franklin, as well as detailing the three meetings that he had held with him and the other commissioners, he cautioned that any trade with the rebelling colonies should be limited to Spain and not its American possessions. He then focused on those possessions. He explained that prior to the Seven Years' War, four European powers had colonies in America. After the war, Spain had retained most of its possessions, while France had lost Canada and Louisiana. England's possessions were now in doubt, and, in Brazil, Portugal had been usurping Spanish territory.

Thus, he proposed that "to conserve its own possessions in America... it is vital that Spain assures and locks in" the loyalty of "that new power by means of a solemn treaty, by meritoriously freeing it of its urgent situation." Aranda correctly assumed that with Spanish and French alliances, the Americans would succeed in their rebellion and independence would result in a well-populated nation of Europeans. This, he theorized, would result in a country indebted to Spain and France.

He found the proposed American treaty to be interesting but bland. Although he had not received the promised, more detailed, proposal, he noted that through secret sources, "whom they do not watch closely," the rebelling colonies wanted nothing for free and they had offered to pay. Perhaps displaying a bias, if not passion, for his position, he left unanswered the question of whether they *could* pay.

An independent nation would be a preferred neighbor to Spain's possessions in America. Aranda described a future country that would be prosperous as well as peaceful because, he emphasized, most of its peoples "are Quakers by way of religion." Then Spain would have a friend bordering its American possessions. Otherwise, if Britain successfully suppressed the rebellion, Spain would be confronted with a traditional and much emboldened enemy neighboring the Viceroyalty of New Spain. Such an outcome would be a worse scenario. "It appears," he concluded, "that necessity now demands assuring to the new Power of America recognition."[25] He added, "I will conclude that securing a favorable treaty from said United Provinces will depend on openly getting them out of their troubles, and on taking advantage of this opportunity to come to agreement with them." Here, Arana the pragmatist argued that now was the time to act because the risks were minimal. Britain would make an enormous effort to suppress the colonial rebellion and defeat any of the colonials' allies; however, using Franklin's argument regarding the current reduction of Britain's naval strength and the already visible drain on that country's resources due to the rebellion, he maintained that the opportunity was now.

He posited that Britain's problems would continue to increase. Its seaborne trade would continue to suffer because of both the loss of its colonies and the aforementioned reduction of its maritime fleet. This would lead to a reduction of available goods and a decline in skilled crafts. Britain's debt would mount, and the only remedy would be to impose unpopular taxes, which would result in civil discord. Aranda concluded that Britain "further suffocates herself" with war.

Then, Spain must consider the presence of France in this scenario, which, by virtue of its just-delivered memorial, was preparing for the possibility of war with Britain.[26] By seeking Spain's input and approval of the memorial, France was tacitly acknowledging that its thinking aligned with Spain's. Although Aranda cautioned that Spain must be leery of France's motives, he acknowledged that the combined fleets of Spain and France would vastly outnumber Britain's weakened fleet. He reported this last viewpoint more than once in the second letter.

As Aranda progressed toward a closing summary, he added further thoughts on how Spain would benefit from the defeat of Britain. Here, he lost a little control of his reasoning. By allying with France in support of the American Revolution, Spain, he argued, would regain the Mediterranean island of Menorca, plus Gibraltar, Florida, and a portion of the Newfoundland fishing rights. Then he boldly wrote that France would regain Canada. This assessment, as history has shown, proved to be overstated. France would not get, nor want, Canada, nor would Spain regain Gibraltar. And the fishing rights in Newfoundland would remain the subject of a series of negotiations invariably tied to the free navigation of the Mississippi River.

Around the same time as Aranda wrote his two letters, the British ambassador to France, Lord Stormont (David Murray, Second Earl of Mansfield), sent an undated memorial to Vergennes. No doubt reacting to information from his spy Edward Bancroft, who had befriended Franklin and secured employment with the American commissioners, Stormont's missive countered most of Franklin's arguments to Aranda.[27] He cautioned that if the rebellion could not be prevented, the colonies would form themselves into a formidable force that would lead them to "attempt the conquest of other Provinces in America richer and better situated." He concluded that "France and Spain have therefore, everything to apprehend for the safety of their colonies, should those of Great Britain succeed in their designs." He hoped that France would quit dealing with the American merchants and "above all it is hoped that Misters Deane and Franklin may be restrained in those measures, which have been gradually unfolded so as to become less and less equivocal." Stormont then claimed to have enough evidence on Deane that "it might reasonably be expected that he should be delivered up." Interestingly, Masserano in London received a copy of Stormont's memorial and sent an English copy with a Spanish translation directly to José Moñino y Redondo, Count of Floridablanca, chief minister to King Carlos III.[28]

Although he never suspected Bancroft, Franklin understood that he was surrounded by spies, and he operated as such. He also had an inkling that Spain favored the American cause. Despite Aranda's formal manner, Franklin understood that the Spaniard never hinted that Spain was unreceptive to the entreaties from the rebelling British colonies. In fact, the Spanish ambassador encouraged him to explain in detail what they wanted. Franklin and his colleagues, however, had no idea of the extent of Aranda's support for using the opportunity presented by the rebels to go to war against Great Britain. Only Aranda's king and his ministers would know of this and, at the very least, reply to him.

 4

An Unofficial Alliance

Jerónimo Grimaldi, Marques de Grimaldi, was an elderly man, simultaneously at the end and pinnacle of a long and illustrious career. Born in Genoa in 1710 and a member of the House of Grimaldi, he had served Spain first under King Ferdinand VI and then under Carlos III. He had been Spain's ambassador to Sweden and Parma as well as to the Estates-General of the United Provinces. Carlos III had named him ambassador to France, where in 1761 he negotiated the Third Bourbon Family Compact that committed Spain to join France in the Seven Years' War. He had also been a signatory to the Treaty of Paris that ended that war in 1763. In September of that year, he was promoted to minister of state, a position in which he devoted himself to strengthening Spain after its loss of that war.

A staunch royalist and reformer, he had voted for and supported the suppression of the Jesuits in 1767. The crown felt that the Jesuit's wealth and influence raised doubt about the order's loyalty. Grimaldi was a member of the group known as the *golillas*, who supported the king's reforms to strengthen and educate Spain's middle classes. He, along with Aranda, had supported the ban on wearing traditional round hats and long cloaks, which was implemented by the Italian-born interior minister, the Marquis of Esquilache, in an attempt to curb robberies and murders. The ban resulted in a public outcry and in riots that led to the subsequent sacking of Esquilache's house.

Grimaldi approved of the covert aid to Britain's North American colonies as well as the daring military move to separate Great Britain from Portugal, its only European ally. This latter action was all the more brazen in light of the relatively recent and disastrous defeat of a large Spanish expedition in Algeria in 1775.[1] That defeat facilitated the announcement of Grimaldi's removal from office in November 1776.

Great Britain's aggressiveness since the Seven Years' War angered the Spanish government. Its loss meant that Spain had to relinquish Uruguay to Portugal, among other concessions. As the antagonists expanded into Spanish territory, Grimaldi, with the approval of his king, initiated a brazen

Figure 7. Pablo Jerónimo Grimaldi, the Marquis of Grimaldi, Spain's minister of state replaced by Floridablanca; oil on canvas, painting by Francisco Javier Ramos. (Location unknown)

policy in which Great Britain and Portugal would be confronted and, possibly, separated.

In December 1776, precisely when Franklin was arriving in France, Spain sent a fleet carrying over nine thousand men to South America under the command of don Pedro de Cevallos. There it would launch a full-scale attack on Portuguese and British establishments. At the same time, another Spanish fleet sailed up the Iberian coast, entered the Tagus River, and, with guns primed, anchored in front of Lisbon. Sabastião José de Carvalho Mello, Marquis of Pombal, who was Portugal's pro-British, anti-Spanish minister of state and who ran the government, had no choice but to receive the Spanish officers with full decorum. He suffered the insult and understood the point being made.

Spain had gambled that Great Britain would not react because they could not afford a war with Spain while they were having problems with their North American colonies. Spain notified the British government that any interference could be considered a reason to declare war: as Spain cleverly put it, the action at Lisbon was an attempt to curtail some illegal merchants and correct some Portuguese affronts. Spain asserted that neither of these motives had anything to do with Great Britain, while postulating that Great Britain would not risk war over Portugal.[2] And the gambit worked. The British did nothing. As history progressed toward the independence of the thirteen British colonies, Spain's neutralization of Portugal would be an important, if unheralded, achievement toward that end.

In 1776, Grimaldi also negotiated a new commercial arrangement with France, wherein France could trade in all of Spain's ports as well as assign French ministers in some of the ports. This policy acknowledged that France and Spain stood together in opposition to Great Britain. It also brought the Bourbon allies closer, helped to curb contraband trade, and muddied the waters for British spies.[3]

Roughly a month before Franklin arrived in Paris, Grimaldi had been notified that he was being replaced in his position and transferred to Rome. Meanwhile, he agreed to remain in place until his replacement, the Count of Floridablanca, who at that time was in Italy, could return to Spain and assume the position.

While Aranda's missives of January 1777, discussed in detail in the previous chapter, noted that France's preparatory plan did not mention Portugal, he committed the same omission in his first report to Grimaldi, in fact writing, "Let us not speak about Portugal" but "focus on England."[4] In the second report, however, Aranda changed his mind. He wanted to remind his king that Portugal had "unmindfully" expanded in Brazil "with usurpations from Spain." Still, the defeat of England outweighed France's objections to Spain's policies toward Portugal. He concluded with the observation that France's memorial did not mention Portugal, "but only England, whose downfall is of such importance."[5]

From Grimaldi's point of view, Spain would not act militarily until Cevallos's fleet had safely returned from South America. Nonetheless, Aranda could not be ignored. In accordance with Aranda's own request that Grimaldi share his reports with Spain's "wisest ministers," his proposals would be considered in appearance, if not in fact.[6] The ambassador's status dictated such treatment. If, as Grimaldi assuredly expected, he would answer his impetuous ambassador's missives with a message of caution, he nevertheless needed the support of his ministers.

King Carlos III had surrounded himself with men who had reached their positions through ability rather than lineage. Ambrosio de Fuentes y Villapando, Count of Ricla, and José de Gálvez were examples of that practice. Fifty-seven-year-old Ricla, Spain's secretary of war, had enjoyed a wide-ranging career that included an ambassadorship to Russia; more importantly, he had been the captain-general of Cuba, where he initiated military defense reforms that permeated Spanish America. A few months Ricla's senior, Gálvez had trained in law and had served as the king's visitor general in New Spain, where he had helped enact some of the Bourbon reforms, including the administrative reorganization of New Spain's northern frontier, then known as Las Provincias Internas. The previous year, Carlos III had also promoted Gálvez to the crucial position of minister of the Indies. Obviously, both Ricla and Gálvez were familiar with American affairs. So it was with good reason that Grimaldi tasked them to review and react to Aranda's reports.[7]

Any conflict involving American colonies and European nations would necessarily include naval forces. And when it came to a confrontation with Great Britain, the command of the high seas would be paramount. Grimaldi wisely called on Spain's secretary of the navy for an opinion. Pedro González de Castejón had spent his life in the navy. In a career that had spanned forty-one years, he had worked his way up from cabin boy to ship's captain to squadron commander. Finally, in 1776, he was appointed secretary of the navy. He would go on to become a strong ally of Grimaldi's replacement, Floridablanca, and a rival to Aranda.

The matter of finances also could not be overlooked. Wars were expensive. Fifty-eight-year-old Miguel Múzquiz y Goyeneche, Marquis of Villar de Ladrón, was one of Carlos III's most favored, if not his most trusted, ministers. He had been a government operative since he was seventeen years old, and after the riots in 1766, he was appointed secretary of state and finance, replacing Esquilache.[8] He relinquished his state duties to concentrate on the nation's finances, and his well-informed words mattered.

Carlos III was a well-read, enlightened man who had made a mistake that he would not repeat—he would not rush unprepared into war again. He had learned a painful lesson from the loss of the recently concluded Seven Years' War, in which he had gone to the aid of France.

The king and his ministers had a common distaste for Great Britain. They were simultaneously curious about and cheered by the colonial rebellion. Anything that weakened or caused problems for Great Britain pleased them. But they dealt with reality and had a healthy respect for the island country's martial prowess.

In addition, the ministers in Madrid had access to more information than did Aranda. Spain had two official observers in the rebelling colonies. Both men were known to the Continental Congress and were friends with many of the colonial leaders.[9] Information also arrived from New Orleans, where

Spanish officials actively received news of the rebellion.[10] As mentioned previously, in 1776, Charles Lee had corresponded with Luis de Unzaga, the Spanish governor of Louisiana. The American commander directly asked in writing if the king of Spain desired the town and harbor of Pensacola, then held by the British, and, if taken, would he "receive possession" from the Americans?[11] Governor Unzaga could not have been surprised, for he had already been arranging clandestine aid with Oliver Pollock, a colonial agent from Virginia.[12]

In London, Ambassador Masserano continued sending clear, matter-of-fact reports back to Madrid. One dated January 31, 1777, undoubtedly reached Grimaldi after the retiring minister had composed his reply to Aranda's January 13 reports. Significantly, Masserano relayed that his cautious informant had told him that British officials were aware of the aid that France and Spain were sending "to the colonists to help sustain the independence," and that Dr. Franklin and the American commissioners had met "with Counts Aranda and Lacy." If nothing else, this reference to the second meeting demonstrates how rapidly news travelled between Paris and London.

Masserano pled ignorance about the information while assuring his informant that his king sought to "conserve peace with England, if that Potency does not attack" or attempt "to make new establishments" in Spain's territories.[13] Masserano's reply about new establishments was an implicit reference to Cevallos's expedition to South America. The astute report by Masserano foresaw the reply that Grimaldi had prepared for Aranda.

Aranda's reports provided a new and official perspective from the rebelling colonies. Unbeknownst to Franklin and his colleagues, they had opened a new avenue of discussion within Spanish officialdom, as the Count of Ricla, José de Gálvez, and the other ministers proceeded to fulfill their duties in detail. By the first week of February 1777, they, as well as Grimaldi, had written out their reactions to Aranda's proposals.[14]

The five men unanimously disagreed with Aranda's desire to enter into a treaty with the colonies. Spain should not be seen as an aggressor, and, moreover, the time was not yet right to go to war. Ricla caustically noted that Spain should not consider a treaty until the rebels started winning some battles.[15] Grimaldi postulated that although there had been a lack of colonial victories, he nevertheless expressed confidence that the final outcome was far from determined.[16] Gálvez observed that time was on Spain's side, and the opportunity to declare war would remain available in the future.[17] Múzquiz concurred and noted that Spain should be careful not to give Great Britain cause to declare war.[18] González de Castejón penned the longest report, which essentially detailed the tribulations that going to war in what he considered haste would precipitate. The complicated entanglements of the various European possessions in America, plus the balance of powers in Europe, must be considered with extreme caution. And he, like the others, wrote that time was needed to prepare Spain's forces. In the process, he could not help but indirectly mock "our ambassador in Paris," without naming him, as a man who should know better from his own experience, but advised for the moment, "*ocurrencias del día.*"[19] Thus, the officials agreed that the opportunity to strike remained in the future, and in the meantime, Spain should support the rebellion with covert aid.

With the opinions of Spain's ministers a matter of record, the king signaled his approval of a reply to Aranda. Grimaldi could write in full confidence, and perhaps anticipation, as he expected his replacement to arrive from Italy at any time. Surely, he must have thought, this letter would be his last official act as secretary of state.

Just two days after his fellow ministers had written their "dictums," and three weeks and a day after Aranda had written his two letters, Grimaldi sat down, quill in hand, and composed an eleven-and-a-half-page draft of the letter that he would send to Aranda.[20] In language disjointed but clear, if not slightly condescending, he wrote a complete refutation of his impetuous ambassador's audacious letters. He had the draft copied and dated on the same day: the only major change was in the introductory paragraph.[21] Unlike the draft, which had immediately brought up the question of the king's opinion about going to war with Great Britain, the official letter referred to Grimaldi's earlier letter (sent on January 27), which relayed the king's stance with regard to the position of Spain and France toward England. He then noted that this current missive was meant to keep Aranda abreast "as to how to effectively help the colonies with precise dissimilation" and leave for another day Aranda's major points contained in his letters of January 13.

Grimaldi addressed Aranda's overriding argument at the beginning. Spain would neither declare war on Great Britain nor enter into a treaty with the colonies. Moreover, to do one would result in the other. Then followed his justifications.

In consideration of Europe's neutral nations, Spain preferred that England be the aggressor. Spain and France could wait, continue to covertly aid the colonies, and strengthen and deploy their own forces, while Great Britain "continues making enormous expenses" incurred from dealing with its rebellious colonies. As such, Spain must strive for a "just and offensive war" against the "common and natural enemy of the House of Bourbon."

Grimaldi effectively spelled out Spain's policy regarding the opportunity presented by the rebellion of the English colonies. He supported that policy with a bit of reality as well as with a hint of what the strategy would be if and when Spain and France entered the war.

He noted that the colonies were not a country and therefore could offer very little with a treaty. Moreover, Spain had its own vast colonial empire to maintain, and no matter what strategy it followed regarding the rebelling colonies, over time "the issue of independence would ... be replaced by common business considerations and cultural ties." In other words, Spanish officialdom had no illusions that Spain's assistance would not result in a new loyal trading partner and friend.

It is "one thing to prepare for an immediate war ... and another to enter when we are ready." Here, the secretary of state noted that time allowed for not only strengthening Spanish forces but also deploying them. On the one hand, if Spain and France entered the war, they would have to keep a "large part" of their naval forces in Europe and "thus distract" the British "from the colonies." In an expression of the moment and possibly to make a point, Grimaldi instructed Aranda to ask Vergennes if the French had sent a fleet to the West Indies to unite with twelve Spanish ships of the line to deter any British intent in that region.

Grimaldi closed by writing that the government could reconsider its position if circumstances changed. Of course, Spain's policy would adapt to the situation as it developed. Aranda should assure the colonial commissioners that His Most Catholic Majesty had ordered aid for them and wished them well in their endeavor. Finally, Grimaldi wrote with a sense of irony, "I conclude by assuring you that the King has seen with appreciation all your observations."[22]

Grimaldi laid out Spain's policy. It included France, as both countries made up "the House of Bourbon." There seemed little doubt that war was imminent. It was just a matter of exactly when it would commence. Grimaldi loosely forecast the strategy that would be used when war came. Confrontations would occur in Europe as well as in the Americas. When the Bourbon allies acted, the North American rebellion would become a world war. Until then, Spain, with France's cooperation, would nibble at the heels of the wounded British leopard. The maxim of *divide et empera* would take effect.

Neither Franklin nor any of the Americans in Paris had knowledge of the effects caused by Aranda's letters and their meetings with him. Only silence greeted them. It seemed that both Spain and France had given them a knowing acknowledgement followed by ... nothing.

And so they waited. Grimaldi's reply to Aranda had undoubtedly been sent to Paris by rapid mail, which, based on the time it had taken Aranda's missives to reach Madrid, would take more than two weeks to arrive. At the earliest, Aranda would have received Grimaldi's letter around February 23 or 24. At least until then, he could not convey any of its contents to the American contingent.[23]

The contingent had become impatient and decided to act before Aranda received Grimaldi's letter. Contrary to what they had verbally agreed to with Aranda, the commissioners decided to send Arthur Lee to Madrid. They would be proactive and press Spain for recognition. Inexplicably, Aranda acquiesced to their plan and gave them what they considered to be a passport and a letter of introduction for Lee. Perhaps Aranda decided to help them because they had particular proposals meant only for Spain. Thus, with passport in hand, Lee departed on his overland journey on February 7, at least a week before Aranda would receive Grimaldi's letter.[24]

The French and Spanish officials in both Paris and Madrid immediately reacted to Lee's departure. Vergennes warned his ambassador in Madrid of the pending arrival of Lee, including the detail of Aranda's letter.[25] Grimaldi did not mince words. In reply to the two additional letters that Aranda had sent to justify his decision to encourage Lee's trip, Grimaldi wrote a short and very curt reply dated February 13. The news of Lee's trip and Aranda's role in encouraging it had displeased the king. Why? "Because, above all it is not necessary," and it ran contrary to the cooperation between Spain and France, which were working in unison "with the three deputies there [in Paris]." Lee's appearance in Madrid would be "be a grave inconvenience to the King" and would cause problems with the English ambassador in Madrid, resulting in "a big embarrassment" for Spain "as well as an annoyance and exasperation to the colonies."[26] Apparently, Aranda's enthusiasm for the colonial cause had led him to make a faulty decision that his superiors did not appreciate.[27]

Left unsaid is the role that Franklin played in the decision to send Lee to Madrid. As the senior member of the delegation, he was universally thought to be its leader. Aranda considered him as such, and the French had no doubt about the matter. Franklin surely knew that Spain had wanted to protect its appearance of neutrality. As such, he seriously miscalculated Spain's reaction. Then again, like many things in Franklin's life, this miscalculation paid unexpected dividends.

Coincidentally, Diego de Gardoqui, an important banker and merchant from northern Spain, had been called to Madrid. His international firm, Gardoqui e hijos, had been founded by his father and had been trading with

An Unofficial Alliance 51

Figure 8. Diego María de Gradoqui, Spanish banker, strategist, and diplomat who arranged for aid for the rebellious colonies and later became the first Spanish ambassador appointed to the United States of America; oil on canvas, artist unknown. (Courtesy of the New Mexico History Museum, Department of Cultural Affairs. ID 11844.45)

New England for decades, including some business dealings with Franklin a few years earlier.[28] The firm was based in Gardoqui's hometown, the port of Bilbao on Spain's northern coast. Gardoqui spoke English and was very familiar with the rebelling colonies. He had done business with many American merchants, especially in New England. With France's knowledge, and apparently because of the lack of recognition Spain had received for the aid delivered by the *Amphitrite,* Spain had decided to covertly supply the colonies on its own, and Gardoqui's company was to oversee the transactions. Most likely, Gardoqui had been called to Madrid to discuss the particulars of his company's role in the new policy.[29]

Grimaldi wasted no time in dispatching Gardoqui to Burgos to intercept Lee. At all costs, the American should be prevented from getting to Madrid. Grimaldi himself would follow Gardoqui to join in a meeting that would be held in secret. Three days after Grimaldi's scolding letter to Aranda, Gardoqui sent a letter in broken English requesting that Lee wait for him and Grimaldi in Burgos, a town in northwestern Spain that was far from Madrid.[30]

Lee agreed to the meeting and for three days, March 3–5, 1777, the three men convened in secret in the town where El Cid is buried. Grimaldi and Gardoqui shared Spain's position in detail with Lee. They revealed that

Gardoqui's company had been assigned to oversee the shipments of armaments and supplies to the colonies. The first of these was being arranged with a 170,000 *livres* line of credit, and this did not include the stockpiled supplies in Havana and New Orleans that were awaiting pickup. In addition, Bernardo de Gálvez in New Orleans had two thousand barrels of gunpowder, lead, and clothing waiting to be delivered to colonial representatives. Lee learned that Spain's northern port of Bilbao would be open to colonial ships. Again, Gardoqui would oversee the particulars, since American prizes, as well as legitimate cargoes of specified goods, would be used as payments for Spanish aid. At that moment, the company was collecting more supplies to aid the rebellion.

While still with Gardoqui in the small town of Victoria Gastiez, which lay northwest of Burgos on the road back to France, Lee could not contain himself. In correspondence gushing with satisfaction, Lee bypassed Franklin and Deane, both of whom he suspected of duplicity, and reported directly to the congressional Committee of Secret Correspondence. He wrote: "I am authorized to assure you that supplies for army will be sent by every opportunity from Bilbao. I can say with certainty, that a merchant there has orders for that purpose. He is now here with me. . . . I am also desired to inform you of ammunition and clothing being deposited at New Orleans and Havana, with directions to lend them to such American vessels as may call there for that purpose."[31]

The naturally suspicious Lee wrote that Spain could not enter into a treaty or otherwise officially recognize the colonies "for very powerful reasons."[32] Moreover, Lee was able to convey the news that Spain, through Aranda, would intercede with Holland on behalf of the Americans about extending credit for their cause. This was important news indeed. Rather than approaching the Dutch directly, the Americans could let Spain do it for them. This in itself necessitated another meeting with Aranda.[33]

Lee's return to Paris during the first week of April coincided with the receipt of new instructions from Congress. His news and the ensuing instructions had resulted in renewed activity, some of which was puzzling. Obviously, the delegation wanted to hear from Aranda about Holland, and Deane took the lead.

Aranda agreed to meet with the American commissioners on Saturday evening, April 5, again "after night fall." Lee began the conversation with a long description of his recently completed trip, and he iterated what he expected from Spain. As Franklin sat by quietly, Lee continued to make veiled threats that if Spain and France did not help, the colonies might be left with no choice but to sue for an early peace.

In response to Lee's request that Aranda help with Holland, Aranda replied that in his report from Grimaldi's replacement, don José Moniño y Redondo, Count of Floridablanca, which had recently arrived, no mention had been made of Holland. Lee expressed disappointment, displaying his exasperation. Aranda, however, assured Lee that if the information had indeed come from Grimaldi, then he could be assured that it was accurate. If Aranda's report of this meeting is accurate, until this point Franklin had said nothing.[34]

After Lee finished, Franklin brought out a sheaf of documents, explaining that he had received new congressional instructions that spelled out what France and, incidentally, Spain, could expect if they entered into an alliance with the rebelling colonies. Conversely, the instructions also detailed some of what the colonies expected. He promised to have copies delivered to the Spanish ambassador.

Franklin took charge of rewriting the instructions, and here he made his second miscalculation by deciding to write two drafts, one each for France and for Spain. Then he decided to deliver the French version to Vergennes a week before he delivered the Spanish draft to Aranda. He should have anticipated that Vergennes would share his draft with Aranda.[35]

France and Spain had more in common than not; thus, it made sense for Congress and Franklin to demonstrate a degree of sensitivity to each potential ally. First, Franklin wrote that Congress understood that to deal with one or the other country meant they were dealing with both and that "for the sake of humanity" they "would not for the Advantage of America only, desire to kindle a War in Europe," the devastation of which could not be foreseen. In these telling sentences, Congress expressed a willingness to tie its goal of independence to the goals of Spain and France.

In the version received by Vergennes, the Americans grandiosely agreed to ally themselves to France in an attempt to conquer "Canada, Nova Scotia, Newfoundland, St. Johns, the Floridas, the Bermuda Islands, the Bahamas, and the West India Islands, which were in Britain's possession." In the campaign to take the "Sugar Islands," Congress would provide 2 millions "of dollars" and six frigates of no fewer than twenty-four guns each. If Spain joined the war, the Americans would join in the conquest of Portugal. In addition, East and West Florida, along with their cities and ports, most significantly Pensacola, would once again become a part of the Spanish Empire.

These conditions were almost laughable on their face. First, the Americans were in no position to offer help, militarily or otherwise. They had just asked for ships the previous month. Both Spain and France had extended credit to them, and, moreover, at that time the Americans had not won any significant victories on their own territory and were certainly not capable of joining alliances in quest of other territories. With Spain at its side, France had just suffered a major defeat to the British in the Seven Years' War. How could a motley group of rebelling British colonists offer a stronger alliance?

Then there was the question of Portugal. While at once demonstrating an understanding of the dynamics among Spain, Portugal, and Great Britain, the colonies exhibited a complete ignorance of the current actions of Spain's fleets in the Río de la Plata in South America and near Lisbon. Apparently, Congress, and Franklin even less so, still had no knowledge of Grimaldi's gambit to neutralize Portugal. In short, Spain did not need colonial support with regard to Portugal.

The differences in the two letters were at once obvious and problematic. That France would use its influence to impede or prevent the transportation of foreign troops into the colonies was a direct reference to Great Britain's use of the Prussian mercenaries that the Americans called Hessians, a name derived from their general place of origin. This was a legitimate request, in that France was better positioned to use its diplomatic influence to slow down or possibly stop the movement of those soldiers. Franklin also noted that the Americans pledged not to approach another government without first consulting with France nor, he added, would Congress do anything to negotiate a peace "without consulting His Majesties Ministers." Surely, Franklin did not want Aranda to see those last two statements. Most assuredly, he misplayed his hand with these letters, for both the French original and its English counterpart ended up in Spain's national archives, a sure sign that, whether or not Franklin believed it to be the case, Spain and France, or at least Vergennes and Aranda, had indeed cooperated with one another.[36]

Franklin signed off on the Spanish letter because he wanted to personally inform Aranda of Congress's official position and to deliver a separate document that appointed him the "Minister Plenipotentiary to the Court of Spain." This is most likely why Franklin thought it best to present separate letters. At the very least, the announcement had to have caught Aranda's attention. Franklin could not represent a country that, in the ambassador's mind, did not exist. Before reading the letter, Aranda replied to Franklin, saying that he "could do no less than persuade him not to carry out this commission at present, since the same reasons that had detained" Lee also applied now. Then he listed three reasons for this policy. First, Spain had to proceed with caution while it remained at peace with England. Second, in reference to the fleet sent to South America to deal with the Portuguese, he stated that "Spain had had a huge deployment of forces committed to her possessions in South America," the success of which needed to be realized. Third, and above all, Spain had "first to prepare."

Franklin bowed and acquiesced to Aranda, stating that he could give Aranda his letter and an official congressional document. At least Aranda had no doubt about Franklin's authority. Aranda quickly returned the official document, insisting that a copy be sent with the letter. He instructed the three Americans not to frequent his home, even in "the dark of night." He insisted "that they make clear . . . their wishes in writing" and said that he would respond in the same way. Again, Franklin agreed, and he sent a copy of the document, along with the letter, in a sealed packet the following evening.[37]

Fortunately, Franklin foresaw Aranda's position, for his letter noted that he understood that his official presence in Madrid "is not at present thought convenient." Neither he nor Congress would do anything to "incommode" a country "they so much respect[ed]." Therefore, he would remain in Paris unless otherwise directed. Or, as he wrote, "I shall therefore postpone that Journey till circumstance may make it more suitable."[38]

The official document that Aranda reluctantly received was large, stamped with a red wax seal, and signed by Congress's president, John Hancock, with his usual oversized signature. In it, Congress named Franklin "our Commissioner," giving him "full power to communicate, treat, and conclude with His Most Catholic Majesty the King of Spain . . . and also to enter into and agree upon a treaty . . . for such purpose for assistance in carrying on the present war between Great Britain and these united states."[39] It went on to say that Franklin would continue "to be possessed of all the powers heretofore given him as commissioner to the Court of France . . . so long as he shall remain and be present in said court." The words "minister plenipotentiary" did not appear in the document.[40] Franklin used those words in his accompanying letter to Aranda.[41] The French document had two changes, the most of important of which named Franklin as a commissioner to France, making no mention of Spain.[42]

The appointment to Spain raised some questions. Why would Congress want Franklin in Madrid and not in Paris, where he was immensely popular? He was deemed the senior member of a diplomatic commission in a country that Congress's Committee of Secret Correspondence considered to be the most important of potential allies. On the face of it, moving him to Madrid did not make sense.

One possible answer to this conundrum might be attributed to Arthur Lee, who suspected both of his colleagues of being something less than patriotic. He came from a powerful family in Virginia and had been educated in Britain. He therefore enjoyed influence. Two of his brothers had signed the Declaration of Independence. At the time, Lee complained to his brothers about Silas Deane, whom he suspected of working with Beaumarchais to skim monies meant to pay for supplies. He had a prolonged dislike of Franklin that traced back to 1770 in Massachusetts. Some of the more radical Patriots suspected Franklin of being a closet Anglophile. Sam Adams had led a contingent in the Massachusetts House of Representatives that opposed Franklin's appointment as that colony's agent in London. Instead, they had backed Arthur Lee. Franklin had won the vote, while Lee was selected as an alternate.

Lee could not contain his jealousy. He despised Franklin's politics and resented his appointment. From 1770 on, he undertook a one-man campaign to discredit Franklin and undermine his influence. His letters found positive acceptance from readers like Sam Adams and John Adams in Massachusetts, as well as from Lee's brothers and friends in Virginia. One of Sam Adams's cohorts in the Sons of Liberty was John Hancock.

Lee sidestepped open accusations; rather, he insinuated slights and wrongdoings. In his mind, Franklin had colluded with the British and was too cozy with the French. His jealousy of the elder man's popularity in London carried over to Paris. Lee considered himself to be a rival to Franklin as America's chief spokesman. Moreover, he felt that he was the only true Patriot among the three men. He believed that Franklin was too complacent about Deane's intrigues. His ultimate desire was to have both Deane and Franklin removed from Paris, leaving him to be the colonies' sole major representative. He eventually succeeded in having Deane recalled to appear before Congress.[43] It is entirely possible that through his influence in Congress, he had conspired to arrange Franklin's appointment to Madrid.

Unfortunately for Lee, as he had just discovered during his own foray into Spain, Madrid would not accept *any* American representative. Franklin clearly knew this, and he parried the plan by graciously writing and telling Aranda that Congress would respect Spain's desire.[44] Moreover, Congress fudged on the appointment by simultaneously appointing Franklin to France and instructing him to remain in France, if, as they probably had surmised, Spain would prefer that he stay in Paris.

After almost four full winter months in Paris, the American Commission had accomplished a great deal: they made initial contact with two potentially major allies, secured critical aid from both countries, and gained access to a key port in northern Spain. The commission, however, had also created some controversy. Lee's trip to Spain had not been appreciated by either that country or France. The constant violations by American privateers entering French ports, which had occurred with Franklin's tacit approval, caused diplomatic problems and compromised France's neutrality.

Lee's paranoia had begun to cause friction within the commission, and that must have been obvious to Aranda, who preferred Franklin over Lee. The latter's suspicion of Deane and, with just cause, Beaumarchais, would result in Deane's recall, thus creating congressional factions.

The French government shared Lee's opinion of Beaumarchais, and Aranda was aware of it. Thus, while Lee was talking to Aranda and Franklin was presenting his diplomatic credentials, Beaumarchais made a plea, which he claimed was on behalf of Vergennes and Jean Frédéric Phélypeaux, Count of Maurepas, advisor to King Louis XVI. Spain should send its aid through him. He knew all about the recent exchanges between the commission and Aranda, for, as Aranda reported, "as a well-spoken person he has gained the favor of the deputies and has become intimate with them."[45]

Aranda listened to Beaumarchais's arguments and refused to make any commitment, neither "white nor black." He immediately reported Beaumarchais's actions to both Vergennes and Floridablanca. Vergennes reminded Aranda that Franklin and Deane had been warned to avoid Beaumarchais when they first arrived in Paris.

Moreover, in the same report to Floridablanca, the Spanish ambassador used the opportunity to plead his case, now reviving his suspicions of France. While the French ministers treated him well and with respect, he noted that France had its own agenda, and he would not broach the idea of interfering with it. He finished his letter by stating that as Spain's ambassador, he had given his honest observations and could appreciate that they were not being accepted. Nevertheless, he was fulfilling his obligation in the service of his king.[46]

As he had done after his first meetings with the American Commission, he sent two reports to Madrid after the April 5, 1777, meeting. The first was an account of the meeting and the second a report on Beaumarchais. Both Aranda and Vergennes decided that it was best to avoid the commission for the time being. And each country would send aid to the colonies separately.

Despite their missteps and internal fighting, the American diplomats had been successful. Ideas had been exchanged, and each side had a good concept of the others' position and potential. Dutch aid was forthcoming,

Figure 9. José Moñino y Redondo, the Count of Floridablanca, Spain's patient minister of state who orchestrated Spain's participation in the war; oil on canvas, painting by Francisco Goya. (Bank of Spain Headquarters, Madrid)

and it would supplement the continuing aid being sent from Spain and France. Not the least of these successes was the news that both countries would be sending another subsidy, this time amounting to 3 million *livres*. Aranda noted that this additional support "should permit Congress to attend to its urgent matters."[47]

By virtue of his double appointment to France and Spain, Franklin emerged as the officially recognized leader of the American contingent. Aranda had tacitly always recognized this. Apparently frustrated by this slight, Lee continued to criticize both Deane and Franklin.

Importantly, all American exchanges between Spain and the colonies would be carried out with discretion and in Paris. They would deal directly with Aranda and through him, with Grimaldi's replacement, the Count of Floridablanca.

Floridablanca had risen to his position at the relatively young age of forty-nine. He came from a middle-class background and had worked as a lawyer. His unyielding loyalty to his king and his opposition to the Jesuits and the Office of the Inquisition had advanced his legal career and attracted the king's attention.

Franklin and his colleagues would have to deal with this man for the rest of the war. Floridablanca was a studious and rational man. He had a clear-minded view of a very turbulent period. He listened and considered all proposals. On occasion, he even repeated them so that the proponent would know that he had been heard. Invariably, the choice was in keeping with a policy of patience and reason. Like his ambassador in Paris, however, he could also throw a fake temper tantrum when it suited his purposes.

Floridablanca would continue the policy that had been initiated by Grimaldi. Spain would take its time to strengthen itself while secretly aiding the Americans. Because in his two letters Franklin had made the veiled threat that an early accommodation might be struck, Floridablanca perhaps believed that diplomacy presented a very real possibility of accomplishing the goals of all of the parties—including independence for the rebelling colonies.[48] On October 7, 1777, the American commissioners were able to inform Congress that the Gardoqui firm in Bilbao had dispatched to the colonies "several cargoes of naval store, cordage, sailcloth, anchors and etcetera" consigned to Elbridge Gerry.[49]

 5

An Interlude of Hope and Persistence

Partially because of Maj. Gen. John Burgoyne's overconfident posturing, British officialdom accepted and approved a plan that was supposed to defeat their American insurgents—the gregarious Burgoyne's "Thoughts for Conducting the War from the Side of Canada." Moreover, he had been entrusted with a major portion of the strategy and been given a command. Such was his confidence that he made a point of wagering that he would be home victorious by Christmas 1777. His bet, placed in the book of the ultrafashionable Brook's Club in London, read, "John Burgoyne wagers Charles [James] Fox one pony [fifty guineas]."[1]

On the face of it, Burgoyne's plan appeared sound. With a huge force, he would sweep south down Lake Champlain out of Canada and take Fort Ticonderoga, after which he would continue his drive down the Hudson River to Albany, New York. There he would be joined and reinforced by another contingent moving down the Mohawk River from Oswego on Lake Ontario. The united forces would then be part of a pincer movement that would meet with a command led by Sir William Howe that was moving up the Hudson River from New York harbor. The result would be either to end armed resistance or to cut off New England from the rest of the colonies, a move that would spell doom for the rebellion.

The interceding months between the American diplomatic commission's first meetings and the eventual outcome of Burgoyne's gambit would be a difficult period for the commission. Both Spain and France thought it best to keep their distance from the Americans. The two countries sensed that war was inevitable, but they wanted to avoid being surprised by Great Britain or being drawn into the conflict at an inopportune time.

As early as the end of 1776, Vergennes and his ambassador in Madrid cooperated with their counterparts in Spain to assess the condition and combined strengths of their respective navies and armies. Floridablanca emphasized that his king felt it necessary to take great care at a time that he considered to be so uncertain; and, moreover, he did not know how the English Parliament would react.[2] The French understood that Spain would not commit to war until the return of its fleets from South America and Mexico, and they concluded that neither country would be sufficiently prepared for war until 1778.[3]

Nonetheless, both countries maintained their support for the colonies. Spain continued sending supplies, armaments, and money through Havana and Bilbao as well as laundering aid through France. As Franklin and his colleagues anxiously waited, Spain was making good on its promise to secure aid from the Dutch. Floridablanca wrote to Aranda that the Americans could expect fifty thousand *livres* from that quarter.[4]

The commissioners could not help but be disheartened by the lack of good news from home. While their initial contact with Spain and France had been successful in arranging for much-needed aid, they still had not won an alliance with any country, much less with France or Spain. The commission also struggled internally. Lee was doing his best to sow dissent within the ranks. He detested both of his colleagues, accusing Deane of corruption and Franklin of incompetence.[5]

Not everything was kept secret. In fact, quite the opposite was true. Spies were everywhere. The British became openly suspicious of the French, while Spain appeared to escape their notice. One obvious reason for this could certainly be attributed to the public presence of the American Commission in Paris. They, and especially Franklin, naturally attracted the attention of the British.

Franklin openly acknowledged the prevalence of spies and assumed that they knew everything that he did. Rather than succumbing to paranoia, he felt that he could use the situation to his advantage. Upon receiving a warning from a patriotic woman living in France, he replied:

> I have long observed one rule which prevents me any inconveniences from such practices. It is simply this: to be concerned in no affairs that I should blush to have made public, and do nothing but what spies may see and welcome when a man's actions are just and honorable, the more they are known, the more his reputation is increased and established. If I was sure, therefore, that my *valet de place* was a spy, as he probably is, I think I should probably not discharge him for that, if in other respects I liked him.

"Truth," he added elsewhere, "is my only cunning."[6]

Moreover, double agent Edward Bancroft's greed knew no bounds; not only was he disloyal to Franklin, but he also extended this disloyalty to his employers in England by speculating on the advanced information he had received.[7] Nevertheless, London received its money's worth when it came to Franklin and the American Commission. As early as the beginning of April 1777, Lord Stormont sent a missive to Vergennes in which he cautioned the French minister not to listen to the Americans. "Above all," he warned, "Misters Deane and Franklin [must] be restrained in these measures."[8]

Aranda had his own sources, one of whom he called a man of greatest confidence. This person gave Aranda a paper written by Franklin that was intended for Vergennes. Aranda proceeded to share its contents with Vergennes and then refused to let Vergennes have a copy because the letter had been written in French and Aranda was sure that the French minister would be receiving his copy directly through normal channels. This, indeed, came to pass.[9]

True to Franklin's words about dealing with spies, the paper contained nothing controversial, nor did it seem to be of much interest. Franklin wrote that France's policy of not getting more involved with the colonies was based on two false assumptions: that England would not weaken itself and that the war would last a long time. Because of this, an early peace would give England an opportunity to turn on France. The only way to avoid this was by "drawing up" an alliance with the colonies rather than "remaining idle spectators of the quarrel and even denying a verbal acknowledgement of their independence."[10]

This same information had been conveyed to Aranda, who reported everything to Floridablanca. On June 3, Spain's minister of state sent Aranda a rather livid reply, in which he complained about the ingratitude of the Americans and, by the way, also of France. Spain, he noted, had been sending aid to the rebels for the past two or three years. Moreover, a goodly portion of the money was being used to purchase supplies in France and then have them shipped to America. Aid had been sent from Bilbao and, now, from Holland. This presented clear evidence of "our support" that "neither Congress nor its deputies" could mistake. While he agreed with Aranda's policy that the Americans should explain themselves in writing rather than in person, Floridablanca was perplexed by the Americans' lack of gratitude, or even acknowledgement, and complained that "even the very court of France" acted as if it were "in ignorance." Floridablanca instructed Aranda to make his position clear to the American commissioners.[11]

Apparently upon hearing from Aranda, Franklin quickly reacted by making a personal visit to the ambassador's residence, after dark, as per his instructions. He thanked the ambassador for Spain's aid, not only in money but also in supplies and equipment. He added his appreciation for the aid being sent through Bilbao. In reply to an inquiry from Aranda, Franklin unequivocally answered that there was no disunity in Congress and that the Continental Army was "well provided with arms and munitions." He added that a ship had arrived in Boston with twelve thousand muskets, and he knew of the arrival of other ships in different ports.[12]

In July 1777, Franklin had another letter delivered to Aranda, this time a copy sent by the normal channels. Franklin repeated the threat that England might sue for peace and declare war on France because of the secret aid it had given to the Americans. He implied that as France's ally, Spain would be drawn into the conflict, and he reiterated that by attaining peace in North America, British forces would be free to attack Spanish and French possessions. He concluded that there had never been a better opportunity to successfully surprise and attack the British forces, exclaiming, "Heaven has rarely offered such a favorable opportunity." He then offered the caveat that "nations are always skillful at imagining special pretexts for the wars they want to engage in."[13]

Franklin did not realize that Aranda agreed with him in full. The ambassador had written as much in his early missives to Grimaldi; however, while he had been very open, possibly even audacious, in expressing his opinions internally, he had been very careful not to share them externally. Aranda worried that the colonies would draw France into the war for various reasons, not least of which was the American corsairs' open violation of French neutrality and laws.[14] At the same time, Masserano, in London, was reporting that the French had replied to English complaints by countering with a complaint about the violent procedures practiced by British warships on French merchantmen, claiming that the British had boarded and abused the French crews.[15]

Through his own sources, Aranda knew that England was pressuring France to stop harboring American ships. He felt that this would be hard to do because, at the least, "the merchants of this realm are so caught up with them because of the immense profits that come to them."[16]

Nonetheless, Aranda's position had not weakened, and now he was inspired to write a new diatribe. Fearing that France had been compromised and could easily be drawn into the war, Aranda penned a twenty-page letter to Floridablanca in which he went into detail about the "crises that could not end well" for France. He included both of Franklin's letters, noting that Franklin did not know that he had one of them.[17]

He volunteered the information that Vergennes had revealed. France was transferring forces to Santo Domingo, Martinique, and Guadalupe, and it would soon have eleven thousand men stationed in the Caribbean. Meanwhile, a placard had been circulating in London with the sole intent of enticing the British government to do something about France's complacency regarding the American corsairs. Not even coal barges were safe. Aranda was "stunned to have observed that this court [France] recognizes the risks to which it is exposed." The only solution for one or the other country to "prevent the other's action" would be "by striking a consequential blow." In other words, Aranda felt war was eminent and whoever strikes the first blow would win.[18]

Otherwise, he parroted Franklin. Great Britain would sue for an early peace and turn on France. England, "so displeased with France ... will lend itself with pleasure ... against her great enemy that she had been reluctant to invest ... on those whom she considered her brethren and compatriots." England's "superior naval power" had given France pause. Meanwhile, the colonial rebellion served "to keep her current forces useful" and ready for any further "misfortune." He then appealed to Floridablanca, while pointing out that the rebellion had diverted England's attention. "If a rupture were to occur," now would be the time "to pounce on the wound when it is opening and from the start, radically destroy the enemy."

At this point, Aranda's letter became passionate: "So that to topple her, would be done in the first instance, and [the goal of] securing her final subjection would be managed solely by keeping our feet over her so that in her extreme distress she would mercifully [be] subject to the law that one would wish to apply to her." After noting that the combined forces of the Bourbon powers, along with the Americans, would "sweep" the British forces "away as though with a broom," he continued with a telling statement: "If the English naval forces were swept from America, those on land would be left cut off from all support."[19] Aranda in fact foretold the strategy that would result in the defeat of the British land forces at Yorktown.

Almost pleading, Aranda postulated that if nothing were done, France would "pay the consequences of leaving her greatest enemy standing." And Spain would have to come to its aid. Spain could not help but foresee this predicament.

Then he audaciously used the 1770 confrontation over the Malvinas Islands, known as the Falklands in the English-speaking world, to prove his point. He stated that England had tested the resolve of both France and Spain, knowing that neither government would stand up to the affront. He hoped that Spain would not repeat that embarrassment.

Aranda ended his impassioned letter by noting that he thought the second of Franklin's letters that he included in the mailing "seems to have been prompted by this Ministry [Vergennes] in order to keep him [Franklin] busy."[20]

The intent and even the tone of his letter were consistent with his earlier reports. In addition, his point of view coincided in spirit with Franklin's arguments. With Lee sent off to Vienna, Franklin and Deane were left with the impossible task of convincing France and then Spain to more openly aid the rebellion when they lacked any positive news to support their positions. For most of 1777, the commissioners anxiously waited, and perhaps feared, what news they would hear about the military actions of Burgoyne and Howe.[21]

France and Spain waited to hear the outcome of the British campaigns as well.[22] In fact, and perhaps incorrectly, Floridablanca sent a letter dated one day after Aranda's long report. The two missives most likely passed each other in transit. Floridablanca's compilation consisted of ten pages that succinctly stated that Spain would not be engaged in complicated situations and that nothing had occurred to cause a change in that position.[23]

So, as the Americans could surmise, both Vergennes and Floridablanca had adopted a policy of wait and see. They would use the waiting time to strengthen their own forces. They hoped the rebellion would last and thus divert and possibly weaken Great Britain. This attitude certainly was true of Spain's minister of state. Vergennes, however, believed that his country was ready for war, and he hoped to make the first strike. Still, he wanted Spain's cooperation and waited for positive news from America. In July, he told Louis XVI that secret assistance was no longer enough. France must either withdraw or do more. The king would not budge without knowing that Spain would join them. Moreover, the news from America was anything but good. Burgoyne took Saratoga in July, and Howe was threatening Philadelphia.

Vergennes did not disagree with the arguments posed by Aranda and Franklin. France was exposed diplomatically for having received the colonial representatives. This in itself could give cause for war. As had been explained to the commissioners, official reception of diplomatic representatives was regarded as a formal recognition of the country that they represented.

Aranda's letter to Floridablanca was clear on this point. Also implicit in his letter was the fact that he had shared his thoughts with Vergennes. For example, he pointed out the problem with the American corsairs using French ports—and here he named them: Dunkirk, Saint Malo, Nantes, La Rochelle, and Bordeaux. This amounted to "an open traffic," where "war goods were being publicly loaded as much on French as on American ships."[24] While he considered this effort laudable, it had forced France into a corner. France could acquiesce to the demands of England and cut off the Americans, or it could give lip service to the British Crown and continue receiving the ships, thus risking war. Aranda concluded that the former surely would result in a British victory and an early peace in America, which meant Great Britain would turn on France. The latter option would mean a continuation of the rebellion, but it gave more than enough reason for the British to declare war at the moment of its choosing.[25] American privateers would remain a continuing problem for Franklin and his colleagues.[26]

So, while having the same outlook as that expressed in Aranda's and Franklin's arguments, Vergennes, like Floridablanca, would wait, but he would wait for a different reason, for he was hoping and waiting to hear positive news and thus be provided with the right opportunity to strike.[27]

At this time, Congress appointed Lee as its commissioner to Spain. As will be explained in chapter 7, this was part of a reorganization of its diplomatic corps in Europe. Lee could not have been surprised to hear Aranda tell him that he would not be welcomed in Madrid. Floridablanca agreed with Aranda, writing that Lee would not be accepted in Spain's capital nor allowed to conduct any business whatsoever, and that the king "would have to make him leave in order that His Majesty continue his protection to the Americans."[28]

Floridablanca and his ministers had a more cautious approach than Vergennes and Aranda. The Spanish minister knew that the Bourbon Compact diplomatically bound his country to France. He also realized that if the rebellion continued and showed any signs of success, the British government quite possibly would seek an early peace. With the threat of the two houses of Bourbon looming, he strongly felt that he could broker peace, thus avoiding war.[29] In the meantime, he would prepare for any eventuality, and this included the potential that France would either declare war or be drawn into it. In Paris, Aranda would have to accept his policy—a policy that Franklin wanted to change.

Franklin continued to concentrate on the priority. He convinced his fellow commissioners to overcome their differences enough to agree to and sign a memorial, which they had their French banker, Rodolphe-Ferdinand Grand, deliver to Vergennes and Aranda. The memorial was a serious attempt at rekindling the support that they felt had been reduced from the level it had been when they first arrived. They did not bother to have it translated into French or Spanish, so Aranda, not trusting anyone in Paris, passed it on to Madrid to be translated there.[30]

The somewhat rambling memorial brazenly requested more aid, including 80,000 suits of clothes, brass cannons, muskets, pistols, and a large quantity of naval stores. In exchange, Congress had purchased "great quantities of Tobacco, Rice, Indigo, Potash, and other produce of the country," which they would send as soon as they could overcome "the great difficulties of procuring ships, and marines for the merchant service, with convoys of force sufficient" to protect them. This was followed by a directive from Congress that the commissioners request a loan of "two millions sterling" at 6 percent interest on the credit of the United States. The end of the memorial contained an "Estimate & expenses" section that had probably been compiled by Grand. It detailed monies received, monies spent, and the estimated cost for additional supplies. Those supplies ran the gamut from the above-mentioned uniforms to blankets, ship repairs, saddles, anchors, and transportation of the supplies.[31]

The body of the memorial acknowledged that both Spain and France had given support but had ceased to answer any inquiries about additional aid. "Spain after furnishing us with 187,500 *livras* in money and some naval stores sent directly to her ports (the value not yet known to us) has desisted." Additionally, neither country had agreed to their proposals to sign treaties of commerce and alliance. They understood that there had been a problem "relating to our armed vessels and their prizes." Still, they believed that "these Kingdoms," Spain and France, would still side with "America," and they understood that the lack of recent support was due to "circumstances of the times" and the "occupation in other great affairs."

As a result, they felt emboldened to make this request for supplies as a loan and not a subsidy. If granted, the trade would benefit the economies of Spain and France and weaken Great Britain "in proportion." More importantly, Congress offered "these advantages, not as putting them to sale for a price, but as ties of the friendship they wished to cultivate with these Kingdoms."

If, however, an early peace had to be brokered, the commissioners made what had to be a surprising proposal. Would Spain and France agree to help the colonies with "their advice and influence in the negotiation, that their liberties with the freedom of commerce may be maintained"? This request was followed by assurances that the colonies were not involved in any talks "for an accommodation" with the court of England. Nor, they stressed, had there been even the smallest overture made by either side.

This proposal and the accompanying assurances directly focused on European concerns regarding Congress's loyalty to its potential allies. To emphasize the point, the memorial added that Congress would agree to terms already laid out, including that it would not enter into a treaty with any other country ("power") that could be considered inconsistent with the propositions made to Spain and France. Clearly, Congress's priority was the support of and alliances with the Bourbon courts.[32]

In a sense, the memorial attempted to reassure both European countries that the Americans would persist. On more than a few occasions, they noted that they expected victory. There was a feeling of American determination that, with or without the requested loan, the Americans would prevail.

Over a month later, in October 1777, Franklin would privately state the same viewpoint. In a conversation with what must have been a surprised Lee, Franklin began with a summary of his view of the revolution. According to Lee, he described it as "such a miracle in human affairs, against insurmountable odds." The colonists had started with nothing against the most powerful nation on earth. In apparent agreement with Lee, Franklin believed that "France and Spain mistook their interest and opportunity in not making an alliance with us now. . . . It is well for us to work out our own salvation." The revolution would succeed because Britain had overlooked the colonies' spirit and inherent determination.[33]

Historian Carl Van Doren summarized Franklin's romantic view of the revolution as mirroring a "grand style by which the humorous philosopher lived" and wrote that it embodied "a [colonial] force which the cynical British ministry could not learn to take into account."[34] Franklin's reality could not have been more evident when he received the horrible news that Howe's forces had occupied his hometown. Instead of bowing to the news that Howe had taken Philadelphia, he replied, "You mistake the matter. Instead of Howe taking Philadelphia, Philadelphia has taken Howe."[35] Whether or not his outlook was shaken, he would do nothing but show confidence about the eventual outcome of the colonial struggle.

The news of Philadelphia had come shortly on the heels of the news that Burgoyne had taken Saratoga. The American commissioners could not have known that Howe's presence in Philadelphia meant that he had not cooperated with Burgoyne in the planned pincer movement. Instead of going up the Hudson River to meet Burgoyne, he had gone south to occupy Philadelphia. There could not have been a bleaker time for Franklin and his fellow commissioners. But the memorial reflected the American "grand style" rather than any depression.

Aranda listened to Grand's verbal synopsis of the memorial, but it would be a few weeks before he would receive the exact gist of the document from

Madrid.³⁶ It would take at least that long before the American commissioners could expect to receive an answer. This would have been especially exasperating in light of the bad news coming out of America.

Meanwhile, Franklin heard that Diego de Gardoqui was asking for payment for shipments that had been sent to the colonies from northern Spain. Gardoqui apparently inquired about this of the commissioners, who, in turn, sent their banker, Grand, to defend them before Aranda. Aranda countered that the Americans should understand the various expenses Spain had assumed, not to mention the current "considerable amount that Spain was spending indirectly to the advantage of the Americans" with their armaments and other needs.

Grand and Aranda decided that the problem did not lie with the Americans or Gardoqui but with the middlemen assigned to carry out the exchanges. Without overtly stating that these French "friends" and "*fermieres*" (i.e., French tax collectors) had dishonestly absconded with the funds, they concluded that the Americans should choose a trustworthy merchant to deal directly with Gardoqui. For his part, Gardoqui needed to be clear on what he would accept.³⁷

Spain reacted to the written disposition that Franklin and his colleagues had presented to both Spain and France. In a long memorial sent to France, Spain clearly spelled out its position, concerns, and aspirations. As such, they deserve the full attention here that they undoubtedly received at the time.³⁸

Spain was not impressed with the American threats about what an early peace would bring about. Rather, that argument was turned on its head. How could the Bourbon kingdoms continue their support without a specific guarantee that the colonies would not secretly negotiate such a peace and leave them hanging? The first step to receive continued aid and obtain an eventual treaty had to be such a guarantee.

Moreover, aid had been sent and continued to be sent, and the new request for a loan of 2 million pounds sterling was reasonable. In the meantime, the colonies must realize that the best use of the alliances would be when France and Spain could combine their strength to make a difference. Specifically, this referred to their combined navies and to the return of Spain's two fleets from America, which, the report detailed, meant 113 completely armed ships in the port of Cádiz, including 20 ships of the line.

The document described ongoing Spanish aid. Beginning with the initial amount sent through the fictitious Roderique Hortalez company, it then pointedly mentioned the money sent to France to purchase arms and materials for shipment to the colonies. The report then cited various shipments

Figure 10. Louis XVI, King of France and Navarre, wearing his grand royal costume; oil on canvas, 1779, painting by Antione-François Callet. (Museum of the History of France, Paris)

from Bilbao, "the total of which we cannot easily put a value [on] because of the different modes and places from which it has been done." Nevertheless, the aid had been substantial and generous and one "can affirm its importance" (*se puede afirmar ser ya de mucha importancia*).[39]

Spain appreciated that France shared its concern because it instructed its ambassador in Madrid, the Marquis d'Ossun, to personally deliver France's hesitancies, and that His Most Christian Majesty, the king of France, did not want to make a final decision without consulting with the king of Spain, "his uncle." He obviously was aware that Spain had other considerations, including "its vast possessions in America."

Even the fact that neither the Americans nor, apparently, the French, understood the extent of aid Spain had been giving, thereby exposing itself to an early entry into war with Great Britain, had not stopped their support.

Spain had no doubt that the revolution continued to weaken Great Britain and that both France and Spain should continue their covert aid, thereby prolonging the rebellion to a time in which they would sufficiently be prepared to enter the conflict: "Time is necessary for the ultimate good."

Therefore, because of "this precise consequence the colonies should be sustained" with effective aid in money and the proper supplies for their actual war.

Continued aid would prolong the rebellion and solidify the reality of Spain and France entering the war, thus accomplishing their ultimate goal in one of two ways: the "Court in London" would realize the enormous expense that they would encounter in a futile effort, and they would thus negotiate a peace or face defeat in a heightened war. Therefore, Spain's interest was to work secretly and with caution, and King Carlos would not enter into an agreement that "is not based on Independence" for the "American Provinces."

The document concluded with six numbered points that repeated the emphases of the overall text, including, perhaps, Spain's biggest complaint—that the American deputies needed to stop their "noxious complaints" and conduct. They wanted Spain to enter the war before Spain had prepared for its own defense.[40]

This amazing document was meant for Vergennes and his king. Hopefully, the French would be able to work more closely with Spain in a spirit of cooperation, and each country could make their respective positions clear to the Americans.

Over a month later, Arthur Lee wrote a cover letter and arranged the delivery of another memorial from the American commissioners to both Vergennes and Aranda. Lee introduced the memorial by repeating its request for a quick treaty while expressing the "great veneration entertained by the United States for this of Spain [and] its people."[41]

The accompanying memorial noted that it had been a year since the delegation first broached the idea of a treaty and suggested that now was the time to form one. Then, to boost their argument, the American commissioners gave the excuse that because of the great secrecy in which they must work, the American people were unaware of "the friendly and essential aids that have been so generously but privately afforded us."[42]

Vergennes could not have been surprised at Spain's position, or that it anticipated the American request and underlying argument. Moreover, the American memorial dutifully recognized Spanish aid, thus in itself anticipating Spain's complaint that they were not being appreciated.

What the American diplomats apparently did not know was that Floridablanca had tired of Aranda's forthright attitude. In September, Floridablanca had informed Aranda that he was to cease talking to the American Commission. Floridablanca felt that Aranda could deal directly with his counterpart, Vergennes, and that the latter should be in charge of relations with the rebelling Americans. Thus relegated to a secondary role, Aranda was instructed only to keep the king and Floridablanca informed.[43] As will be seen, this was a policy that neither Floridablanca nor Aranda followed.

None of the diplomats had real-time information about what was happening in America. Distance affected the time news took to travel, and wartime hazards resulted in further delays. Under the most favorable circumstances, it could take between six weeks and two full months for information to cross the Atlantic Ocean. A major consideration was the state of belligerency and the potential capture of news-bearing ships by British men-of-war. As a result, approximately one-third of the correspondence failed to reach its destination.[44]

The American commissioners had no way of knowing that even as they compiled their request for more support and voiced their complaints that Spain had ceased in its support, Bernardo de Gálvez, the Spanish governor and captain-general of Louisiana, had sent a missive to the Congress. He informed them that he had a warehouse full of supplies and armaments waiting to be picked up.

Nor could the commissioners know that in that same month of October 1777, Congress had appointed an agent to oversee the exchanges in New Orleans.[45] They could not know that a few months later, Patrick Henry—or Patricio Enrique, as the Spanish called him—would be thanking Gálvez for his "friendly help" in supplying the Continental Army on various occasions.[46]

As the war progressed, George Washington felt obligated to profusely thank Spain for its "estimable care [and] cordial and affectionate friendship and support." He acknowledged the "friendship of His Majesty" and stated that he "only wanted to express the gratitude" for the help with which Spain had "honored him."[47]

No one in Europe would have been aware of the outcome of Burgoyne's march out of Canada when Francisco Escarano, Spain's ambassador in London, sent a letter to Floridablanca in which he described the joy of British officials upon hearing about Burgoyne's occupation of Saratoga. Escarano reported that the British felt victory was near.

In the same letter in which Escarano described the premature celebration, he noted a complaint about Franklin possibly traveling to Madrid. Lord Mansfield, Britain's chief justice of the King's Bench, told the Spanish ambassador that he could not believe that a man so astute would undertake such a journey "without the certainty of being very well received." Escarano ignored the diplomatic implication and replied that Franklin was "a man of wisdom, whose works grant such honor to the republic of letters, and whose reputation is so firmly set in that kingdom." A man like Franklin, he continued, should be welcomed anywhere.[48] Did the exchange remind Escarano of his fond memory of Franklin and the glass armonica?

Nothing seemed to be going well for the American Commission. Franklin could have become despondent. For all he knew, both Fort Ticonderoga and Philadelphia had been lost. Then he had to deal with the zealousness of the American privateers and with Lee's mechanisms, which had resulted in the recall of Deane (who did not receive notice until March 1778)—ostensibly to report to Congress on the progress of the commission, but in reality to answer to Lee's accusations.

Ironically, between the day Escarano wrote his letter to Madrid on October 3 and the day it arrived in Spain on November 7, Burgoyne had surrendered at Saratoga and been taken prisoner.[49] News of Burgoyne's ultimate defeat would not reach Europe until early December 1777.[50] Eventually, Burgoyne would be returned to London in disgrace in a prisoner exchange.

Thus, on a December's day, Franklin had reason to expect more bad news when a rider who worked for the commission rode into the courtyard at Passy calling for Franklin. What now? he must have thought. Then, as if to soften the blow, Franklin spoke first, turning his back on the man and asking with a look of foreknowledge if the rider had heard that Philadelphia had fallen. The answer came quickly: "Yes." But the messenger would not be deterred. "But, sir, I have greater news than that. General Burgoyne and his whole army are prisoners!"[51]

Franklin rejoiced for two reasons. This was a major colonial victory, and one that left Howe isolated in Philadelphia. Could this mean that overall victory was near? Only time would tell, and Franklin would not waste that precious commodity. Now was the moment for direct diplomacy.

 6

Saratoga and a Diplomatic Gambit

Burgoyne lost his bet to Charles Fox. Almost from the beginning, his plan went awry. A lack of coordination among British forces combined with misjudgment of his foe and a series of misguided decisions resulted in very slow progress south, where a series of conflicts depleted his army both physically and mentally. And Howe never moved north to meet him. Burgoyne found Ticonderoga abandoned by the Americans, and he claimed victory only to be defeated further south at Saratoga. His force of around 8,400 men had been reduced to 6,200 when he surrendered to Horatio Gates and Benedict Arnold at Saratoga in October 1777. He returned to London in disgrace.[1]

In London, Masserano and Escarano reported the progress of Burgoyne's invasion of the colonies as news reached them. Escarano noted the euphoria brought about by the news that Ticonderoga had been occupied, which was followed by the surprise, if not disgust or disbelief, at the news of its ultimate abandonment by the British army. Escarano even detailed Burgoyne's less than welcoming treatment upon his return to London.[2]

Subsequent historians of the revolution have written that the colonial victory at Saratoga was the turning point of the war. Not only was it the rebels' first major military victory, but it also provided legitimacy to the colonial cause. Historians have written that Burgoyne's defeat resulted in the release of the international aid that the patriots so desperately needed. What generally has been overlooked was that this aid was already being sent and that France and Spain were in the process of planning for war against Britain. True, more aid was needed, but, more importantly, here was an opportunity to achieve international recognition.[3]

The American commissioners were ecstatic at the news of Burgoyne's defeat. They also felt that the military success would help them in their efforts, as it provided a golden opportunity to leverage France and Spain for the recognition that they so desperately sought. As the commissioners' leader, and recognized as such by Vergennes and Aranda, Franklin would not waste any time.

Franklin quickly and calmly, if not joyously, compiled a news release that overstated the reality of the American victory, claiming that there were "9200 men killed or taken prisoner." More importantly, he added that General Howe was in Philadelphia, "where he is imprisoned" and "all communication with his fleet is cut off." While the whole release greatly exaggerated the events, it would play well in his upcoming diplomatic exchanges.[4]

He obviously felt that now he could operate from a position of strength, thereby manipulating the French public, and then the governments of France and Spain, to openly side with the rebelling colonies. He may have surmised that Aranda and the French, if not the more stoic Vergennes, already agreed with his position. Indeed, he was encouraged when Aranda told him that he believed "the moment had come" for Spain to act.[5]

The French had been preparing for this moment for over a year. They and the Spanish had believed all along that their countries would be ready for war after the New Year. The French already had a plan in place as early as July 1777, when Vergennes, through Louis XVI, asked Carlos III's advice regarding the decision to pursue war. France's policy of limited intervention had already very nearly led to war. At the time, Spain promised full aid if France were attacked. The tension between France and England had increased to almost uncontrollable levels.[6]

In *The French Navy and American Independence,* Jonathon Dull writes, "Diplomatically, Saratoga served not as a cause for France to abandon her neutrality, but as an excuse."[7] Although the American Commission tried to frighten Vergennes with the possibility of a quick Anglo-American peace, which would save Britain from the loss of its commerce with the Americans, such impetus was unnecessary. Franklin pretended to be interested in an early accommodation and openly met with British emissaries, while Vergennes, in turn, attempted to use the information to scare Floridablanca into supporting France's position of going to war. These ploys did not work.

Spain remained unconvinced that the colonies would or could negotiate an early peace. Rather, Spanish sources in London told them that Parliament was split, and the king was adamant against peace. London, they reported, wanted to "reduce the colonies and their leaders as they were before." Spain's officials correctly surmised that the colonies would accept nothing less than independence and that their British opponents were not ready to acquiesce on that point.[8]

Instead, given Spain's position of entering the war if it must, its leadership saw a renewed opportunity to use the threat of a prolonged war against the two houses of Bourbon to force a negotiated peace upon the British.

Two days before Christmas 1777, Floridablanca penned, as he put it, "the King's resolution." He asked Aranda to share it "with complete frankness" with the French ministers and, "with major circumspection," the American deputies. An important caveat was repeated twice: Spain would not consider entering war or signing a treaty until its fleets from the Americas had safely returned.[9]

He added, rather, that now was the time to gather information and be more secretive. The American delegation in Paris needed to forego writing memorials because the British knew everything that they were doing. The king of Spain did not want any surprises and understood that the colonies had their own interests in mind. As a result, His Majesty had sent commissioners to the colonies "to prepare other methods for frustrating their enemy militarily and diplomatically." Spain was positioned to "have the capability of reaching an agreement with the English" that would achieve the "absolute liberty that the colonies desire" (*absoluta libertad que pretenden las colonias*). The defeat of Burgoyne had presented an opportunity for Spain, through careful planning, to negotiate a suitable peace.

Floridablanca continued, "The King will maintain his Royal Dignity." He felt that he could best help the colonies by negotiating a peace treaty that would recognize colonial independence. The king would use the next three months to study and clearly understand "what England might desire." He would support the propositions as put forth by the American deputies.

"If the colonies want his help and protection in negotiations, the King will do all in his power to help." He understood the colonial position and believed it could be achieved without causing more war. Floridablanca and King Carlos had received a letter, supposedly sent by Franklin, that asked for money. Spain would help within its means but noted that it had sent the colonies "a good quantity" in the last month and much more during the previous six months. The Spanish government was secretly sending "no less than three million *reales*" via the ship *San Julian* and would send another 6 million on a separate ship.[10]

Spain's treasure fleet, as they called it, from Mexico was not expected until spring at the earliest, while the fleet from South America also had not yet returned. The ever-cautious Floridablanca again consulted with his ministers as he had done before.

Aranda sent a report that probably crossed paths in transit with Floridablanca's missive. He wrote that the British ministry felt that the colonies were ready for peace and that they had sent orders to General Howe to sound out the Congress. Meanwhile, the American delegation needed assurances. Congress needed to know "the fidelity" or indisposition of the Bourbon courts and whether England could send more forces off the American coast. This information was being sent on an American ship, on a French commercial ship, and on a more secure French royal frigate, the *Belle Poulle*. He added that Franklin's colleague, Silas Deane, would be returning to America aboard the same frigate.[11]

Then Aranda reported that Edward Bancroft—whom he described as a well-known scientist and trusted, prudent man, and of whom he said that none were more qualified to deal with England—had been sent to London to learn of the sentiments there. After six days, the spy returned to report that the colonies were weak and could not refuse to negotiate. Vergennes met with Aranda to share Bancroft's letter, which Aranda sent to Floridablanca along with his report. Like Franklin, neither Aranda nor Vergennes suspected Bancroft of being the double agent that he was.

Aranda closed his report by relaying Escarano's belief that the British ministry was tired of the conflict and that independence "is definite." Aranda concluded that England needed to reevaluate its position, secure what it could, and not lose the opportunity to consider the House of Bourbon.[12]

On January 13, 1778, Floridablanca drafted a series of points that he wanted Aranda to read and share with the king of France, noting that "the consequences" of the two kingdoms' cooperation could "be so beneficial or so fatal," after first noting that Spain still did not find itself "at the point of going to war."[13] He sent a separate letter dated the same day solely to Aranda, in which he unequivocally stated that Aranda should not let his "fiery" impatience cloud his judgment. Spain would not allow itself to be dragged into France's foibles, and Aranda should understand that Madrid had other sources of information, both in the colonies and in London. Floridablanca then went into detail, demonstrating how much he knew about the situation in America.

In a telling paragraph, the minister wrote that he understood that England would love to secure a quick peace, with the strict condition of a commercial monopoly with the colonies (*"bajo el pie de un comercio exclusivo"*), after which it, together with the colonial forces, would attack the possessions of Spain and France. However, he continued, the colonies would not agree to such an arrangement, for that would not be independence. Also, the colonies would be tired of war and would not trust Great Britain. None of Britain's claims would be possible once the colonies established their independence.[14]

The draft listed a number of points reiterating Spain's position. Those summaries could be grouped into general concerns, such as Spain's relationship and planning with France, Spain's relationship with the colonies, Great

Britain's current and potential situations with their ramifications, and the stability of the balance of power in Europe.

Spain would not rush into a decision with France without some clarity that included France's plans and goals. Together they should set out an effective plan that would achieve "a gratifying result." This meant that throughout the process, the two countries would maintain a mutual trust that cemented the "close friendship of the two courts." This strategy needed to consider many facets, not the least of which was the balance of powers in Europe. If Russia decided to take advantage of the situation and invade the Ottoman Empire, France could be drawn into that conflict and thus abandon its commitment to the war against England. This would leave Spain and the colonies to fight England without allies.[15] The Spanish ministers wanted assurances from France. The latter had abandoned Spain in the past while fighting the English—most notably at the Battle of Toulon in 1744. Unstated was a long-held belief and an underlying suspicion that France coveted trade with the Spanish colonies as much as England did.[16]

Spain's ministers placed a strong emphasis on trust and guarantees that no alliances would be broken. This also extended to the Americans. They wondered if France and Spain should negotiate a treaty that would be kept secret until a designated moment, when it would then be made public.

Above all, however, Spain wanted more clarity about colonial plans. As a matter of good policy, they would wait to hear from their recently appointed emissaries in the colonies.[17] Also, they inquired if the American representatives in Paris had sent requests for updated instructions, "as reported." They wanted to be careful while maintaining a robust relationship with the rebels. They would patiently collect information as long as they could be assured that the Americans would not betray them.

The draft clearly expressed Spain's desire for a good relationship with the colonies. The ministers wanted "to count [on] the fidelity and forces of said Provinces," to develop a plan "about the manner and substance" in which to deal with them. Importantly, the plan did not advocate abandoning them until they were "recognized as an independent state."[18]

The draft, however, added that the return for Spain's support must be spelled out. And, more importantly, that as an ally, the colonies could be "entrusted . . . with our ideas" and strategies. What role would Spain play, when the North American colonists were a people who had so many relations of nationality, kinship, and even economic interests with Great Britain? The two European courts would have to know what campaign each participant would undertake and how they would do so. In other words, they wanted to delineate specific strategy. Would they fight together or separately? What role would the colonies play, even if "only the diversion of forces"?

With all of this spelled out, Spain listed its goals for entering a war and asked that France do the same. The draft, here repeated, stated, "Spain has no further objective than to recover the humiliating usurpations of Gibraltar and Menorca" and "expel from the Gulf of Mexico, Bay of Honduras, and the Coast of Campeche" some troublesome English settlers. These settlers were in fact illegally trading (i.e., smuggling) and expanding into Spanish territory. At the least, Spain insisted that France, in conjunction with Spain, prepare a plan "to defend ourselves, and inflict harm on our enemies in any anticipated action" and while doing so, always "be suspicious and avoid any evil consequences."[19]

These suspicions were in reference to the British government. And this was yet another reason to be patient. The Spanish wanted to wait and see what Parliament would do. While the Spanish ministers felt that the revolution was taking a toll, they also realized that King George III "wished to test fortune" and was not agreeable to peace. Therefore, whatever England would do depended on the prime minister and Parliament. This raised the question as to whether France and Spain should let Britain negotiate with the colonies in the confidence that the colonies would not give in. The Spaniards correctly believed that the British government did not have an appetite for granting the Americans independence, which was a deal-breaker.

Around the same time that Aranda's draft was being compiled, Armand Marc, Count of Montmorin, the French ambassador in Madrid, received word from Vergennes that George III had sent a Moravian friend of Franklin's to Paris. James Hutton met an hour with the king before departing from London. In Paris, his first meeting with Franklin lasted more than two hours, and, the letter noted, another meeting was scheduled for the next day. Nothing was speculated regarding the results of the meeting. Vergennes instructed his ambassador to convey the information to Floridablanca.[20]

Nothing came of the meetings. Hutton probably had not expected success. He had another motive, which was for Franklin to write a letter to colonial leaders asking them not to persecute the Moravian community, who were pacifists.[21] If, however, as the draft postulated, a hostile British administration were to take over, could we "initiate and carry out our negotiations with vigor" for an agreement with the colonies? No matter what, Spain and France should be prepared for any British surprise.

The draft and cover note repeated that, at the very least, Spain would not act at all until its fleets had safely returned to Spain. The fleet from South America and the large land force it transported were not due until July. This implied that there was more than enough time to thoroughly plan a coordinated strategy.[22]

Floridablanca clearly understood that Vergennes feared an early peace that would be harmful to France. The French minister of state did not want England to become reconciled with the colonies. The American victory at Saratoga had increased his anxiety. Only a treaty between France and Spain and the colonies would prevent such an outcome, and signing such a treaty would be an act of war. Vergennes needed two things. He already had the first, which was a colonial guarantee that Congress would not abandon France. He did not, however, have the second. Spain had made clear that it would not join France in the conflict but would instead bide its time. Both Vergennes and Floridablanca knew that France could not take on Great Britain alone.

Vergennes clearly understood that Floridablanca did not believe in the preeminence of a British-American settlement. Moreover, the Spanish minister would not be rushed into war when the ends could be met through negotiation. Spain would not act until it had "more clarity about" Great Britain's "designs" and could "make its decisions without rushing."[23]

An important aspect of Floridablanca's hesitancy to rush into war had to do with the precarious balance of powers among European nations. He feared that a wrong move could result in war breaking out in Eastern Europe and thus negate any opportunity to influence the conflict in America. France used its alliance with the relatively weak states of Sweden, Poland, and Turkey to counter the expansionist tendencies of Russia and Prussia. France and England, in an age-old rivalry over European supremacy, stood at the pinnacle of this balance. Both countries had to be aware of the potential for disrupting this uncertain stability and throwing all of Europe into war. Any of the weaker countries could seek an advantage and cause that war, thus forcing both France and Spain to pursue a compromising arrangement with England. "A prejudiced and shameful peace," Floridablanca called it. The two countries needed to be careful and strengthen their positions by asking the Dutch to join them. The Spanish minister knew that the Dutch had become discontented with the British.[24]

The ever-astute Franklin knew all of this. He could have drawn two conclusions. First, Floridablanca, unlike Aranda and Vergennes, did not rise to Franklin's ploy but rather had a clearer grasp of the situation. Second, while Vergennes was more amenable to Franklin's entreaties and had actually become concerned about a quick peace, Spain's position had created a problem. Would France ally with the colonies without assurances from Spain?

In addition, the death of Maximilian Joseph, the Elector of Bavaria, on December 30, 1777, heightened tensions on the continent. This was a serious concern, and a breakout of war became a real possibility. Vergennes was under pressure from more than the colonial requests.

The French minister answered "Spain's gigantic demands," writing that France wanted nothing more than to gain trade with the colonies and strike a serious, if not damaging, blow to England.[25] Vergennes had become frustrated with Spain. He felt that he had a window of opportunity to deliver that blow. His impatience caused concern in Madrid. Spain became suspicious of Vergennes, and Floridablanca felt that his French counterpart had become secretive about his private negotiations with the colonial delegation. As a result, in early February 1778, Aranda received instructions to be careful about what he said to Vergennes.[26]

Any disappointment the Americans may have harbored over Spain's position was overshadowed by France's open willingness to take up the American cause. As early as the first week of December 1777, Franklin wrote a renewed proposal for a French-American alliance, which resulted in a quick meeting with Vergennes, who agreed to full recognition of the colonies. At this moment, he still sought the approval of Spain. Soon after that, Vergennes's representative, Conrad-Alexandre Gérard, asked the commission what France needed to do "to give such satisfaction to the American commissioners as to engage them not to listen to any proposition from England for a new connection with that country?"

Franklin answered that only the long-sought treaty of amity and commerce would satisfy. An immediate conclusion of that treaty would turn Congress from any British proposals of peace, which, Franklin noted, "have not for their basis the entire freedom and independence of America."[27] Gérard countered that the two countries should not only agree to a commercial treaty but also to a treaty of military alliance that would leave France to decide when to go to war.

Word came back quickly. The king would agree to the treaties, but with the added stipulation that the colonies could not make a separate peace with Great Britain. While expressing the hope that France's entry into the war would be sooner rather than later and voicing their disappointment that France could not speak for Spain, the commission agreed to the terms.[28]

Such an agreement was a French gamble. France hoped that an element of surprise would be to its advantage and would result in a quick victory. If not, Vergennes knew that only the combined naval fleets of Spain and France could match or, in fact, outnumber Great Britain's fleet.

Spain would officially remain out of the conflict; however, Vergennes hoped that the Third Bourbon Family Compact of 1761 would provide some security. Both the Americans and the French recognized Spain's demonstrated willingness to help; thus, perhaps to placate the Spanish as well as to reinforce that supposed security, the American Commission and the French agreed to include a clause in the treaty that permitted Spain to enter the conflict as a full partner. This meant that if Spain were to join the war, it would be considered an equal partner, and its goals would have to be considered in any negotiated peace. No one, neither the American commissioners nor Vergennes, doubted that if Spain eventually did join the fighting, victory would be at hand and colonial independence would only be a matter of time.[29]

Franklin and the other commissioners met with Vergennes and signed the two treaties in Paris on February 6, 1778, just two months after word of Saratoga had reached Europe. Louis XVI made the treaties official by receiving the commissioners at Versailles on March 20. Franklin felt at the time that the treaties were perhaps the crowning achievement of his diplomatic career. Subsequent historians have gone further, proposing that they were "the greatest diplomatic victory the United States ever achieved."[30]

Aranda reported about a letter that Louis XVI sent to Spain's Carlos III. The French king tried to justify his decision to sign the treaties with the Americans as "an indispensable step." Moreover, he had confidence that he could maintain good relations with Russia, while the treaties gave Holland a reason to withhold its stipulated assistance to England. He then added a veiled plea to Spain by claiming that Holland wanted other countries to recognize independence.

Aranda reported that he had met with Maurepas and had told the elderly French minister that he would end his days with glory if France were successful, and that France would enter its "epoch of greatest power." Maurepas, in turn, shared the information that Deane, who had been recalled, had been replaced by John Adams, "one of the famous partisans of independence." The Frenchman believed that the cause for the change "was gossip about disagreement among the deputies." Aranda added his own observation, which was that Franklin would meet with the French king and his ministers, but not while Lord Stormont was present.[31]

Aranda's comment about Stormont not being present is curious, because the latter had announced on March 16 that he had been recalled. This was three days before Aranda's letter. And, on the same day as Aranda's letter, France's ambassador to England was withdrawn. Vergennes had sent a copy of the treaty of commerce to his ambassador in London with instructions to present it to King George. The king received it on March 13, and three days later, the reaction was clear.[32] The first treaty now became a matter of public record.

Thanks to Bancroft, London knew of the treaties before Louis XVI ratified them. Vergennes's element of surprise had never existed. Both Britain and France needed time to prepare for what seemed to be inevitable. Vergennes sought a clear reason to declare war. He hoped that somehow his element of surprise could be maintained and that Britain would commit an act that would give him a legitimate reason to declare war. Ideally, this would happen before the French fleet arrived and surprised the British fleet at New York.

The French fleet of twelve ships of the line and five frigates, under the command of Admiral Charles Henri Hector, Count d'Estaing, sailed in April 1778. D'Estaing carried sealed orders to open hostilities once he reached America. With the element of surprise, he could capture or neutralize the British fleet in North America, cut off aid to their troops, and achieve a quick victory. At the same time, France planned to reclaim its territories in India.

Fortunately for Vergennes, his hope that Britain would provide a cause for war came about on the high seas when a British convoy attacked three French frigates, two of which were captured and one of which, though badly mauled, managed to escape. This was just the belligerent act that Vergennes needed. He had his *causas belli* but not his surprise.[33]

Spain closely monitored Great Britain's reaction to the French alliance with the colonies. The French fleet to North America was sent with Spain's knowledge and approval. Both ploys failed. D'Estaing proved to be a disappointment. He declined to engage the British at New York and left North America with the British fleet not only intact but even reinforced. News from the Indian Ocean was also disastrous. Every French post in India had been lost by the spring of 1779.[34]

Almost a month after Great Britain declared war on France, Escarano reported from London about British ship-building activities and, more importantly, about the fact that English ministers currently still wanted to avoid actual fighting with France and were sending envoys to negotiate with Congress. Moreover, they secretly sent a Mr. Pulling to France talk to Franklin, and he "has returned very unsatisfied."

Escarano also told Floridablanca that while the British were making every attempt to reconcile with the colonies, they still would not agree to independence; and, Escarano stressed, they would have to agree eventually. He continued that the war effort was costing them dearly, and if war with France broke out, their "national debt would have to be increased."[35] Edward Gibbon, then in the process of writing his multivolume history of the Roman Empire and a member of Parliament, remarked that "the two greatest countries in Europe were fairly running a race for the favor of America."[36] But war would not be avoided, and France needed Spain.

Vergennes knew all along that if France failed in its initial attempts to surprise the British, and if Spain's attempts at negotiating a peace failed, France could not defeat Great Britain on its own. France needed Spain. Its only hope of matching the firepower of Great Britain's navy and of obtaining a favorable balance of forces was the active participation of Spain and its navy.[37] He appealed to his king: "It is a fact that His Majesty cannot struggle long on equal terms with the English and that a prolonged war ... could entertain the ruin of his navy and even his finances, and finally that His Majesty reduced to his own means would be less able to make his enemies feel the need of peace." An alliance with Spain must be made "for the establishment of combined operations, which one cannot hasten too much to prepare."[38] His ambassador in Madrid was more succinct, "Be sure, Sir, that in whatever manner France is dragged into the war, Spain will follow."[39]

 7

A Declaration of War and a New Focus

With Great Britain, France, and the colonies committed to their respective positions and about to engage in combat, Spain had a great diplomatic advantage. Spain could determine the outcome through either negotiation or active participation, and it preferred the former. The Americans and the French did not doubt that Spain's allegiance meant victory.

The two representatives France and Spain sent to Congress arrived in Philadelphia within two weeks of each other in the summer of 1778. Conrad-Alexandre Gérard arrived with d'Estaing's fleet and operated openly as France's diplomat to the United States. Juan de Miralles y Trajan, who came to Congress disguised as a merchant from Cuba, did not have official diplomatic status but operated as an observer. As long as Spain remained neutral, Gérard was used to officially express Spain's position.[1] As information came from abroad that the negotiations were not going well, congressional delegates such as Samuel Adams and Henry Laurens noted that Spain was preparing for war—and that meant victory.[2]

There can be no doubt that Franklin, John Adams (who had replaced Deane), and Arthur Lee had as much, if not more, knowledge than Congress of what Spain was doing. From existing correspondence, it appears that the commission had decided to let history run its course. For all intents and purposes, the commission's work became routine after the treaties of alliance were signed.[3] The active pressure to involve Spain in the conflict had paused.

If Spain could achieve its political goals without an expensive, ruinous war, it was obliged to try. Floridablanca tried to win peace diplomatically by offering Great Britain mediation. He insisted that American independence should be accepted because antebellum considerations were not part of the exchange. Great Britain would have some hard choices: either accept Spain's conditions for staying out of the war and accept the loss of its colonies, or try to win them back through a prolonged war. At best, if England considered some of the enumerated concessions to Spain, such as the return of Gibraltar and the Mediterranean island of Menorca, Spain might remain neutral. The government in London was resistant, although a great many British subjects in positions of influence knew that Spain's participation would mean defeat.

Spain continued to receive detailed information from London. In May, Escarano relayed an account of Burgoyne's questioning in the House of Commons. Burgoyne, who was taken prisoner after his surrender at Saratoga, had been sent back to England "with permission of Congress."[4] In the spring of 1778, he stood before the House of Commons to explain what had happened. This resulted in a serious rift between Lord Germain and James Luttrell, with the latter defending Burgoyne. The argument devolved into personal insults, and thereafter pandemonium ensued. It took the Speaker some time to restore order.

With feelings already frayed, a Mister Hartley, recently returned from Paris, stood up to speak. Hartley, a friend of and correspondent with Franklin, had visited him there to seek a means to reconcile Great Britain with the American colonies. Franklin told him that if England did not concede American independence, then there could be no reconciliation. Hartley made two proposals, the second of which suggested that the House make "a request of the King expressing to His Majesty the wish that reconciliation with the Americans take place as soon as possible." And in that effort, the House of Commons would help.

Hartley's proposals resulted in shouts of disagreement. The opposition suspected that this was a move to allow the ministry the opportunity to declare the colonies as independent, "if it deemed it necessary for reconciliation." Hartley withdrew the second proposal, after which the House rejected the first proposal: that Parliament not close but rather, given the gravity of pending business, that it remain in session from "one day to the next."[5] Clearly, the leadership of Great Britain was divided over what to do. Just as clearly, Spanish authorities did not see an American-British reconciliation coming any time soon.

Meanwhile, Juan de Miralles kept the Continental Congress informed, and through Gérard, he formally recommended that it was time for Congress to select a delegate to send directly to Spain to participate in the ongoing negotiations. Spain now had no problem with welcoming an American diplomat in its capital. Not only would this person be important for successful negotiations, he would be equally so if they failed. The time had become critical for a congressional representative to work with Spain to assure Congress's continued role, whether that be as an active participant or otherwise. In the latter case, Spanish support would be crucial to the continued war because it "could give the States credit in Europe equal to their wishes" and because France needed time to financially recover enough to "be more competent to war."[6]

The necessity of bolstering the Americans' faltering and almost worthless currency and credit could be accomplished only via Spain's economic support. Colonial currency would come to be strengthened by and based on the Spanish *peso fuerte* (or, as was printed on paper money, the "Spanish dollar"). Spanish coins were sometimes called "pieces of eight," two parts (or "bits") of which equaled a fourth or quarter. Some of the colonies made Spanish coin their legal tender. The first issue of Continental paper money on May 10, 1775, noted that it was payable in "Spanish Milled Dollars or the value thereof in gold or silver."[7] There could be no clearer message to the Americans that Spain was working toward independence for the rebelling colonies.

From the American point of view, Carlos III had become a broker for a "just and lasting peace," meaning independence. While somewhat skeptical, American public sentiment leaned toward and perhaps hoped for a negotiated peace. Irrespective of the political intrigue in Congress and within the American Commission, Spain continued in its attempts to negotiate with London, which occasionally seemed willing to talk. Some in the British government hoped to avoid war by means of diplomacy, and that was precisely Floridablanca's position. The Spanish minister hoped that Great Britain would be willing to make a concession (i.e., turn over Gibraltar) to avoid an expansion of hostilities.

Lord Weymouth, one of Great Britain's secretaries of state, made overtures to Spain's chargé d'affaires in London. He wanted to know if Spain would mediate in the dispute. Floridablanca quickly agreed. France did not like the idea, but Spain left it no choice in the matter. The mediations hit an impasse, however, when Great Britain asked Spain to have France retract its American treaties. The Spanish government reportedly dismissed the idea, saying that Spain "could not suggest such an indecent proposal." Upon hearing that the negotiations had collapsed, Floridablanca endorsed France's plan to surprise the British.[8]

Franklin presumably shared the same confidence in Spain as his patriotic colleagues in Congress, and he thought that those "fruits" would bear the sweet juice of independence. After all, he knew that Aranda had advocated his position and that Spain's strategy, as conveyed by the ambassador from Floridablanca, assured Spain's support.

Neither France nor Spain cared for Arthur Lee. Moreover, he had become more than an irritant for Franklin. As described by historians, he was a jealous, suspicious person who never ceased his backbiting and rumormongering. He bred trouble if he could not find it.[9] Fiercely patriotic, Lee did not like Franklin, and his insane jealousy led him to write letters to his brother, Richard Henry Lee, as well as to Samuel Adams, accusing Franklin of duplicity, corruption, and incompetence. His behind-the-scenes subterfuge had already resulted in Deane's recall, as well as in a reorganization of the diplomatic corps that had posted Lee's other brother, William, to Berlin and Vienna and appointed an ally, Ralph Izard, to Tuscany. Congress had named Lee as the emissary to Spain. However, none of those countries had officially recognized the colonies, so the appointees stayed in Paris and joined forces in demeaning Franklin by whatever means they could.[10] Izard joined Arthur Lee in writing letters to Congress that were critical of Franklin.

Lee's letters resulted in a controversy that divided Congress, and eventually, in September 1778, Congress decided to abolish the commission, leaving Franklin as the sole representative to deal with France, if not Spain. (Aranda preferred to deal with Franklin.) Word of the move reached the commissioners in February 1779, having been personally delivered to Franklin by the Marquis de Lafayette, who had returned to Paris on a leave of absence. Lee sulked but would not quit. He campaigned for and expected to be named as the sole congressional representative to France. He even plotted to have Franklin and Deane assigned to another post, such as Vienna or Holland. Moreover, because France had recognized the colonies and had sent its official emissary to America, Franklin was officially named as the minister plenipotentiary to France.[11]

Although Franklin's friends and family members informed him about the poisonous campaign that was being waged against him, he acted as if he did not know.[12] He wrote that his popularity allowed him to "grieve those unhappy gentlemen; unhappy indeed in their tempers and in the dark uncomfortable passions of jealousy, anger, suspicion, envy, and malice. . . . They are vexed at everybody's good luck, can never be happy. . . . Let them remain in the miserable situation in which their malignant natures have placed them."[13] When Lee, his brother, and Izard eventually were recalled by Congress, Franklin wrote, "No soul regrets their departure."[14] He dashed off a note warning a trusted member of Congress about Lee: "I caution you to beware of him; for in sowing suspicions and jealousies, in creating misunderstandings and quarrels, in malice, subtlety, and indefatigable industry, he has I think no equal."[15] Meanwhile, Spain's strategy proved uncannily correct. American success at Saratoga did not amount to a victory that would put an end to the war. France needed Spain's commitment, and Great Britain had been stalemated. As a result, Spain benefited from a commodity it wanted most—time. The last of the Spanish ships returning from South and Central America came into port in September 1778, and Mexico was producing silver to fund the war effort.[16]

Spain continued to support the American cause as the war stagnated. In Paris, Aranda and the American commissioners focused on Spain's aid, which had become even more crucial. Henceforth, France's assets would be needed to fund its own efforts. Just a few weeks before the signing of the treaties, Arthur Lee went to Aranda's residence to acknowledge that the colonies had received a shipment of supplies and money. The shipment had passed through Havana, and it was the first of three equal shipments that had been scheduled. Lee received assurances that Spain would continue to do what it could.[17] Congress reflected this knowledge as it continued to ask Spain for aid.[18]

Obviously, the rebelling colonies would have preferred for Spain to forego its neutrality and actively join the war. On the other hand, they understood the value of Spain's financial support. Robert Morris and William Smith expressed their pleasure with Spain on at least three different occasions. Patrick Henry, in his letter to Bernardo de Gálvez in January 1778, wrote of Spain's "friendly help"; and George Washington added his praise of the "good will" and "respect" for the "friendship" of the king of Spain.[19]

With France now in the struggle, Benjamin Franklin, through Aranda, secured permission from Spain to recommend that Continental naval captains place themselves under the auspices of Gardoqui's company in the neutral northern Spanish port of Bilbao. Gardoqui had used his family's banking firm as a cover to protect Spain's neutrality, and he was working directly with the colonial commission in Paris.[20]

The Americans and the French needed Spain. American praise and appreciation for Spain's financial assistance was authentic, but the real, underlying motive was to enlist Spain into joining the war. Congress sent word that they had resolved to cede West Florida to Spain and that the colonies would assign three thousand troops to help Spain gain control.[21]

Floridablanca had remained in contact with the British government, which, on occasion, continued to show interest in some sort of mediation. Never losing sight of preparing for actual war, Floridablanca kept France apprised. In November, his ambassador in London wrote a detailed, twenty-seven-page report that was sent to Spain's minister of the Indies, José de Gálvez. The diplomat theorized that Spain needed to support the colonies to curb the new country's future appetite for expanding into Spanish-American territory as well as to demonstrate to its own possessions that Spain understood the plight of the English colonists. He felt that their independence was inevitable and that its realization would forever change the relationship between the two continents. In addition, in his cover letter, he expressed his belief that their friendship "will be one of the most worthy objects to occupy Your Excellency's superior talents" and "untiring applications."[22]

On the one hand, Spain's untiring applications for a negotiated peace were not bearing fruit, while on the other hand, the country was preparing for war. With its treasure ships safe in home ports with the return of the South American fleet, the fleet and Spain's officials throughout its American empire were put on notice to prepare for war. France's ambassador in Madrid warned Vergennes not to alienate Floridablanca. The French ambassador correctly predicted that Spain would declare war sometime in 1779, adding that Spain would not officially recognize the United States until peace had been established.[23]

Apparently informed in early 1779 (by either Gérard or Miralles, or perhaps by both), Congress understood that Spain would be sending what could possibly be a final ultimatum to Great Britain. In February 1779, Gouverneur Morris, a congressional delegate, published a letter in the *Pennsylvania Packet* in which he conveyed a clear understanding: "And those who know the connection between the Courts of Versailles and Madrid, their enmity to that of St. James, and their national interests, cannot but perceive that Spain will soon be joined in this contest, unless it be terminated agreeably to our interests."[24] Morris added, perhaps reflecting on the financial support being given, that Spanish aid would make the colonial currency strong.

Spain's position and the knowledge of a forthcoming ultimatum reinforced confidence among the colonial leaders. Gérard submitted a letter to John Jay, president of the Continental Congress, stating that Spain would be sending an ultimatum, or, as he put it, Spain was about to offer England a final chance to settle the conflict through mediation, adding that if this offer failed, Spain would enter the war on the side of France and the colonies. Gérard's letter, read to Congress on February 12, 1779, stated that the king of Spain had made "the independence of the United States the preliminary article to the general pacification."[25]

Congressman William Henry Drayton immediately sent a letter to King George III stating that now was the time for him to take the "harsh prescription" and grant independence to the American colonies. Apparently unaware of the timing, he wrote that he knew that Spain's ambassador had delivered Spain's ultimatum to him, which he emphasized as being a "REMONSTRANCE of a very serious and decisive nature."[26]

Congress resolved that the king of Spain was working in their interest and that he had forced Great Britain either to accept independence as a condition of peace or to face the prospect of Spain declaring war on them. Franklin wrote from Europe that Spain's negotiations with England had been ongoing for a while and that Spain had insisted on American independence. But Spain's efforts had been rejected. He added in a letter to Patrick Henry that he hoped "Spain is now near declaring against our enemies."[27]

Spain sent the ultimatum to France and England. Written in Spanish, the nine-page document, dated April 3, 1779, enumerated Spain's position as to what it wanted, while insisting on American independence. Madrid warned London that time was running out and that Great Britain should not delay; rather, it should give serious consideration to the points offered for peace. Great Britain must end hostilities with France and the colonies, and within a month the belligerents must select a location for negotiations. Moreover, the colonies must "be treated as Independent in fact" and should be represented by one or more of their commissioners in the negotiations.[28]

The British king received Spain's offer; however, both he and his government wasted no time in refusing it. Pedro Luján Jiménez de Góngora, Marqués de Almodóvar, Spain's newly appointed ambassador to England, quickly reported that the British government would not accept the idea of treating the colonials as equals.[29] The written answer from London came soon thereafter, and on May 4 an extract was penned and sent to Congress.[30] Besides their refusal to treat the colonials as equals, the British would also not consider having colonial representative seated at the negotiations. They could not accept Spain's insistence that the colonies be treated as independent, neither in appearance nor in fact, even during the negotiations. They felt that each of the belligerents, meaning Great Britain, France, and Spain, should have representatives at the talks that would determine the destiny of the new country. King George III and his government were not yet ready to accept this "harsh prescription."

Floridablanca gave Great Britain an opportunity to avoid an expanded war. His other target was France, who had to agree to help Spain gain Gibraltar, Menorca, and the Gulf of Mexico's northern coast. He probably never expected Britain to agree, since he had secretly worked out an alliance with France while awaiting Great Britain's final offer. Upon hearing of the British refusal, George Washington wrote to John Jay, stating that England's failure to accept Spain's offer of mediation "is more strongly tinctured with insanity than she has done in the course of this contest." He added that Great Britain's "obstinacy" was the only reason for its reaction.[31]

Carlos III had no further options but to declare war. According to the secret clause of the treaty that had already been signed by the colonies and France, Spain would assure that military victory included independence for the colonies. Spain would enter the fray, but it would not yet formally recognize the colonies so as to avoid problems in its own colonies.

Perhaps the logic of acknowledging a rebellious nation before it had won its independence, thereby creating a free nation, played on the minds of the king's advisors. Nevertheless, France had no choice but to accept Spain's conditions for an alliance. France knew, as subsequent historians have observed, that it was "almost inconceivable that France and the United States could have defeated Britain without Spanish help."[32]

On April 12, 1779, the Franco-Spanish alliance was signed at Carlos III's summer palace at Aranjuez. France ratified it at Versailles on April 28. Without becoming an official ally with the colonies, Spain had tied itself to their independence. Upon hearing of the treaty, Great Britain had one last opportunity to agree to the terms, but as expected, it refused. Colonial leaders were very pleased, even happy, to hear of the alliance, and they were even happier to learn that on June 21, 1779, Spain declared war on Great Britain.[33]

Now under investigation by Congress, about to be recalled, and perhaps feeling pressured, Arthur Lee took it upon himself to send two audacious letters to the court of Spain in which he put forth his own strategy for a Spanish victory. He sent his first letter a couple of weeks before the Spanish declaration of war and the second letter four days after. By any norm of the times, especially those for a diplomat representing a country seeking recognition, his letters were unusual. He cautioned Spain against privateers and suggested that the key to victory would be a major naval victory in the Mediterranean Sea.[34] The letters ended up on Floridablanca's desk, and he waited a month and a half before he replied, giving Lee's affront the short shrift that it deserved.

The Spanish minister merely acknowledged receiving the letters and nothing more.

By then Lee was also in disfavor with his own country. Within weeks of Floridablanca's reply to him, Congress recalled Lee, and after an extended

Figure 11. John Jay, sent to Madrid and called to Paris where he secretly negotiated with the British during the peace talks; oil on canvas, 1794, painting by Gilbert Stuart. (Courtesy of the National Portrait Gallery, Washington, DC. Accession number 2009.132.1)

debate, it named John Jay minister to the court of Spain. In addition, Congress asked John Adams to return to France to help negotiate a peace treaty with Great Britain.[35]

Floridablanca must have considered Lee's advice superficial. The preparations for war that had been undertaken by the minister and his government far exceeded Lee's imagination. The colonial leaders understood that Spain's military might, especially its navy, would secure victory. Carlos III's proclamation was translated and published in the colonial newspapers on August 23. George Washington read the account in a newspaper, describing it as "most interesting and agreeable." He knew that the conflict would spread beyond the colonies and that independence had come closer to reality.[36]

John Jay, who had been the president of the Continental Congress, now prepared to cross the Atlantic to represent the colonies before the Spanish government. After Spain's declaration of war, the presence of an American representative in Madrid no longer posed a problem. Jay travelled to Spain with his wife, young nephew, brother-in-law, and two slaves, adding an Irish serving women while in Cádiz, before travelling overland to Madrid. He stayed in touch with Franklin, keeping him informed of his progress in reaching the Spanish capital and then about his activities while there. Jay started requesting payment of bills while he was in transit to Spain, and he continued doing so throughout his stay in Madrid.[37]

His expenses had initially been paid by Congress, but that quickly changed. Funds were short in the colonies, and there were other priorities. Jay then solicited the Spanish government to pay his expenses, apparently with some success at the beginning. But when the Spanish government heard that Congress had decided not to reimburse his expenses, it also refused any further payments. Jay's somewhat exorbitant lifestyle may have had something to do with this decision. Also, from the Spanish point of view, Jay's constant insistence that Spain pay his expenses had become overbearing, as was his unfounded criticism that Spain was being niggardly in its support of the revolution.

Spanish officials, Floridablanca among them, made themselves scarce to the American diplomat. Jay naturally turned to Franklin, who reprimanded him about his exorbitant living expenses while in Madrid. Jay's situation "mortified me exceedingly and the Storm of Bills which I found coming upon us both has terrified and vexed me to such a Degree that I have been deprived of Sleep." He continued, "Forbear the practice of asking Spain for your expenses."[38] Yet, inexplicably, he later told the same man that Spain had "taken four years to consider whether they should treat with us. Give them forty and let us mind our own business."[39] Nevertheless, he sympathized with Jay: "I do not know to what Amount you have obtained Aids from it [Spain]; but if it is not considerable, it were be wish'd you had never been sent there, as the Slight they put upon our offered Friendship is very disreputable to us, and of course hurtful to our Affairs elsewhere. I think they are short sighted, & do not look very far into Futurity."[40]

Aside from his financial problems, Jay became bitter and critical of the Spanish, because he felt that their declaration of war against Great Britain had not been sufficient. He wanted nothing less than full recognition and an alliance. Never mind that Spanish blood had been spilled and their money spent. No. In his view, acknowledging that would be tantamount to prostituting American independence to Spanish goals. It did not matter that America's attachment to Spain's goals had previously been readily approved by Congress, over which he had presided, in the secret clause of its treaty of alliance with France. Moreover, that same clause had bound Spain to American independence.

8

Corsairs and Intrigue

Taking prizes on the high seas must have been exhilarating. The first excitement would be generated by the sight of sails on the horizon. Then followed putting spyglass to eye to discern the type, size, and armament of the vessel. Next came the critical assessment of whether it was a friend, a foe, or a neutral, and, finally, determining its intent: Was it maneuvering to avoid capture or coming in pursuit? If the captain decided that it was worthy of capture, the chase would begin. Once the prey was in cannon range, it would hopefully not put up a fight and have to be forcibly boarded. The general rule of privateering was never to attempt to take on a more heavily armed ship—or even one that was equally armed. The idea was to capture ships and their cargoes as prizes with minimal risk.

Franklin had firsthand knowledge of this dangerous occupation, and, when necessary, he approved of the practice. With his grandchildren in tow, he had witnessed the process twice while traveling to France in late 1776. No doubt he watched this key aspect of the war with a combination of anxiety and curiosity. He would learn that such activity could and would be troubling, for there was only a vague line between a loyal corsair, or privateer, and a pirate.

Historians have chimed in over the hazy and often overlapping definitions. Spanish historian Carlos Cólogan Soriano wrote that the difference between a corsair—*corsario* in Spanish—and a privateer or pirate is that the former had a contract, called a Letter of Marque, which was a commission of service or patent to sail under a specific country and its flag. The corsair's job was to pursue and capture enemy ships and collect their cargoes. It was hard, however, to determine just where legal privateering ended and piracy began. The same ship could be considered a corsair by friends and a pirate by enemies.[1] John Paul Jones, who had a shady past, refused to be categorized as a privateer, because "public Virtue is not the characteristic of the concerned privateers." He considered privateers nothing more than "licensed robbers."[2]

Historian H. W. Brands noted that privateers, which was another name for corsairs, were a colonial alternative to the British blockade and sea power. They were licensed pirates who needed crews for dangerous but potentially lucrative work. In an article for the National Park Service, John Frayler described "Letters of Marque and Reprisal" as a way to legitimatize privately outfitted men of war. Without such documentation, privateers' activities were considered acts of piracy.[3] Bruce Lancaster, in his history of the American Revolution, described American privateers who "swarmed out of every port, returning with booty." He continued, however, that the windfalls were of little benefit to the colonies as a whole, because Congress had no way of channeling specie into the national treasury.[4]

Moreover, the colonies had inherited Britain's sea policies and a history in which the British had "relied" on these "licensed pirates" since the days of Sir Francis Drake in the sixteenth century. Knighted by the queen of England, Drake wrought havoc upon Spanish ships, towns, or any other location he visited. Although neither England nor Spain had been at war, the queen semi-secretly approved of his activities. To the rest of the world, he was considered a pirate and was known in Spain as *El Draque*. His most complete biographer called him "a pirate, largely because he was untroubled by a conscience that in most men would murmur against theft and murder." Henry Kelsey subtitled his biography of Drake "The Queen's Pirate."[5] Drake died of dysentery in 1596 and was buried at sea after unsuccessfully attacking San Juan, Puerto Rico.

The rebelling colonies had turned this practice against Great Britain. American corsairs preyed on Britain's maritime trade, cutting into its revenues, increasing the cost of insurance, and gaining prizes that sold for desperately needed hard currency.[6] In addition, the strategy was intended to lure the Royal Navy away from its blockade of the colonies' Atlantic Coast.[7]

Great Britain's reaction to privateering was to start boarding ships—irrespective of their country of origin—that it suspected of aiding the colonies. This policy also led to abuses. As a result, in 1780 the Empress Catherine II of Russia initiated the League of Armed Neutrality to protect neutral shipping from what Russia and the countries that joined the league considered England's wartime policy of unlimited searches of neutral shipping.

John Paul Jones, a native of Scotland, had come to Franklin with a checkered career and an overbearing personality. He was a swashbuckler and womanizer who reveled in feats of daring on the high seas, and his indiscriminate deeds would take his patriotic actions into that vague gray area between legality and piracy. Jones, who became legendary in the annals of US naval history, would become involved with Franklin after both France and Spain had entered the conflict. His actions, though, never conflicted with Spanish interests.

The concept of privateering was not new to Franklin. After all, he had grown up in two American port cities, and he had also spent time in London, where the concept was known. In addition, as a recent member of the congressional committee to investigate and find methods for financing the Continental Army, he had recommended that George Washington arrange for the sale of vessels and cargoes that had been captured by American ships that were outfitted at the expense of Congress. The proceeds from these sales would be used to support the war effort.[8] In other words, privateering would help fund the revolution. Franklin also carried a sheaf of blank Letters of Marque that he dispersed to American captains in France; in fact, he dispersed so many of these letters that he ran out and had to request more.[9] Franklin would become one of the overseers of American privateering activities in Europe, thus earning the appellative the "patriarch of corsairs" by one historian.[10]

At some point, however, Franklin's sense of practical politics—what was needed for the cause—conflicted with his humanity. It is unclear when he came to believe that the practice of privateering was an "ancient practice" that, no matter how it was justified, remained nothing more than a heinous business based on theft and ending with murder. Unarmed ships and merchantmen became the main prey of these scavengers.[11]

After the war ended, Franklin and his colleagues tried to include clauses outlawing privateering in the treaties that they drew up with European countries. He believed that such a change would be a "happy improvement in the law of nations," adding that "it is high time, for the sake of humanity, that a stop be put to this enormity." He wanted to prohibit "the plundering of unarm'd and usefully employed people." Perhaps his attitude stemmed from his work in trying to arrange prisoner exchanges. Most of the American prisoners in British prisons were sailors who had been captured from American privateers. The English treated them as common felons—that is, as pirates. Franklin argued that they had sailed legally and should be treated as prisoners of war. Such an argument walked a fine line that only someone with Franklin's command of language and diplomatic skills could finesse.[12]

He had previously met with Robert Morris about arranging shipments to the colonies, and upon his arrival in France, he had boarded with a partner of Pierre Penet, who no doubt educated him on the nuances of getting shipments to the continent. A shadowy figure, Penet was a private commercial agent who acted as a special messenger. At the time, he was in France arranging shipments from Nantes to the revolutionaries.[13]

Franklin also must have realized that prizes such as those taken by Capt. Lambert Wickes were being sold illegally in friendly ports and that the revenues from them rewarded the captain and his crew and paid for the shipments to be sent back to the colonies.

Still, there were problems. Shipments to America were already leaving the northern French port of Nantes. In 1776 and 1777 the departures doubled, and over fifty ships were outfitted as privateers.[14]

Both Franklin and Deane carried with them copies of printed commissions, and they had the authority to appoint captaincies in the Continental navy. As one historian has surmised, the American navy was made up of ex-privateers and adventurers.[15] The appointment pertained to the individual captain and not necessarily to the ship, since captains frequently changed ships.

In fact, the status of a naval vessel under the authority of a Continental captain could be hard to ascertain. The vessel could be owned in part by Congress, by the government of one colony, by a private investor, or it could be the property of a combination of the three.

Even the commissions sometimes came under suspicion.[16] Privateering could easily be considered a form of stealing, a decriminalized form of piracy. Most of the American privateers were merchantmen and adventurers, many of whom dealt in the slave trade. All of them had been smugglers dealing illegally, as Robert Morris's company had done, with Spain, the Middle East, India, and the Caribbean, including Cuba.[17]

Nevertheless, the activity of American privateers commissioned into the Continental navy played a key role in the eventual success of the revolution. As attested by the exploits of Gustavus Conyngham, no matter how controversial were their activities, they did pose a diversion to the Royal Navy and British trade. Honor, as well as profits, motivated hostility toward Britain.[18]

American privateers plagued enemy shipping along the Florida coast and into the Caribbean Sea, where they disrupted trade with British-held Jamaica.[19] Revenue from privateers' prizes purchased all-important armaments and supplies for the Continental land forces; they partially supported the nascent navy; and by severely disrupting British commercial shipping, they greatly increased the cost of insurance coverage to British merchants. The latter aspects gave rise to the opposition by Great Britain's middle and business classes of their government's pursuit of the war.

A neutral country's support of privateering could be considered an act of war. In the case of France, this was problematic. Franklin faced a huge task, the goal of which was to secure the alliances of France, Spain, Holland, and any other country he could solicit. The main target was France, followed closely by Spain, as he would learn from necessity. He knew that the Continental navy, as personified by Captain Wickes, had orders to pursue British shipping and seek the protection of French ports. He also knew that France and Spain, were ostensibly neutral countries that risked war by harboring belligerents. Moreover, both countries were providing clandestine aid under the umbrella of their neutrality.

Although the Americans needed an alliance with France, the overaggressiveness of their navy could alienate their most important potential ally. The practice of "gunboat diplomacy," as one historian labeled the privateers' use of French ports, could be very problematic.[20] Persisting in the use of French ports to sell off prizes had the advantage of supporting the cause financially as well as militarily. This activity, however, could push France into a war with Great Britain. If France did not consider itself ready for war and was embarrassed too deeply, however, this practice could turn against the colonies.

French and Spanish merchants continued to trade with British merchants. This created an additional dilemma. Just because a ship had sailed from a British port or was heading into a port in that country did not mean that they were eligible targets. Complicating matters even further, as Franklin would learn, was the practice of changing the ships' flags of designation.

Major merchant houses involved in the Atlantic trade had existed before the war and continued to trade during the war. Some of these international companies were based in Spain. As noted, the firm of Gardoqui e hijos was already involved in supporting the colonies. Other Spanish firms included the Houses of Lassare in Cádiz, of Lagoanere in El Ferrol, and of Cólogan in Tenerife. These organizations had international networks, some of which had offices or branches in Great Britain. In addition, American merchants like Robert Morris, who had served on the Committee of Secret Correspondence with Franklin and would be appointed as Congress's superintendent of finance while also serving as the agent of marine in charge of the Continental navy, was dealing with these firms. Based in Philadelphia, Morris's firm had operated before the war as Willing, Morris & Company; during the war, it was called Willing, Morris, & Swanwick.[21] Morris's alcoholic half-brother Thomas initially held the position of commercial agent in Nantes and had authority over American shipping and prizes in France.

Figure 12. Gustavus Conyngham, a continental naval captain who dabbled in piracy; eighteenth-century print after Louis Marie Secardi. (Courtesy of the US Naval Historical Center)

His activities and his refusal to cooperate with the American Commission in Paris remained problematic until his death in January 1778.[22]

Franklin's collusion with Captain Wickes was the beginning of a policy that expanded the activities of American ships into European waters. The use of French ports could not be avoided. Congress depended on French acquiescence, but its commissioners, especially Franklin, had to tread softly. As the colonies' director of naval affairs and judge of admiralty in Europe, any problems would be brought to his attention.

Wickes's activities during Franklin's voyage to France were only an indication of the captain's loyalty, daring, and successful career as an American corsair. Almost immediately upon Franklin's arrival in Paris, the commission sent Wickes out with the *Reprisal* and some smaller ships. Within a month, the enterprising captain brought in five British prizes, which, despite British protests, were sold in Lorient.[23] Wickes immediately set sail again, this time with two other ships. Like his previous foray, he sailed up and around Ireland, frightening the coastal towns and capturing another eighteen prizes. Of the twenty-three total prizes, he sank seven, released two that belonged to smugglers, and sold the rest in France.[24] With his small, rapid schooner, the *Reprisal,* which boasted eighteen 6-pounder guns and a crew of 130 men, Wickes would become one of the three most successful American sea captains during the War for Independence. The other two were Gustavus Conyngham and John Paul Jones.[25]

At the same time Wickes was attracting France's attention, Conyngham was insulting the French as well. After he embarrassed France by taking his prizes to Dunkirk, the French government ordered him to stay in port while the commissioners were arranging for a new ship to be outfitted for him. Instead, he lifted anchor and escaped, under orders to sail directly to America. Naturally, and probably under secret orders from the American Commission, he continued to take prizes. British authorities knew that French complicity had allowed for his escape.

Then, the British recaptured one of Conyngham's prizes and found that most of the crew the American captain had placed in charge of the prize was French. This incensed the British government, from the king on down. French complacency (and complicity) was obvious.

A special British envoy was immediately dispatched to confront Vergennes with nothing less than a threat of war. Whether it was a ruse or not, Vergennes took the threat seriously. As mentioned in an earlier chapter, the American commissioners were told as much. Although he favored the Americans, Vergennes would not let the American corsairs push his country into war.[26] Aranda had kept abreast of these events and considered that the Americans' activities, with France's acquiescence, had pushed France dangerously close to war.[27] Franklin felt that the problem of privateering had hampered the commission's efforts to get more aid from both France and Spain.[28]

Nevertheless, while Franklin could not help but admire the daring of the American captains, he saw the difference between capturing British prizes in an act of war and taking them to neutral ports to sell them. Such an act could draw the neutral country into the war.

In a letter to John Jay, he noted that a small cutter fitted out at Dunkirk, the *Black Prince,* had captured over thirty sails within three months. Franklin exchanged the captured prisoners for captured American and French crews, the latter of which had come from Conyngham's recaptured prize. While American privateers had caused him "a great deal of trouble," the activities of the *Black Prince* and John Paul Jones "make me more willing to encourage such armaments, tho' they on occasion [cause] a good deal of trouble."[29] And that trouble, he knew, included the safety of American merchantmen. He pointed out to Vergennes that the problem was multifaceted, because American ships also had difficulty in transporting because of the "treachery of seamen."

Even as he soothed ruffled French feathers, he received complaints from Aranda about American privateers capturing Spanish ships. Franklin believed that the basis for those captures was not the fault of American captains but rather of British ships falsely flying American colors. Nevertheless, he agreed to investigate these matters and assured Aranda that if American captains were culpable, they would be punished and reparations would be made.[30]

However, Conyngham, a native of Ireland, personified the dichotomy of licensed corsairs who had trouble delineating between friend or foe when taking their prizes. He thereby created problems in Spanish and colonial relations. To be sure, other American-commissioned privateers existed. These men primarily operated along the North American coast and in the Caribbean. Others had preyed on shipping in Europe. Conflicts occurred and Congress received complaints, some of which reached Franklin in Paris. This was especially the case if Spanish merchants were the aggrieved parties.

Franklin had to draw the line between legal seizures and piracy. He had commissioned the American privateers, who were using French and Spanish ports as bases for raids against British ships and the British coast. When they returned to France, he served as judge in the proceedings of condemnation and sale, a task he disliked in part because of his distaste for the system.

As outlined below, those prizes were challenged numerous times—in this case, by Spain and its merchants. And Franklin knew that the colonies needed Spain at their side beyond the secret aid that was already being given. By June 1780, he hoped that the League of Armed Neutrality would extend its stand on free ships and free goods to "ordain that unarmed trading ships, as well as fishermen and farmers, should be respected, as working for the common benefit of mankind, and never be interrupted in their operations, even by national enemies."[31]

Nevertheless, Franklin had to deal with the reality of privateering and remain sensitive to the feelings and positions of Spain and France. After the treaties of alliance, American corsairs selling their prizes in French ports were no longer a problem in terms of French diplomatic relations with Britain. Once France declared war, its harbors openly welcomed American ships, and those same ports now became subject to British attack. Meanwhile, Spain maintained its neutrality, which provided cover for its continuing secret aid to the colonies. Thus, Congress turned its attention to making sure that the American captains seized enemy vessels and not neutral or allied ships.

After France's declaration of war against Britain, the focus turned to maintaining good relations with Spain. As a neutral nation, Spain could trade with any of the belligerents of the current war. Moreover, maintaining that neutrality provided Spain with a solid bargaining position as well as a cover for the clandestine aid it was sending to the colonies.

At times, American privateers would test those relations. For example, in early 1779, before Spain had declared war, American privateers took two ships to Boston to be sold. Captured in December 1778, both ships were sailing from Cádiz and destined for London, carrying cargoes of wines, oils, and cochineal, the latter highly prized for creating red dye especially used by royalty. Joaquín García de Luca and José de Llano, captains of the respective ships, wrote to Miralles in America, who passed their complaints to José de Gálvez, Spain's minister of the Indies. Miralles also had Gérard deliver two memorials to Congress.

In response, Congress formed a special committee to study the matter, but in the end, Miralles received word that Congress could do nothing. As with another incident, when the American ship the *Sally* seized a Spanish ship carrying British prisoners from Pensacola, Congress took the position that the colonial ships had sailed under commissions from the various states, and it would not overrule them.

In November 1782, long after Spain had entered the war, an American privateer, the *Patty*, captured the *San Antonio*, a Spanish prisoner exchange ship. In this case, Spain's complaint was settled—not by Congress but by the owners of the privateer, who paid the Spanish captain $1,000.[32]

It is unclear whether Franklin heard about every one of these problems. However, the record shows that he continued to be involved with some of the incidents and that the British played into the issue. In May 1777, Aranda received two letters from Floridablanca describing an American attack on a Catalan ship in the waters around the island of Santo Domingo and another on a Spanish packet boat that had sailed from Tenerife and was destined for La Coruña. Three offending ships were named in the two attacks: *Resolution, Plymouth,* and *Petite Resolution,* all of which were from the French port of Nantes.

Floridablanca instructed his ambassador to make this information known to "the Representative of the Americans ... in the terms that are judged helpful." Aranda took the complaint to Ferdinand Grand so that he might make it known to Franklin. This, indeed, was a serious matter. Franklin sent an inquiry to his grandnephew, who now held the position of American commissioner in Nantes in place of Thomas Morris. Jonathon Williams's only task was to oversee shipments to America. His reply was copied and given to Aranda, who attached it to his report to Floridablanca. Williams wrote to his great-uncle that he had never heard of the three ships "that supposedly left" Nantes. Moreover, he concluded that they were "English privateers" who had boarded "Spanish ships under the American flag . . . with the intention of passing themselves off as subjects of this nation and all of us as pirates." He found such action to be an abhorrence, "the honor and the reputation of my right-minded compatriots being so strongly threatened."[33] Aranda passed on Williams's letter without comment, which in itself implied that Franklin had confirmed Williams's observation and Aranda was satisfied.[34]

The practice of British privateers posing as Americans complicated matters. On the other hand, American privateers did indeed act like pirates on occasion. One of these instances occurred before France signed the treaties of trade and alliance, and the second instance occurred afterward, but before Spain declared war. First, an American corsair had captured a French ship destined for Spain that was carrying a cargo that had originated in England. *La Fortunée* was seized and taken to Boston, where its cargo was disposed of and sold. The incident outraged both France and Spain. Spanish authorities, presumably Floridablanca, sent Aranda a note dated October 23, 1777, in which the latter was informed that because the American seizure was "prejudicial" to Spain, the king had suspended "the consignment of money that he was going to give them."[35]

Don Ignacio Heredia, the secretary of the Spanish legation, received the note during Aranda's absence. Heredia immediately shared his king's displeasure with Vergennes. Aranda soon returned and confronted Grand about the matter. One can only imagine how that meeting went. Grand quickly took the news to the commissioners, who recognized the gravity of the situation and immediately sent Grand back to Aranda with a response. Grand appeared before Aranda in a "most submissive" disposition, telling the Spanish ambassador that the commissioners would petition Congress for complete restitution for the ship and its cargo. Additionally, they would have Congress order that all American corsairs stop partaking in such activities, and they would send orders to all agents in European ports to inform the American captains to be more cautious.

Perhaps underscoring the seriousness of the matter, the commissioners sent Grand back to Aranda the following day with a rough draft of a memorial that apologized for the seizure of the *Fortunée*. It continued that the ship and its cargo, the "value thereof would be returned." Vergennes received and acknowledged the draft and wanted news of it suppressed.[36] He already had enough problems dealing with American privateers without the British becoming aware of this case.

Aranda dutifully conveyed the commissioners' reaction and the drafted memorial to Madrid, where Floridablanca, presumably, wrote in a marginal note that the Americans' request for the loan and their reaction to *La Fortunée's* seizure had met with royal approval. The "American representations" have "earned the pleasure of His Majesty," and, as a result, the king would continue to support their cause. He would not, however, "bind himself to promises or contracts because of the aid he is giving." The marginal note continued with the observation that the king had many considerations in Europe and would not get his country entangled.[37]

The whole episode, beginning with the request for additional funds and ending with the apology for the seizure of *La Fortunée,* smacks of Franklin's sense of diplomacy as well as his grasp of the problems created by privateering. Deane secretly had been encouraging American captains to take prizes and dispose of them in French ports. He had hoped to draw France into the war and obtain an alliance. Lee suspected Franklin of complacency toward France and all Europeans. Only Franklin seemed to have a nonconfrontational approach.

Franklin and Aranda had ceased meeting with one another after France's alliance with the colonies. Instead, Ferdinand Grand had become the intermediary. For example, in July 1778, Franklin received a complaint from the Spanish government that an American captain's agent had been detained in the Canary Islands. Grand delivered the complaint. Gustavus Conyngham had been charged with capturing Spanish ships for their prizes. In other words, rather than respecting a neutral country on the high seas, he was taking advantage of his American commission to enrich himself. When his agent, Graciano Sieulanne, tried to transport one of Conyngham's prizes away from the Spanish port of Santa Cruz de Tenerife, the authorities took him and the ship into their possession. The agent had complained to Franklin because he wanted compensation.[38]

Franklin apparently heard complaints from the Spanish authorities that such incidents had not been limited to Conyngham. In a letter sent to Floridablanca through Grand, Franklin detailed the measures that the Congress had taken to prevent privateering and "the wrongful conduct on the part of our ship owners and seafarers." To justify such actions when they occurred, he rationalized, "It would surprise us that [England's] annoying example finds supporters among some individuals of a nation that they have offended against so strongly." In other words, some captains may have chosen to copy the acts of their adversaries. He added that this did not excuse Conyngham. It was "a crime to have attacked a nation for which Congress feels respect."[39]

Even as Franklin received Sieulanne's complaint, Floridablanca wrote to Aranda complaining about Conyngham's "atrocities," which he "continually commits along our coasts." The Spanish minister had heard about the same incident involving Sieulanne from Tomás Cólogan, a Spanish merchant based in Tenerife. Cólogan wrote that Conyngham, "as a pirate," had "unjustly" taken a Swedish ship, the *Henrica Sofia*, with a cargo belonging to the "vassals of His Catholic Majesty."[40] Franklin received a copy of this letter, along with Sieulanne's complaint.[41]

Probably more telling was a missive that Diego Gardoqui sent to Arthur Lee, then serving as the commissioner to Spain. Gardoqui noted that Conyngham's capture of the *Henrica Sofia*, the same Swedish ship chartered by a Spanish company and heading for a Spanish port, had caused major disgust in Spain. He recommended that the ship be returned and that Conyngham be heavily fined. Gardoqui continued, announcing severe repercussions. Spain was closing its ports to Conyngham because he did not act like a proper American corsair. Instead, he managed a crew of "French adventurers" and carried out attacks in violation of the law of nations. The commissioners could not help but realize that the incident had put Spanish aid in jeopardy.[42]

Apparently finding the waters closer to Britain too dangerous, Conyngham started prowling the Atlantic from the Iberian Peninsula to the Canary Islands. By so doing, he had access to the friendly confines of Spanish harbors as well as contact with agents for American companies in places like La Coruña, Cádiz, and Tenerife. Conyngham had also arranged for or hired his own agents, either in port or traveling to meet him: Graciano Sieulanne was one example. As Conyngham's "prize master" in Tenerife, it was his complaint about being "unfairly" detained and about the prize ship in his charge being taken by Spanish authorities that had reached Franklin.

Spanish merchant Tomás Cólogan Valois (or "Walsh" in English), a second-generation Irishman and now Spanish subject who ran an international firm from Tenerife, had done business with England as well as with the thirteen colonies. He had chartered the *Honoria Sophia* [*Henrica Sofia*] for a shipment of goods that were to be picked up in London and taken to Tenerife. Cólogan's brother had a company based in London.

When the ship did not arrive on schedule, Cólogan became concerned. He wrote to his brother that he feared that "the Americans" had taken the *Henrica Sofía*. Unaware of who the captain was, he noted that an American corsair was sighted among the islands. He had surmised correctly. It was Conyngham's ship, the fourteen-gun *Revenge,* that had spotted and captured the Swedish ship somewhere off the Portuguese coast. Conyngham had boarded the captured ship and taken some goods for himself and then assigned a part of his crew to take the prize to Boston or Philadelphia. He then continued on to the Canary Islands.

Because the *Henrica Sofía* had originated in England, Conyngham could have made an honest mistake. Nevertheless, he had captured a Swedish boat charted by a Spanish company with a Spanish cargo that had departed from London.[43] He could have listened to the ship's captain, noted the crew, or checked the manifests. In addition, he had chosen not to take his prize into a more convenient Spanish port, as he had done with another prize.

While sailing to the Canary Islands, Conyngham captured a British brig, *La Contesse de Monton,* and had it taken into Santa Cruz de Tenerife while he waited offshore to make sure things were safe.[44] One of the captured crew from the *Henrica Sofía* who was aboard the *Contesse de Monton* escaped and swam ashore, where he told of the plight of his ship. Thereupon, the Spanish authorities detained Sieulanne and took possession of *La Contesse de Monton.* They also wanted to detain Conyngham, but he escaped, sailing for America while leaving his "prize master" to deal with the authorities. He would later be captured and imprisoned in England.

Floridablanca had ordered Aranda to demand of the American representatives that "they should make arrangements for due restitution; and for making amends for Conyngham's conduct." Once again, Aranda went to Grand who, in turn, went to Franklin. Grand came back to the Spanish ambassador with a congressional proclamation and a letter that Franklin had addressed to Floridablanca.

Actually, it appears that Franklin had sent a proclamation signed by Henry Laurens, president of the Continental Congress, and an "Extract from the Minutes" signed by Charles Thompson, the congressional secretary. The documents were dated within two days of each other, and Franklin attested to them as being true copies with his signature.[45] The earlier document expressed Congress's disgust with piracy, especially by "American armed vessels" that bring "dishonor upon the national character of these states." It went on to announce that such acts would not be tolerated, instructing the American captains "that they do not capture, seize or plunder any ships or vessels of our enemies being under the protection of neutral, coasts, Nations or Princes." If caught doing so, they "shall not be considered as having Rights to claim Protection from these States" but will suffer punishment from the offended nations.[46]

The extract of the minutes dealt with the capture of a Portuguese ship on its way to Brazil. The ship, named in the document as *Our Lady of Mount Carmel and St. Anthony*, was taken as a prize and sent to Massachusetts. Realizing that a violation had been committed, Congress ordered that the cargo be sold, since it was perishable, and that the ship be sold because its bad state of repair prohibited it from returning to Portugal. Also mentioned was the likely possibility that it would fall prey to British privateers if it tried to depart. The net proceeds from the sales were ordered to be deposited "in the public funds of these United States," in the account of the Committee of Foreign Affairs. That committee would transfer the funds to the American commissioners in Paris who, in turn, would return them to "the lawful and rightful Owners." The document finished with a statement that nothing in "the foregoing Resolutions" barred further action being taken against "the Master or Owners of the private armed Vessel."[47] Aranda sent Franklin's letter and the two congressional documents to Floridablanca.[48]

In the case of Sieulanne's complaint, Franklin recognized that Spain's patience had run its course with Conyngham; they had taken possession of an English ship that Conyngham had legally captured in exchange for one that he had taken illegally. Franklin understood and accepted the act, adding, "We will not inform the Congress of the reasons for the complaint . . . to His Catholic Majesty." He signed off with the hope that with the "wisdom" of this solution, the king of Spain will have faith in this expression of the colonials' feelings toward him and that "he in turn will deign to show us their fruits."[49]

If, however, the continuing exploits of American corsairs like Gustavus Conyngham were any indication, Spain's disapproval most likely was made known to Franklin. Conyngham was problematic, especially with regard to Spain. Conyngham was good at his profession and truly wanted to help his adopted country, but his inexperience in diplomacy and politics left bitter feelings.[50] Not to be overlooked, however, was his greed. Obviously, he had all the traits that were needed to be a licensed corsair-privateer (or pirate). One historian called him Franklin's corsair.[51]

The *Henrica Sofía* was not the only ship carrying cargo owned by Tomás Cólogan's company that had run afoul of a corsair, or, in reality, two corsairs.

In 1779, soon after Spain declared war on Great Britain, a British corsair legally captured the *Goude Ross,* or *Golden Rose,* which was sailing under a Dutch flag and in transit from Hamburg to Tenerife. Holland, the name commonly used for the seven provinces making up the Netherlands, of which Holland was only one, also had entered the war against Great Britain. The ship and most of its crew were being taken to British-occupied New York when it was recaptured by the *Holker,* a sixteen-gun American corsair under Capt. George Geddes.⁵²

The *Holker* and its one-hundred-man crew hailed from Philadelphia and were being financed by Blair McClenachan, a native of Ireland. Captain Geddes, who had worked for McClenachan since before the war, had congressional patents (i.e., Letters of Marque) to operate specifically as a corsair. He only recently had been released from a British prison in New York. His second-in-command, twenty-six-year-old Matthew Lawler, had served two years with Conyngham, as had a good portion of the *Holker's* crew.

Geddes took the *Golden Rose* and another prize, a British ship, to Philadelphia, where he arrived on October 12, 1779. The admiralty court immediately held a hearing that easily dispersed the second prize, but the court had questions about the *Golden Rose.* Juan Miralles became involved. He, in turn, conferred with Robert Morris. The Spanish observer claimed part of the cargo on behalf of Cólogan. The cargo consisted of anchors, rope, clothing, and, as claimed by Cólogan, one thousand *fanegas* of cacao.⁵³ The authorities determined that its disposition must be under the jurisdiction of Pennsylvania. McClenachan protested, perhaps too much, for his efforts resulted in his denouncement and in fines.

Back in Tenerife, Tomás Cólogan was working on multiple fronts. He had his lawyer in Madrid talking to Spanish officialdom, he was writing directly to Morris, and he was sending instructions to his brother in Paris. Juan Cólogan left London and traveled to Ostend, Belgium, where after Christmas he reported to Tomás that Grand had sent a response regarding the issue of the *Golden Rose* and its cargo. Grand would pay the 6 percent on the loan. Juan explained that he had paid the bills drawn "on Congress or others accepted by Doctor Franklin." He then noted that with the recent entry of the Dutch into the war, the value of the continental currency should increase.⁵⁴

In early June 1781, Tomás Cólogan wrote to Juan, who had arrived in Paris. Seeking to get some leverage with his petition in Madrid, he asked his brother to secure letters of recommendation from various influential people in Paris, including Aranda and Franklin, "who must have connections in the Spanish Court." Once acquired, he was to send them to his lawyer in Madrid, don Fermín Sánchez de Muniaín.[55] Then Tomás commented on just how convoluted war and international trade could be when he wrote, "The insurers we think should be answerable to us for any deficiency we should suffer."[56] Who were these insurers? In a subsequent letter to his brother, Tomás made reference to "settling with the underwriters" in "your government," meaning Great Britain, where Juan had his company. Tomás expected English insurers to pay the cost of the cargo that he could not get reimbursed from America.[57]

A day later, Tomás wrote to Robert Morris regarding the "sundry vouchers" with the *Golden Rose*. His brother in Paris had neither heard about nor received any payments. He then suggested that Morris purchase loan bills payable by Grand and accepted by Franklin. "We are assured Franklin uses this method for his own private affairs." Tomas's attempt to get retribution in Madrid had failed, and so he proposed that Juan get the money from Franklin.[58]

While in Paris, Juan Cólogan met with Franklin at least twice. During the first meeting, he was hesitant to bring up the issue of the *Golden Rose*. He assured Tomás, however, that he would do so at the next opportunity, when he and his wife were invited to dine with Franklin. Whether or not he brought up the subject, he wrote his brother that nothing had come of it.[59]

A despondent Tomás replied to his brother that nothing was left to do but wait on Morris. If he did not respond, perhaps Juan could draw a draft from Grand or Franklin that they could fulfill when they heard that the payment had been made in America. Then almost as an aside, Tomás noted that Morris owed him for 125 gallons of wine.[60]

Meanwhile, working through an intermediary company, Morris was able to come up with a solution that prorated the sale of the portion of cargo that Tomás Cólogan had claimed. The solution stipulated that the cost of the cargo would be considered as a loan from Cólogan, to be repaid at 6 percent interest. Juan Cólogan received a letter dated August 4, 1781, from Morris's business associate that explained the situation. The Cólogans would be receiving 57,000 plus 6 percent in Continental paper money. The money would be paid out in Paris to Juan's "friend."[61] Tomás would receive his funds, and Franklin, who was responsible for the actions of the American corsairs as well as for the dispersal of such funds, no doubt had given his approval to Grand.

This information was sent to Juan, who passed it on, the letter assuredly arriving in Tenerife weeks after Tomás penned his sanguine letter. Morris never corresponded with Tomás. Morris, in fact, had larger issues on his plate. In the final days of September, French and Continental forces had engaged a trapped British Army at Yorktown. The British surrendered on October 9, 1781.

Although historians agree that Yorktown effectively ended the war, peace did not come at once. Hostilities continued around the world until the Treaty of Paris was finalized on September 3, 1783. Meanwhile, as Franklin worked to have Conyngham's sentence in England reduced from the charge of piracy, rumors spread that Franklin and his colleagues were about to issue Letters of Marque directing American corsairs to attack Portuguese ships and ports.[62] This concerned Spain, as a lot of Spanish trade and merchandise passed through its neighbor's now peaceful country and ports. If the rumors were true, Aranda wanted to confer with Franklin to make sure that Congress would protect the goods that belonged to the Spanish.

To broach the topic, Aranda used the occasion when the diplomatic corps were gathered and awaiting an audience with the king's son. He sallied up to Franklin and asked him about the rumor. As Aranda related it, Franklin "responded in a natural manner that he neither knew about it or believed it." Franklin explained that for him, England was enemy enough, and the colonies did not need to look for others. When asked if American ships were entering Portuguese ports, an act prohibited by the queen of Portugal, Franklin replied in the negative. He understood, however, that ships under the French flag were welcome and that while American captains knew this, up to now, no one on the American side had taken advantage of it. He added that these "said notions" had originated in London merely to create confusion, and he concluded that he had no knowledge, nor did he believe them to be true.[63]

By this time, both Franklin and Aranda had something more important on their minds: the hope for a cessation of hostilities and negotiating a peace.

9

Betrayal and the Making of Peace

Little did the Cólogans, or probably anyone else in Europe at the time, know or understand that the combined American and French victory at Yorktown would have been impossible without Spanish acquiescence and without its financial support being supplied by way of Cuba and Mexico.[1] Surely, Franklin and his fellow commissioners had no idea. But with time and some hindsight, they may have realized that their diplomatic efforts had something to do with that key victory.

Inexplicably, Franklin and his cohorts chose not to acknowledge the role of Spain regarding the Yorktown victory. The Americans had been profuse in their praise and enthusiasm when Spain entered the war. At one time, congressional representatives had offered to help Spain take Pensacola—a major victory that Spain accomplished on its own. As he noted in a letter to the governor of Cuba, George Washington had openly opined that victory would be at hand once Spain declared war. John Adams wrote to the president of Congress in March 1779 that Spanish assistance would be the key to victory. Spain, he wrote, was "powerful and influential." After Spain's entry into the war, Samuel Adams had declared that Great Britain would have to concentrate on Europe and withdraw its troops from the colonies, thus leaving the colonies to their own fate.[2]

The financial value of Spain's aid was incalculable, including, but not limited to, the covert assistance and use of its ports before it entered the war. Even Spain's attempt to negotiate an early peace, about which Franklin confidently reported to Congress, helped the cause of independence. Spanish historian Martha Gutiérrez-Steinkamp points out that funds came from various sources and were not always recorded: loans, subsidies, gifts, tradeable assets, ship repairs, and payments in various currencies over the years.[3] Diego Gardoqui's biographer, Calderón Cuadrado, estimated that in 1777 alone, Spanish aid had amounted to 5.9 percent of that country's income.[4] She wrote that no one in revolutionary America seemed to recognize Spain's help, and she cited an Aranda letter complaining that the American commissioners did not believe Spain had sent aid to the colonies.[5]

This raises the question as to what Spain's expenses were during its actual participation in the war. What was the cost of sacrificing Lt. Gen. Juan de Lángara's fleet to successfully hamper Admiral George Rodney's attempt to lift the siege of Gibraltar? Or the cost of the armada and soldiers for the victories at Mobile and Pensacola? Or the monies paid to cover the expenses of the French fleet in the Caribbean? Neither is much made of Spain's myriad victories in its successful defense of Central America, nor of its wresting of the Mediterranean island of Menorca from Great Britain. The expenses incurred from the war-long siege of Gibraltar were paid, in part, by France, but Spain bore the bulk of the costs.

Moreover, until recently, historians in the United States have echoed the American Commission in Paris and overlooked the important part that Spain's military prowess played in the eventual American victory. One historian complained that not a word was said by Congress when Spain sent British prisoners captured at Pensacola to New York for exchange; no comment was made about the blow to British prestige for losing that port. This hinted at a sense of ingratitude that has permeated US-Spanish relations throughout the years.[6] Even Carl Van Doren, in his unequaled and most comprehensive biography of Franklin, quite incorrectly claimed that Spain had given scant support during the war; he wrote that Spain had been of "little help" to France.[7] Another Pulitzer Prize–winner highlighted France's monetary contributions without mentioning Spain's aid at all. Gordon Wood's *The Americanization of Benjamin Franklin* did not even list Spain in its index, and he mentioned the country sparingly in his text.[8] Jonathon Dull, on the other hand, cited an all-too-common American self-righteous contempt for other nations.[9] More recently, Larrie Ferreiro cited Dull and added that Vergennes feared that the insurgents would likely lose without direct intervention. He wanted to avoid a reunited Britain.

Franklin's attempt to commiserate with John Jay contrasted with his earlier correspondence with Aranda. He did not voice much appreciation to Jay regarding Spain's contributions to the war effort. Quite the contrary. He ignored everything he certainly knew or should have known about Spain's role. As noted throughout his negotiations with Spain, he found many opportunities to acknowledge its help, not just to Aranda or Floridablanca but also to operatives such as Diego Gardoqui. For example, he wrote, "I have long been made sensible by many instances of your friendship for America and the kindness you have shown my countrymen. I beg you to accept my thankful acknowledgements."[10]

In the more than two years he spent in Madrid, Jay managed to alienate almost everyone, with the possible exception of the French ambassador. His apparent distaste for Spain and its people was surpassed only by that of his wife. He either consciously refused to acknowledge Spain's continuing aid to his country, or he did not know of it. This lack of knowledge is difficult to understand. He had to have been aware of Spain's efforts while he was in Congress. While he was in Spain, the Spanish press had reported on all Spanish, French, and American activities. In Madrid, Jay could have read of the capture of a sixty-one-ship British convoy on its way to the West Indies, and of Spanish victories at St. Joseph (Michigan), on the Gulf Coast, and in Central America and Menorca. Spanish silver even subsidized the victory at Yorktown.[11] Perhaps his inability to read Spanish was an excuse. His secretary, William Carmichael, was fluent in Spanish, but Jay suspected Carmichael of being disloyal.

As mentioned above, Jay's exorbitant living expenses led him to become an embarrassment, and he blamed the Spanish government for the resulting indignities.[12] It was with good reason that Floridablanca met with him only sparingly and for the most part tried to avoid him. Perhaps Jay was affected by the death of one of his daughters. Whatever the reasons, Jay's efforts resulted in a relatively unproductive two and a half years in Madrid.

At Franklin's summons, Jay left Spain and traveled to Paris. As one historian understated the matter, Jay arrived "a little out of humor with [the Spanish] court."[13] As noted earlier, while Jay was in Madrid, he had lived off the generosity of the Spanish court until they cut him off. Then he sought funds from Franklin, which gave rise to Franklin's consternation.[14]

In March 1781, Jay informed Franklin that Floridablanca had promised him a loan of 3 million *pesos fuertes,* and Franklin received a letter from Gardoqui that said the money would be used to pay for goods already purchased; the balance would be settled by paying the remaining debt, deducting what had already been paid. In other words, the money would be used to pay off the bills and loans Jay had run up.[15]

Franklin complained that he was perplexed by the "storm" of bills evident throughout his correspondence with Jay.[16] At one point, in a long letter dealing with Jay's finances, Franklin complained to Jay about being forced to spend too much time with "extraneous" stuff, such as bills of exchange and money matters.[17] On another occasion, he wrote the "cursed Bills ... do us infinite Prejudice."[18] This last comment was written after the Spanish minister of finance, Francisco Cabarrús, had given Jay a $30,000 line of credit.[19] Two months later, Franklin informed Jay that Cabarrús's loan had been paid in full and, moreover, he had received a promise of "six million" more for the year to be paid quarterly.[20] Finally, in the very letter in which Franklin had asked Jay to leave Madrid and move to Paris, he announced that all of Jay's bills had been paid.[21]

Franklin did receive an up-to-date report on the battle of Yorktown by means of private correspondence; however, the information omitted Spain's role in the conflict, and apparently no one in Spain bothered to share that information with Jay.[22] The latter first heard rumors of the allied victory at Yorktown; this was followed by a report detailed enough to list 6,000 troops and 1,899 sailors and Blacks taken prisoner, the capture of 170 canons (of which 75 were bronze), and the burning of a large ship along with a number transports. Still, he heard nothing of Spain's role in the affair.[23]

This discrepancy brings us back to Yorktown as a particular illustrative point. The battle would not have taken place had it not been for Spain. Upon Spain's insistence and promise of support, the French fleet under Admiral de Grasse had sailed north out of the Caribbean Sea. The promise, which was made by Spanish strategist Francisco Saavedra de Sangronis, assured the French admiral that the Spanish navy would protect the French possessions in the West Indies against British incursions.[24] But money was needed to pay for the effort, both for American and French ground forces as well as for expenses incurred by de Grasse's fleet.[25] Saavedra had solved this problem by collecting the necessary funds in Spanish Puerto Rico and Santo Domingo, although most of it came from Havana.

In Cuba's capital, Saavedra and local officials collected and packaged 500,000 *pesos* and sent the funds north with de Grasse to Yorktown. The money had been collected from the city's merchants. In addition, Bernardo de Gálvez had arranged for another million *pesos* to be sent to de Grasse. That money originated from Mexico.

In short, Spain helped pay for the battle of Yorktown and eventual defeat of the British.[26] Saavedra would later write that de Grasse and he agreed they "could not waste the most decisive opportunity in the whole war."[27] Lest there be any doubt, upon his arrival in the Chesapeake Bay, de Grasse wrote to Washington that he had come with 1.2 million *livres* from Havana.[28] Comte de Rochambeau, who had placed his French troops under Washington's command, wrote that upon receiving the news that de Grasse's fleet had arrived and thus closed the sea approaches to Yorktown, he saw Washington "waving his hat at me with demonstrative gestures of the greatest joy."[29] Moreover, de Grasse later wrote that the victory at Yorktown had been enabled by Spanish money, which might in truth be regarded as "the bottom dollars" upon which American independence was based.³⁰

The Spanish and French understood Spain's key role in the war, but when time came for a peace agreement, the American commissioners, led by Jay and Adams and acquiesced by Franklin, deliberately omitted any mention of it. In a letter to Jay, Franklin wrote that Great Britain appeared to want to negotiate with the United States "exclusive of France, Spain, and Holland, which, so far as relates to France, is impossible; and I believe they will be content that we leave them the other two." He added that "since Spain does not think our friendship worth cultivating," Jay should find out what is owed and pay them off quickly.³¹

News of Yorktown could not be ignored in London. The loss of the battle eventually led to a motion of no confidence for Lord North, and the prime minister was forced to resign. The new government—led by the Marquess of Rockingham and then, upon his death, by the Earl of Shelburne—sought to end the hostilities and quickly let it be known that American independence would be acceptable. Franklin took advantage of the opportunity. For a few months in 1782, he was the only designated congressional representative in Paris. John Adams was in Holland, and Henry Laurens had been captured and imprisoned in the tower of London.

This is when Franklin asked Jay to move to Paris, stating that "there is much talk of a treaty proposed" and that Jay "would be of infinite service." He noted the absence of the others, specifying that Laurens was on parole.³² On the advice of Vergennes, to avoid any appearance of a slight to Spain, Jay's secretary William Carmichael was left in Madrid.³³

A little over two weeks after Jay's arrival in Paris in June 1782, Franklin submitted his conditions for a peace treaty to London. He framed his missive with a list of necessary and advisable articles, implying that the former were nonnegotiable. The necessary articles included full and complete independence, withdrawal of all British forces, acceptable American boundaries between the independent states and loyal colonies, and fishing rights off Newfoundland and elsewhere, including the right to fish for whale. The advisable articles included a British acknowledgement of war guilt, the receipt of compensation, the cessation of Canada, and freedom from British customs duties for American goods and shipping. His conditions, especially the necessary articles, would be the basis for the eventual treaty.³⁴ While Jay and Adams have come under criticism for disassociating the interests of America from those in Europe, it is important to note that Franklin was the first to do so. Except for the suggestion that Canada be ceded to the new United States, he shared his view with Vergennes.³⁵

Within days of Jay's arrival in Paris, Franklin took him to meet Aranda. Surely, the importance of Spain was not lost on either of them. Otherwise, why arrange such a quick meeting? As the appointed representative to Spain, Jay would be left to negotiate with Aranda. Nevertheless, to prove the point, Aranda hosted both commissioners for an afternoon dinner in his residence. Aranda hoped to create a friendly atmosphere in which they would all better understand one another.[36] In a subsequent letter to the French ambassador in Madrid, Jay wrote that Aranda "appears frank and candid as well as sagacious."[37]

Yet Aranda preferred to negotiate with Franklin. As late as September 1784, and long after a treaty had been signed, Aranda still referred to Franklin as the plenipotentiary minister of the North American States.[38] They knew each other, and Aranda felt more comfortable with him.

But Jay's presence presented Aranda with a new player. He asked if both men had the authority to negotiate with him and if Franklin had superiority among the commissioners. Franklin and Jay assured him that only Jay would be representing the United States to Spain. They also added that Franklin fully agreed with Jay's positions regarding a future treaty.[39]

From this point forward, Franklin had little to do diplomatically with Spain. The final negotiations for ending the war were left to Jay. Direct correspondence between Franklin and Spanish officials after 1782 is relatively nonexistent.

When the rebelling colonies first sought aid from and alliances with other countries, that was all they wanted. Their very survival depended on France—and Spain. And independence had been their goal. Now that independence was a reality, other matters came into focus. Franklin's articles initiated the American position. The boundaries of the new country were an issue, as were navigation on the Mississippi River, fishing rights, and trade agreements, among other things. The other belligerents also had goals beyond American independence. Spain, for its part, had been very clear; France wanted complete control of Dunkirk. Holland sought the return of its lost possessions in India and hoped to be the center for European trade with America.

Each country negotiated on its own with Great Britain and with one another. Vergennes tried to keep some sense of order in the matter. He agreed that each country could negotiate its own treaties as long as they went "hand in hand" and were signed on the same day.[40] Those first formal meetings among Aranda, Jay, and Franklin set the stage for negotiations, but then Jay became bedridden with a serious case of influenza, and he remained incapacitated for the rest of July.

Aranda had no choice but to wait. Time seemed to be on his side, and the Americans sensed it. Early on, they had realized that, as Jay put it, Spain was "not tired of the war." They wanted Jamaica and Gibraltar, while "Mahon would be a trump card in their hands."[41] By then, news would have reached Europe of Spanish military victories at Menorca (or Mahon, as Jay referred to the Mediterranean island), on the Caribbean island of Roatan in Central America, and in the Bahamas off the Florida coast. Aranda anticipated similar news regarding Gibraltar, where a combined Spanish and French force continued to lay siege to the rock. Overlooked by subsequent histories was a joint Spanish-French plan to invade Great Britain's most important West Indies port of Kingston, Jamaica.[42]

No doubt, Franklin and Jay presented the American position. As he had done in Madrid, Jay insisted on immediate Spanish recognition. He also stressed that his new country's western boundary would be the western bank of the Mississippi River, which meant free navigation of that river.

Regarding the first matter, Aranda saw it as being of little concern. The opportunity to benefit from the granting of independence had passed. Independence would be fully recognized with the signing of the final treaties. As Spain's ambassador, he would treat Jay as an equal. The second matter, however, was more complicated, and it would have to be negotiated.

Not surprisingly, both Jay and Aranda kept diaries of their respective participation in the negotiations. Over time, historians have drawn the conclusion that one or the other had left a slightly incomplete history.[43] Aranda had a "big picture" mentality. He was a pragmatist who looked into the future and questioned what would result from any current agreement. He believed that Spain's military prowess had won the Gulf Coast. Its victories on the Mississippi River and at Mobile and Pensacola were significant. He saw the Mississippi as a valuable asset. Control of the Gulf Coast and the Mississippi River would secure Spain's possessions from Central America north into what is today Texas and the southwestern United States. Moreover, control of the river, including New Orleans, would prevent corsairs from seeking safe and sound refuge in the area.

In this context, Gibraltar was not a priority, and news at the end of September of a failed attempt to wrest it from British control made it even less so. The recent Spanish victory on Menorca became an excellent consolation in the Mediterranean.[44] But Aranda's instructions insisted that he must not give up Gibraltar. He eventually received a reiteration of that position, even after he had agreed with Vergennes to forgo Gibraltar.[45]

Aranda had authority from Madrid to negotiate but not to conclude. He felt himself to be handicapped, and he felt that Madrid had not given him clear guidance. The Spanish court had wavered between its distaste for England and the dangerous precedent of helping rebel colonies on the American continent. Yet he would do what he could.

On August 3, a recovered Jay met with Aranda to begin their negotiations, which would continue over a series of meetings and dinners. The well-prepared Aranda supplied maps and supporting documents to bolster his position. He reputedly was the only emissary during the negotiations who had brought such supporting visual aids to the table. In one meeting, he drew a line along the 30th latitude to delineate the northern boundary of the Floridas. Jay did not hesitate to disagree, relying on congressional instructions that specified a border farther south; Congress also insisted on the Mississippi River as being the new country's western border. Jay argued that naming the river the western boundary was not only logical but natural. In effect, with Franklin's concurrence, he argued for a concept that a few decades later would become known as Manifest Destiny.[46]

Aranda pointed out Spain's military victories and would not acquiesce. The real conflict was over the free navigation of the Mississippi River, and neither side was willing to budge. Jay constantly used the excuse that he was bound by his instructions, while Aranda, limited by his own government, became frustrated. Jay and Franklin complained to Vergennes, who, in turn, talked to Aranda about seeking a compromise.[47]

When Franklin became incapacitated by various ailments, Jay became the prime negotiator with Great Britain. Aranda knew that Jay was talking with the British, but what he may not have known was that Jay was not letting his instructions impede him. Jay suggested to his British counterparts that Great Britain should recapture West Florida. This was an immense breach of trust, if not honesty, for he encouraged a foe to attack an ally to help him have an improved bargaining position over that ally.

One United States historian has described Jay's action as being "extraordinarily shortsighted" and "an act of bad faith."[48] Another historian merely stated that Jay had innocently offered the idea and that he had "allowed his own perturbation" over Spanish objections to the western boundary and free navigation "to color his judgment." Perhaps more clear-minded, the British were hesitant about the offer. Thus, while petitioning Vergennes for help, he compounded the French minister's task of bringing together the "precarious bundle of alliances."[49]

Although he went along with the final product, Franklin felt that Jay's duplicity had caused him "pain that the Character for Candor and Fidelity to its Engagement, which should always characterize a great People should have been impeached thereby." He worried that he and his colleagues had sown "seeds of Enmity to the Court of Spain."[50]

As Jay negotiated the final preliminary treaty with Great Britain, there can be no doubt that his controversial suggestion resonated. The finished preliminary treaty included a secret clause that ceded West Florida to Great Britain. On the morning of November 30, Jay, Adams, and the recently recovered Franklin went to the British emissary's suite in the Grand Hotel Muscovite, and they signed the preliminary treaty between the United States and Great Britain.[51]

Franklin, who was left with the task of trying to placate the French and Spanish, was quick to point out that neither the treaty nor the terms therein were formally binding "until the terms of a peace shall be agreed upon between Great Britain and France," which of course also meant Spain. And, if there could be no agreement and no further aid were forthcoming, "the whole edifice sinks to the ground."[52] He added that if Parliament hesitated, then perhaps "a little more success in the West Indies [i.e., Jamaica] this winter might totally turn the heads of that giddy nation."[53] Of course, any such success would necessarily involve Spanish forces, for he could only be referring to the Spanish-French plans and preparations for an invasion of Jamaica.

Naturally, the preliminary treaty had an impact on Aranda. Like Vergennes, he knew that the eventual peace had to include France and Spain. Nevertheless, Aranda astutely recognized its importance. He, too, had been negotiating with the British. As mentioned, he was offered Gibraltar for the Floridas. In reference to Franklin's hint about more success in the West Indies, a possible French and Spanish invasion of Jamaica still loomed.

Taking England's only, and extremely important, possession in the Caribbean had been planned ever since Spain entered the war. The city and port of Kingston stood at the center of Great Britain's West Indian trade. But when France's Admiral de Grasse was defeated and taken prisoner while on his way to supplement the armada preparing for the attack on Kingston, some doubt surfaced.

Not to be daunted, Spain sent Francisco Saavedra, the individual who had been key in the strategy and financing of the Battle of Yorktown, to France. He spent a little over two weeks in Paris in June 1782, and he was escorted by Aranda to meet with King Louis XVI, Vergennes, and various other French officials. Saavedra's task was to convince the French of the positive feasibility of resurrecting the plans for a successful attack on Jamaica. After being favorably received in Paris, he traveled to Madrid with a tentative plan of action that now was being fulfilled.[54]

Historians to date have tended to overlook or belittle this attempt by the Spanish and French to regroup for an invasion of Jamaica. For example, US diplomatic historians Thomas A. Bailey and Richard B. Morris do not mention it at all in their monographs.[55] Jonathon Dull gives a detailed account of the French and Spanish plan for the capture of Jamaica, "which of itself might drive England to peace."[56] But he documents it without mentioning Saavedra's presence in France or the fact that Saavedra returned to Spain with the French-approved plan of attack.[57]

A closer look at Saavedra's fifteen days in Paris in 1782 would seem to indicate that a possible attack on Jamaica had played a more significant role in the ongoing peace discussions than previously thought. From June 1 to the 15, he visited with the king twice and with Vergennes three times, including a June 13 meeting in the minister's residence that included the French ministers of state, marine, and treasury, along with Aranda. He dined or met with Aranda a dozen times, and, finally, he was sent to Spain with a plan of action that included gathering forces in the Spanish port of Cádiz with the intent of joining forces in the West Indies.[58]

The combined armadas would amount to seventy-five ships of the line and 25,000 troops. A French admiral, Count Jean Baptiste Charles d'Estaing, had followed Saavedra to Spain and eventually to Cádiz to command the expedition. D'Estaing selected Lafayette, who had arrived in Cádiz two days before Christmas 1782, to command the land forces. The Marquis de Lafayette would also be made the governor of Jamaica should the invasion succeed.[59] According to Dull, d'Estaing was ordered by the French Council of State to delay sailing as long as possible while France tried to convince the Spanish court of the dangers of the attack. Dull went into detail about the planning and seriousness of it, concluding that peace had come just in time to prevent the most massive naval operation undertaken up to that time. He also noted that the British were elated over de Grasse's capture but were keeping an eye on the buildup in Cádiz.[60]

In October, the treaty talks stalemated. A frustrated Aranda reported to Floridablanca that Jay had no authority beyond his instructions, and, in that context, he was a "hiccup." He continued that the Americans were angry because Spain had never officially recognized them and that while in Madrid, the American diplomats were treated as lackeys. This complaint had to come from Jay. Moreover, the Americans had also slighted Spain's aid when compared to their praise of France's contributions. Aranda added, "I will not hide from the King that these American deputies are very alienated from our court."

The ambassador questioned how he should react. He noted that he had tried to befriend Jay, treating him well. "I have visited with him and his wife three or four times: having eaten with them in my house." Contrary to normal diplomacy, the preliminary treaty struck by the Americans with their British adversaries created difficulties for further negotiations between Great Britain and Spain. Aside from their actions, Aranda complained that his own country's "delays and vacillations" had left him "helpless" when confronting the Americans. Still somewhat favorable to them, he reported that the opportunity for a good treaty had been lost. The Americans did not take offense but only wanted a just treaty. Aranda felt that the negotiations had failed with no thought to the future.[61]

Floridablanca blamed Jay and then inquired whether he should ask Congress to remove Jay and authorize Carmichael to conclude the treaty. Aranda advised against it. Likewise, going to Franklin, who they felt was "more intelligent, more imaginative, and more flexible than Jay," was not an option. The ambassador now believed that it was too late and that trying to replace Jay would result in embarrassment. Instead, he would concentrate on his talks with Vergennes and the British representatives.[62]

On the one hand, as much as Jay tried for or wanted immediate recognition, Aranda was limited by Floridablanca's instructions. Despite this, however, Aranda would still manage to steadfastly represent what he thought was best for Spain. At one point, Floridablanca authorized Aranda to explore the possibility of what Spain would get in lieu of pursuing Gibraltar. Aranda shared this with Vergennes to pass on to the British. Vergennes considered the proud and sometimes agonizingly difficult Spaniard to be "an estimable man. He knows his duties; he is exact in filling them and it is not possible to carry any further his love and attachment for his country."[63]

Both men knew that the English had lost their appetite for prolonging the war. When a favorable reply came back, Aranda agreed with Vergennes, who asked the Spanish ambassador, in effect, to violate his instructions and strike a deal foregoing Gibraltar. England would agree to cede East Florida, thus giving Spain both Floridas. In addition, Spain could keep Menorca in exchange for returning the Bahamas, and Great Britain would be granted timber-cutting rights in Yucatán.[64]

Three days after Aranda agreed with Vergennes to forgo Gibraltar, Floridablanca sent instructions to him not to sign any preliminary agreement without obtaining Gibraltar, but these instructions arrived too late. Floridablanca was livid. Perhaps justifying his actions to his minister of state, Aranda wrote on New Year's Day 1783, "Respect and obedience bound me to blind submission but the loyalty of a good subject and an awareness of the real situation compelled me to do what was right." In reference to Gibraltar, he openly questioned Floridablanca. How long "will one rock trouble three empires?"[65]

A little over a month later, the preliminary agreement was signed at Versailles on January 20, 1783. In so doing, Aranda had parried Jay's audacity and violated his own definite instructions: Spain obtained the Floridas and Menorca by ceding Gibraltar and trading back the Bahamas. He had secured the Gulf Coast and both banks of the mouth of the Mississippi River. But more importantly, Jay's secret article had been eliminated from the treaty between the United States and Great Britain.[66]

Aranda's decision seemed astonishing for the times. Backed into a diplomatic corner, he had taken advantage of the moment and exercised an authority that he did not possess to solve the problem confronting him; and he had chosen peace, thus ending a war. Moreover, he had fulfilled a personal belief in protecting the future of Spain's presence in America. Aranda and the Duke of Manchester signed the final treaty on September 3, 1783.

Aranda was happy and perhaps surprised to receive a communiqué from Carlos III through Floridablanca. His Majesty wrote, "I am very pleased with your services and very certain that you will continue them for me. I the King."[67] Apparently, the king and his advisors realized the legitimacy and benefit of Aranda's action. Or perhaps there was another, more reasonable justification. Historian Eric Beerman writes in *España y la independencia de Estados Unidos,* his definitive history of Spain's role in the independence of the United States, that all along, Carlos III's priority and orientation had been the Americas. The blockade of Gibraltar and the projected French-Spanish invasion of the British Islands had been mere diversionary tactics.[68] Aside from the independence won by the North Americans, Spain had come out of the war surprisingly well.

As mentioned, after Franklin initiated talks with the British, he had left the concluding negotiations to Jay and Adams. A period of illness from various causes kept him away from the actual talks for two months. No doubt he was made aware of and approved the process, including knowledge of Jay's indiscretion. Nevertheless, Franklin still had to deal with what he must have considered tiresome, if not mundane, details, along with soothing the intercommission rivalries documented in detail elsewhere[69] and being designated as the person to explain to Vergennes the bilateral preliminary treaty that left out France and its allies. For example, one such problem had come to Franklin's attention immediately after Spain declared war. An American citizen who had received his papers from Franklin was arrested in Alicante, Spain. The Spanish mistook him to be British, and his arguments otherwise had proved of no avail.

Franklin received the letter, and even as he dealt with the Sieulanne and Conyngham matter, he passed on a plea to Aranda, who forwarded the complaint with his opinion to Floridablanca. Without disagreeing, he merely noted that Franklin had affirmed that the man was "a person in favor of the United States."[70] Not only ships could be mistaken for their country of origin—so, too, could human beings.

Upon being notified of peace, Congress immediately assigned Robert Morris to expedite the necessary orders to all its ports commanding all American corsairs to cease their wartime activities. Congress also sent word to French and American land forces to cease hostilities.

Throughout these trying times, Franklin had remained the respected and trusted American diplomat. Now that peace had come, he was undecided about returning to his homeland. At the very least, he had survived to witness what he had written about to the Spanish prince those many years before: that the result of the pending rebellion, "the Event of this great Contest" would "likely soon to act a Part of some Importance on the Stage of Human Affairs."[71] But more work remained.

Epilogue

Hostilities had ended and colonial independence had been achieved. John Adams thought that Spain had received more than it deserved. Back in America, James Madison had a more clear-minded appreciation of Spain; yet more work remained.[1] The elderly and ill Franklin would not return to Philadelphia until 1785, and Aranda would not be recalled until 1789.

William Carmichael replaced Jay in Madrid in April 1782. Ten years later, George Washington named him the US ambassador to Spain. Floridablanca shared the information that Carmichael would remain in Madrid, writing to Aranda that "yesterday Carmichael was presented to the King as the Thirteen Colonies' representative."[2]

Francisco Rendón, who had replaced Juan de Miralles as Spain's congressional observer upon the latter's death, wrote that in an effort to save money, Congress decided to appoint Franklin, Adams, and Jefferson as its ministers plenipotentiary to Europe. Rather than sending an ambassador to each European country, they were instructed to work out of Paris to propose treaties with "most of the maritime powers of Europe."[3]

This very odd policy was perhaps an indication of the major problem of the Continental Congress. Its constitution had established the United States as a collection of thirteen sovereign states, each with an equal vote in a governing body that had little or no ability to enforce its actions. Now that the goal of independence had been achieved, the more serious problem of governance became paramount. Congress was an imperfect instrument for solving the problems of interstate rivalries, domestic unrest, and, most importantly, the country's dire financial problems.

All of this underlined the more serious question as to whether the colonies would remain united or become a series of separate states, not unlike small countries. Historian Thomas A. Bailey writes that after the war, the country "consisted of thirteen separate entities" and that the word "'United' seemed at times merely an ironical adjective."[4] None of the newly independent colonies' pressing needs would be resolved until after the painstaking process of drawing up and accepting a new constitution and creating a government was completed in 1789. Until then, Europe and the colonies would deal with each other somewhat awkwardly, and this included the oddity of having three diplomats in one city. This perhaps also contributed to the short American memory regarding Spain's role in the achievement of independence.

Upon receiving their new appointments and instructions, the three American "deputies" went to work. Along with making contact and beginning talks with other countries, they sent Aranda a formal note along with their instructions, "to treat and negotiate" with "His Catholic Majesty" a treaty of amity and commerce and send it to Congress for its final ratification.[5]

As per their request, Aranda dutifully sent the missive on to Madrid. Within a week, however, Aranda responded that while he appreciated the Americans' desire to negotiate a friendly treaty, he had to remind them that the proper channel for doing such things was to meet in one or the other capital of the involved countries. He referenced the difficulty of the recent negotiations in which more than two countries were involved, concluding that it would be more efficient to negotiate in Madrid rather than in a third country, which could complicate matters. He then inquired if it would be possible for one or more of the American deputies to travel to Madrid? He simply desired that a "satisfactory" result for both countries would come from your "good intelligence and friendship."[6]

A month later, the three Americans sent a reply with a copy of their congressional instructions. Franklin almost certainly composed the letter. They explained that Congress thought it more efficient to conduct its European diplomatic work in Paris. They understood and appreciated Aranda's concerns, but they had already made contact with other countries and begun their work. It would be difficult to leave Paris until they finished what they had started, and that "may take up much time." Hopefully, the court in Madrid would understand and make an exception to their general rule.[7]

Floridablanca, with the king's approval, and perhaps with magnanimous attention toward the new country, notified Aranda of a different solution. Instead of trying to convince the American representative to go to Madrid, the Spanish government chose to send its own representative to the United States. The king appointed Diego de Gardoqui as Spain's first official minister to the United States. Carmichael immediately reported Spain's actions to Franklin, noting that Gardoqui was well "known to Mr. Adams and your Excellency." He added that "the choice of him . . . may be considered as a proof of the good disposition of the Court, which tho' hurt by the Silence of Congress, has manifested much attention to the Objects relative to the interests of Individuals of America for which I have had recourse to its Interference."[8]

Gardoqui had full power to negotiate any treaty of commerce and amity directly with Congress. This included the unsolved problem of free navigation of the Mississippi River. This solution rendered null any negotiations in Paris.[9] Ironically, Gardoqui ended up befriending and negotiating with Jay, who had returned to the United States to become the new country's secretary of foreign affairs. Contrary to his stance while in Europe, Jay eventually acquiesced to Gardoqui and recommended that Congress give up any rights of navigation of the Mississippi River in exchange for more agreeable trading privileges, which appeared to favor New England. Representatives from the southern states, which had western claims to the river, rose up in Congress to block approval of the treaty.[10]

Although their official business seemed done, both Franklin and Aranda continued to enjoy the copious attractions offered to them by Paris. Although the record is scant, they no doubt remained in contact. It is known that Franklin invited Aranda to attend at least one party that included the other dignitaries.[11]

In July 1783 Franklin passed along two booklets to Aranda. The Spaniard described one booklet as being half-sized and the other as being quarter-sized. Each contained the printed "constitution of the thirteen United States." Franklin wanted the larger booklet to be given to the king, and the smaller one was meant for Aranda to keep. The ambassador deferred to Floridablanca and sent the smaller one to him. A grateful Floridablanca dutifully passed the larger booklet to the king, who ordered that it be kept in the archive of the secretariat. He asked if it would be convenient to get three or four of the quarter-sized copies. Aranda complied with the request.[12]

Aranda was most likely the person who informed Franklin about Spain's Royal Academy of History and who introduced him to Pedro Rodríquez Campomanes y Pérez Sorriba, Count of Campomanes, a Spanish statesman, economist, and writer who had written over thirty publications. A student of law and ancient languages, including Arabic, Campomanes was a colleague of Aranda's and, at that time, director of the Academy of History.[13] Campomanes, Aranda, and Floridablanca had collaborated in the expulsion of the Jesuits from Spain and its possessions in 1767.[14]

As early as June 1784, Campomanes and Franklin exchanged some of their publications. Franklin thanked the Spaniard, sharing that he had learned a lot from reading his works, and he encouraged him to continue his work in "reforming the ancient Habitudes, removing Prejudices, and promoting the Industry of your Nation." He added that Campomanes would be amazed at what one good man could accomplish through persistence. Apparently referring to an exchange that they had begun, Franklin criticized what he called the two "mischievous Effects in Europe; that work is dishonorable, and that Families may be perpetuated with Estates." He extolled that neither of these maladies existed in America. He had some of his own publications sent to the Spaniard through his "very much and esteemed friend" William Carmichael. He especially noted a piece he had authored entitled "Information to those who would remove to America." The article detailed his thoughts about European maladies.[15]

Meanwhile, Franklin was impressed enough with his new friend that he had him inducted into the American Philosophical Society, an organization that Franklin had founded. On January 16, 1784, Campomanes became the first Spaniard accepted in the society.[16] Diego Gardoqui may have been the second Spaniard to be inducted, as his membership was proposed in 1788.[17]

On July 9, 1784, the members of the Royal Academy of History in Spain listened as one of its members noted that Franklin had given a collection of his political works to their president. He then read a letter that Carmichael had sent noting that the society's president, the Count of Campomanes, had been accepted as a corresponding member of the Philosophical Society in Philadelphia. Campomanes then nominated Franklin to receive a corresponding membership in the Royal Academy of History, justified by "the wide fame justly acquired by Dr. Franklin as a celebrated politician and intellectual, and by virtue of his being a member of the major academies of Europe." There was no further discussion, and the nomination was approved by acclamation. Among those approving Franklin's membership were Gaspar Melchor de Jovellanes, one of the most important figures of the Spanish enlightenment, and the Duke of Almodóvar, the recently returned Spanish ambassador to Great Britain.[18]

A long laudatory letter was soon penned by Campomanes. He began by acknowledging that Carmichael had delivered Franklin's writings. In a letter full of praise for Franklin, the count countered Franklin's earlier observations by sending a tract that he had written in 1765 about the "amortization and gradual extinction" of law, pointing out the differences between a constitutional monarchy and democracy, between ancient states and new ones. He would love to "amplify these reflections if time permits." Regarding the wonderful news of his induction into the American Philosophical Society, he wrote, "I have the good obligation to manifest my gratitude to you as its dignified President." He continued that he had proposed that Franklin be admitted to Spain's Royal Academy of History, making him the first person to be named as an honorary member. He exclaimed how wonderful it was to include Franklin, a "gentleman and man of letters," who had been a prime mover of "one of the most memorable revolutions of our time."[19]

Franklin left France in July 1785. His last months in Europe involved getting his affairs in order, suffering the full rounds of saying goodbye to all his Parisian friends, and enjoying some time in England, where he met with his estranged son for the last time. William Franklin's staunch loyalty to Britain throughout the recent war had alienated his father. Franklin felt that he had been betrayed and could not forgive his son, even though the son had requested the meeting to reconcile their differences.[20]

The long trip back to America caused a delay in the correspondence between Franklin and Campomanes. Finally, writing from Philadelphia in December 1786, Franklin composed a letter to Campomanes that accompanied his certificate of membership in the American Philosophical Society. The society had only just begun issuing certificates of membership two years before, and Campomanes was among the first recipients. Franklin also sent Campomanes the second volume of the society's transactions. Franklin wished the count every success, "particularly that of constant success in your continued laudable endeavors for the Service of your Country."[21]

Campomanes thanked Franklin for his letter, for the certificate, and for the volume of transactions. He said that he was very much indebted to Franklin and that he would endeavor to keep contributing to the advancement of knowledge. He was pleased to reciprocate by sending Franklin the first dictionary of Spanish, Latin, and Arabic that the Royal Academy of History, under his direction, had printed, and in which he wrote about the usefulness of the study of the Arabic language. And, he added, more volumes that were still in press would be forthcoming.[22]

Franklin was more popular in Europe than he was in his own country; nevertheless, his affection for Europe did not influence his judgment. He knew that America was not another Europe but something different. As his correspondence with Campomanes demonstrated, he believed in the American experience. He worked to keep America separate from Europe. Among his plethora of letters, articles, and notes, he remained silent about the key role Spain had played in the birth of his nation.

After his return to Spain, Gardoqui wrote a letter in which he expressed his belief that Spain's role in the colonial struggle for independence had been very important, maybe even decisive.[23] Perhaps a little more insightful, Aranda predicted that the first effort of the new United States toward expansion would be to take the Floridas and dominate the Gulf of Mexico.[24] Vergennes agreed, for he wrote, "We shall be poorly paid for all that we have done for the United States ... and for securing to them a national existence."[25]

Correct predictions aside, Franklin's popularity in Spain equaled that in the rest of Europe. Probably the first published biography of him was written in Spain by Pantaleón Aznar. Published a little less than eight years after Franklin's death, Aznar wrote that he was offering this biography of Franklin because he had been a person who "should not be forgotten among the geniuses of Europe that have distinguished this century."[26]

The library of Francisco Saavedra, who inexplicably did not meet Franklin while he was in Paris, contained books in many languages and subjects, and Franklin was well represented. Along with books and writings by Adam Smith, Edward Gibbon, John Locke, William Shakespeare, as well as classics in Greek and Latin and John Adams's 1787 publication entitled *Defense of the Constitution and Government of the United States of America,* Saavedra had French copies of Franklin's *Autobiography* and *Memories of His Private Life Written by Him* (1781). Notable as well, Saavedra had a copy of Campomanes's *Histories of the Templars* (1747).[27]

The question arises as to why the role of Spain in the independence of the United States has been overlooked. The memory of it did not fade over time but almost immediately. In part, the new United States worried over its own existence and under what form of government it would operate. Then there was the matter of the country's heritage, which is widely considered to be English and which speaks to an attitude inherited from England that has come to be known as the *Leyenda negra* (Black Legend). This notion was born out of Europe's Reformation and Counter-Reformation, in which England took the lead in the movement to "reform" the Catholic Church with the acceptance of Protestant religions, while Spain defended the Church. This conflict resulted in national rivalries and wars, and the prejudices it evoked eventually embedded themselves in the attitudes of the populations. The British colonies shared Great Britain's attitude toward Catholics in general and Spain in particular.[28]

Anti-Catholic sentiment spilled into nationalistic jingoism and even surfaced in the colonies when the Quebec Act of 1774 granted the people in Canada a Catholic bishop and guaranteed the free practice of Catholicism. So embedded was anti-Catholicism in the fabric of American thought that the act became one of the "Intolerable Acts" that precipitated the American Revolution. Not even the Revolutionary War could erase it. President Thomas Jefferson's lifting the embargo against Spain in 1809 would be the new nation's last positive gesture toward Spain for a long while. Jefferson allowed aid to go to Spain as its government fought for its independence against Napoleon, whose armies had occupied the country.[29]

It would not be until 1925, over a century and a quarter after Franklin' death, that the first history of Spain's involvement in the birth of the United States would be written and published. The first part of that book was a narrative and the second part an anthology of documents from the archives of Spain that were pertinent to the revolution. An American did not write this history, nor was it published in the United States or in English. Spanish historian Francisco Yela Utrilla wrote and compiled this first account of Spain's key participation, which had guaranteed the success of that struggle. In 1992, US historian Eric Beerman wrote the first overview and detailed history of Spain's role in the independence of the United States, but it was published in Spain, in Spanish.[30] While the various American representatives were mentioned in both books, diplomacy was not their focus.

The classic, 781-page biography of Franklin by Carl Van Doren, first published in 1938, is still the standard-bearer. Spain is mentioned in passing, almost grudgingly. Van Doren's meticulous research and penchant for detail could only surmise Spain's involvement in the war as being "of little help"—France was "the one real source of help."[31]

Today, as more information becomes available and historians look beyond the heretofore myopic view of how thirteen British colonies succeeded in their rebellion, the colonial connection to Spain and Spaniards cannot be overlooked. America's first commissioners not only witnessed the "event of this great contest," they also played a key role, and Spain, along with France, shared with them that "stage of Human Affairs."

The Americans went to Paris with little to offer but friendship. Yet they received the aid that resulted in the independence of the United States. Spain's covert and subsequent open aid resulted from the success of those first diplomatic contacts between the rebelling British colonies and Spain.

Notes

Abbreviations

AG	Archivo de la Familia Gasset, Papeles del conde de Campomanes, Fundación Universitara. Madrid, Spain.
AGI	Archivo General de Indias, sections Santo Domingo and Indiferente General, Seville, Spain.
AGP	Archivo General del Palacio Real, Infante de Don Gabriel, Madrid, Spain.
AGS	Archivo General de Simancas, sections Estado and Secretaría de Estado: Inglaterra, Valladolid, Spain.
AHN	Archivo Histórico Nacional (de España), section Estado. Madrid, Spain.
AHPTF/AZC	Archivo Histórico Provincial de Santa Cruz in Tenerife/Archivo Zárate-Cólogan, Canary Islands.
BL	Rochambeau Papers and Rochambeau Family Archive, General Collection Beinecke Rare Book and Manuscript Library, Yale University. New Haven, CT.
BS AHFT	Biblioteca de Francisco de Saavedra, Archivo Histórico Facultad Teología, Fondo Saavedra, Universidad de Granada. Granada, Spain.
PBF	The Papers of Benjamin Franklin, Founders Online, https://founders.archives.gov/about/Franklin.
RAH	Archivo de la Real Academia de la Historia. Madrid, Spain

Introduction

1. Gordon S. Wood, *The Americanization of Benjamin Franklin* (New York; Penguin, 2004); H. W. Brands, *The First American: The Life and Times of Benjamin Franklin* (New York: Doubleday, 2000); and Walter Isaacson, *Benjamin Franklin: An American Life* (New York: Simon & Schuster, 2004).
2. Carl Van Doren, *Benjamin Franklin* (1938; reprint, New York: Garden City Publishing, 1941). Special thanks go to Richard "Doc" Weaver of Santa Fe, New Mexico, who gave me his copy of Van Doren's book.
3. Larrie D. Ferreiro, "El legado de Gálvez en los Estados Unidos," *Desperta Ferro: Historia Moderna* 59 (2022): 56–61; and Gabriel Paquette and Gonzalo M.

Quintero, eds., introduction to *Spain and the American Revolution: New Approaches and Perspectives* (New York: Routledge, 2019), n.p.
4. Benjamin Franklin, *The Papers of Benjamin Franklin*, 44 vols., eds. Leonard Larabee et al. (New Haven, CT: Yale University Press, 1959–), hereafter cited as *Papers of Franklin* (Yale), with volume number; and Benjamin Franklin, *The Papers of Benjamin Franklin*, Packard Humanities Institute, franklinpapers.org (hereafter cited as *Franklin Papers* online). As noted in the citations below, the editors of that project discovered many of the documents in the Spanish archives. The citations will clarify which documents used here are in which collections.

1. On the Stage of Human Affairs

1. Isaacson, *Franklin: An American Life*, 276.
2. At the time, Escarano was in charge of the embassy while the ambassador, the Prince of Masserano, recouped from the gout in Madrid. See note 23, this chapter.
3. Escarano reported that Marianne Davis claimed that her father invented the glass armonica, a fact that has not been corroborated in the known literature. Escarano to Masserano, London, January 13, 1774, Archivo General de Simancas (hereafter AGS), Estado, legajo 7016-5, Valladolid, Spain.
4. Celia López-Chávez, "Benjamin Franklin, España y la diplomacia de una armónica," *Espacio, Tiempo y Forma: Revista de la Facultad de Geografía e Historia* 4, no. 13 (2000), relates the story of Escarano's attempt to get an armonica from Franklin. Nevertheless, the original documents cited by her are cited here for clarity. López-Chávez writes that Marianne Davis and her sister, Cecilia, were Franklin's close friends. Franklin especially enjoyed listening to Cecilia singing.
5. Escarano to Masserano, January 13, 1774, AGS.
6. Isaacson, *Franklin: An American Life*, 275; and Brands, *First American*, 469.
7. Accounts of Franklin's appearance before the Privy Council in the Cockpit are related in all of his biographies. The account given here is taken from Brands, *First American*, 469–75; and Isaacson, *Franklin: An American Life*, 276–78. The quotes are taken from the former.
8. Isaacson, *Franklin: An American Life*, 278.
9. The timing of the visit is taken from the date of Escarano's letter to Madrid reporting on his visit, February 1, 1774.
10. Escarano to Masserano, London, February 1, 1774, AGS, Estado, legajo 7016-7.
11. Ibid.
12. Escarano to Masserano, London, February 18, 1774, AGS, Estado, legajo 7016-6.
13. Escarano to Masserano, London, March 11, 1774, AGS, Estado, legajo 7016-9.
14. Ibid.

15. Escarano to Masserano, London, February 18, 1774, AGS.
16. Ibid., March 11, 1774.
17. Masserano to Duke of Bexar, Madrid, April 6, 1774, Archivo General de Palacio, Infante de don Gabriel, Madrid (hereafter AGP), legajo 501.
18. Escarano to Masserano, London, March 18, 1774, legajo 7016-10; and April 1, 1774, legajo 7016-11, both in Estado, AGS.
19. Quoted in Brands, *First American,* 483.
20. Quote in ibid., 484; and Isaacson, *Franklin: An American Life,* 288.
21. Miguel Ángel Ochoa Brun, "La misión diplomática de Benjamin Franklin a Europa y las relaciones internacionales," in *La ilustración española en la independencia de los Estados Unidos: Benjamin Franklin,* eds. Gonzalo Anes Álvarez and Eduardo Garrigues (Madrid: Marcial Pones, 2007), 67–68.
22. Escarano to Grimaldi, London, March 31, 1775, AGS, Estado 7016-53, no. 470.
23. Victor Amédée Philippe Ferrero Feischi, Prince of Masserano (1713–77), was the Spanish ambassador to England. His title refers to his connection to the principality of Masserano, near Biella, Italy, which was made a princedom in 1598 by Pope Clement VIII. He died on October 26, 1777, while returning to Spain from London.
24. Masserano to Grimaldi, London, June 27, 1775, AGS, Estado, 6990-15.
25. Ibid., September 19, 1775, AGS, Estado, 6991.
26. A handwritten note on the flyleaf of the book traces the route of the book from the London embassy to Philadelphia.
27. Jonathon Williams Jr. to Doctor Franklin, London, June 7, 1775, *Papers of Franklin* (Yale), 22:61–62. The translation is housed in the Franklin Papers, call number 467+17725, Beinecke Rare Book and Manuscript Library, Yale. A note written on a blank front page says that the book is a present "from Don Gabriel Infant of Spain, the Translator to B. Franklin." It continues that it was given to "Mr. Williams, Jr." by the Prince of Masserano. In an otherwise meticulously researched book by Light Townsend Cummins, *Spanish Observers and the American Revolution, 1775–1783* (Baton Rouge: Louisiana State University Press, 1991), the book is mistakenly described as being translated into English (55).
28. *Pennsylvania Gazette,* August 16, 1775, cited in Cummins, *Spanish Observers,* 55.
29. This information is quoted by Thomas Leech in the colophon included in Thomas E. Chávez, *Doctor Franklin and Spain: The Unknown History* (Santa Fe: Press of the Palace of the Governors), 61.
30. Benjamin Franklin to don Gabriel de Borbón y Sajonia, Philadelphia, December 12, 1775, AGP, legajo 501. This is the original copy received by the prince. A transcript of this document was published in *Papers of Franklin* (Yale), 22:298–99. This is based on a letterpress copy in the Library of Congress. The

editors note that a second copy is in Yale University Library. It has some minor differences from the original used here. A facsimile of the original is in the limited-edition Chávez, *Doctor Franklin and Spain.*
31. Franklin to don Gabriel de Borbón, December 12, 1775, AGP.
32. Quoted in Isaacson, *Franklin: An American Life,* 328.
33. Ibid., 321.
34. Escarano to Grimaldi, March 31, 1779 [1775]; Masserano to Grimaldi, June 27 and September 19, 1775, both in AGS.
35. Cummins, *Spanish Observers,* concentrates on the Spanish system and methods for gathering information before and during the revolution. For above, see pp. 18–25; the quote is on 53.
36. George Gibson to Luis de Unzaga y Amézaga, Governor of Louisiana, n.d., Archivo General de Indias, Santo Domingo (hereafter cited as AGI), legajo 2596.
37. Cummins, *Spanish Observers,* 49–50.
38. Franklin to William Temple Franklin, September 10, 1776, as quoted in Cummins, *Spanish Observers,* 29. The original is in Paul H. Smith, ed., *Letters of Delegates to Congress, 1774–1789* (Washington, DC: Library of Congress, 1976–91), 5:132.
39. Brands, *First American,* 510.
40. Thomas Paine, *Common Sense,* Online Library of Liberty, https://oll.libertyfund.org/pages/1776-paine-common-sense-pamphlet.
41. Brands, *First American,* 508.
42. John Ferling, *Independence: The Struggle to Set America Free* (New York: Bloomsbury, 2011), 290; and Van Doren, *Franklin,* 549.
43. Isaacson, *Franklin: An American Life,* 316.
44. Masserano to Grimaldi, London, June 18, 1776, Estado, legajo 6994-30, no. 294; and December 17, 1776, legajo 6995-77, no. 411, both in AGS.
45. Isaacson, *Franklin: An American Life,* 320.
46. Van Doren, *Franklin,* 564.
47. Isaacson, *Franklin: An American Life,* 326.
48. See the conversion chart in appendix 3, "Money at the Time of the Independence of the United States," in Thomas E. Chávez, *Spain and the Independence of the United States: An Intrinsic Gift* (Albuquerque: University of New Mexico Press, 2002), 234.
49. Regarding Gibson, see ibid., 29–30, 49. Regarding the Royal Order, see Letter from Madrid to the captain-general of Havana and to the governor of Louisiana, December 24, 1776, AGI, legajo 2596.
50. Francisco Saavedra, quoted in Chávez, *Spain and Independence,* 43. Also see Francisco Morales Padrón, "Editor's Introduction," in Saavedra, *Journal of don Francisco Saavedra de Sangronis, 1780–1783* (Gainesville: University of Florida Press, 1989), xx, xxiii.

51. Chávez, *Spain and Independence*, 43.
52. Troy S. Floyd, "Bourbon Palliatives and the Central American Mining Industry, 1765–1800," *The Americas* 18, no. 2 (October 1961): 106, 108.
53. Chávez, *Spain and Independence*, 19, 23, 25, 27.
54. Ibid., 76–77. For example, Floridablanca to Aranda, January 13, 1778, El Prado, Archivo Histórico Nacional [de España], Madrid (hereafter AHN), Estado, legajo 3884, folio 69. Also see Larrie D. Ferreiro, *Brothers at Arms: American Independence and the Men of France and Spain Who Saved It* (New York: Knopf, 2016), 121.
55. Quoted in Brands, *First American*, 527.
56. Van Doren, *Franklin*, 564–65.
57. Ibid., 565.

2. To Cultivate the Good Will

1. The titled people discussed throughout this book had given names as well as titled names. On occasion the two names matched; however, in most cases they do not. I use their titles here since that is how they are known to history. Pedro Pablo Abarca de Bolea, 10th Count of Aranda, discussed in these pages, is not to be confused with Abarca de Bolea, the Spanish writer.
2. As a result of wounds received in Italy, Aranda lived with a slight inclination of his neck and a perceptible deviation in one of his shoulders. His remains were exhumed two hundred years after his death and, in part, were identified by the evidence of his wounds. See Luis M. Farías, *La América de Aranda* (Mexico City, D.F.: Fondo de Cultura Económica, 2003), who cites José Ignacio Lorenzo Lizalde (21): "Hallazgo de la tumba del conde de Aranda: Su identificación y reconstrucción fisiognómica," in *El conde de Aranda y su tiempo* (Zaragoza: Instituto Fernando de Católico, 2000), 409–35. Aranda's many portraits give evidence that he also had a right "lazy eye."
3. Quoted in Joaquín Oltra and María Ángeles Pérez Samper, *El conde de Aranda* (Barcelona: Promociones Universitarias, S.A., 1987), 96; regarding Aranda's many decorations see, Farías, *La América de Aranda*, 19–20.
4. Oltra and Pérez Samper, *Aranda*, 113–20.
5. Dr. Jacques Barbeu-Dubourg (1709–79) translated into French and published many of Franklin's works, including Franklin's testimony before the British House of Commons in 1766. Aranda condensed his name to "DuBourg," which has been retained here. Various historians have conveyed his name as DuBourg, Dubourg, and du Bourg. Dubourg is the common spelling for English publications.
6. Aranda to Grimaldi, Paris, June 28, 1776, AGS, Estado, legajo 4603, no. 753. Also published in Spanish in Francisco Yela Utrilla, *España ante la independencia de los Estados Unidos* (Madrid: Ediciones Istmo, S.A., 1968), 562–64.

7. Aranda to Grimaldi, Paris, December 14, 1776, AGS, Estado, legajo 4605, no. 83.
8. Antonia Sagredo, "Personal Connections between Spaniards and Americans in the Revolutionary Era: Pioneers in Spanish-American Diplomacy," in *Legacy: Spain and the United States in the Age of Independence, 1763–1848,* eds. Mercedes Agueda Villar et al. (Washington, DC: Smithsonian Institution, 2007), 48–49.
9. See Jonathon R. Dull, *A Diplomatic History of the American Revolution* (New Haven, CT: Yale University Press, 1985), 56.
10. Aranda to Grimaldi, Paris, January 13, 1777, AHN, Estado, legajo 3884, no. 938 and no. 4. Also in Spanish in Yela Utrilla, *España ante la independencia,* 582–91.
11. Ibid.
12. Ibid.
13. Ibid.
14. Ibid.
15. Ibid.
16. Van Doren, *Franklin,* 566–67.
17. Aranda to Grimaldi, Paris, January 13, 1777, AHN, Estado, legajo 3884, no. 938 and no. 4.
18. Aranda to the Vergennes, Paris, December 28, 1776, attachment A to his January 13 letter to Grimaldi cited in note 17. Aranda wrote the letter in French.
19. Vergennes to Aranda, Versailles, December 28, 1776, attachment B to ibid.
20. Franklin, Silas Deane, and Arthur Lee to Aranda, Paris, December 28, 1776, attachment C to ibid.
21. Aranda to Grimaldi, Paris, January 13, 1777, ibid.
22. Aranda to Grimaldi, January 4, 1777, AGS, Estado, legajo 4609, no. 932.
23. Ibid.
24. Ibid.
25. Ibid. Some histories have claimed that Arthur Lee was fluent in Spanish and French. Aranda's report would seem to refute that claim. See Samuel Flagg Bemis, *The Diplomacy of the American Revolution: The Foundations of American Diplomacy* (Bloomington: Indiana University Press, 1957), 31. Silas Deane's instructions included the curious advice that he would spend time "acquiring Parisian French." See Committee of Secrete Correspondence: Instructions to Silas Deane, Philadelphia, June 2, 1779, Papers of Benjamin Franklin, Founders Online (hereafter cited as PBF).
26. Franklin, Deane, and Lee to Aranda, Paris, December 28, 1776, attachment C Aranda to Grimaldi, January 4, 1777, AGS, Estado, legajo 4609, no. 932.
27. "Señor conde de Aranda, que parece bien dispuesto hacia nosotros." As quoted in Spanish in Oltra and Pérez Samper, *Aranda,* 142.
28. Aranda to Grimaldi, January 4, 1777, AGS, Estado, legajo 4609, no. 932.
29. Aranda to Grimaldi, January 13, 1777, AHN, Estado, legajo 3884, no. 938 and no. 4.

3. Intrigue and Contact

1. Aranda to Grimaldi, January 13, 1777, AHN, Estado, legajo 3884, no. 938 and no. 4.
2. David McCullough, *John Adams* (New York: Simon & Schuster, 2001), 302. Abigail Adams also noted that the British ambassador had fifty servants.
3. Aranda to Grimaldi, January 13, 1777, AHN, Estado, legajo 3884, no. 938 and no. 4; January 4, 1777, AGS, Estado, legajo 4609, no. 932.
4. See Kristine L. Sjostrom, *Fernando de Leyba (1734–1780): A Life of Service and Sacrifice in Spanish Louisiana* (Seville: Privately published, 2022), 124–25, in which are cited documents dated January 18–April 24, 1777, AGI, Cuba, legajo 1227, nos. 143, 1135, 1138; and Bernardo de Gálvez to José de Gálvez, May 16, 1778, AGI, Cuba, legajo 223B, no. 111v–115v. These armaments and supplies were received by Capt. James Willing, commissioned by the colonial government, who had traveled down the Mississippi River to New Orleans. See Chávez, *Spain and the Independence*, 104–7.
5. Dull, *A Diplomatic History*, 80–81.
6. Aranda to Grimaldi, Paris, January 13, 1777, AHN, Estado, legajo 3884, no. 939 and no. 6. This is the second of two long reports that Aranda sent to Grimaldi on the same day.
7. Vergennes to Aranda, Versailles, December 28, 1776, attachment B Aranda to Grimaldi, January 13, 1777, AHN, Estado, legajo no. 938 and no. 4.
8. Aranda to Grimaldi, Paris, January 4, 1777, AGS, Estado, legajo 4607-5, no. 932.
9. Ibid.
10. The memorial delivered to Vergennes is dated January 5, 1777, the day after this meeting. See Brands, *First American*, 530 and footnote 530, p. 735.
11. Aranda to Grimaldi, January 13, 1777, AHN, Estado, legajo 3884, no. 939 and no. 6.
12. Ibid
13. Ibid.
14. Historian Reyes Calderón Cuadrado did an excellent survey of American documents regarding the *Amphitrite's* shipment and the lack of acknowledgement of Spain's involvement. See Calderón Cuadrado, *Empresarios españoles en el proceso de independencia norteamericana: La Casa Gardoqui e hijos de Bilbao* (Madrid: Unión Editorial, 2004), 236–38; and Calderón Cuadrado, "Spanish Financial Aid for the Process of Independence of the United States of America: Facts and Figures," in *Legacy: Spain and the United States*, ed. Agueda Villar, 68.
15. Calderón Cuadrado, "Spanish Financial Aid," 66.
16. Aranda to Grimaldi, Paris, January 13, 1777, AHN, Estado, legajo 3884, no. 939 and no. 6.

17. Edward Bancroft, who befriended himself to Franklin, became, on Franklin's recommendation, the American delegation's secretary. He spied for and was under salary of the British government. See Brands, *First American*, 608–11.
18. Aranda to Grimaldi, Paris, January 13, 1777, AHN, Estado, legajo 3884, no. 939 and no. 6.
19. Ibid.
20. Quote from ibid. See also Chávez, *Spain and the Independence*, 56–57.
21. Aranda to Grimaldi, Paris, January 13, 1777, AHN, Estado, legajo 3884, no. 939 and no. 6; and Vergennes to Aranda, December 28, 1776, attachment B, AHN, Estado, legajo no. 938 and no. 4. For a detailed overview of the role of the French and Spanish fleets and their respective preparations, see Jonathon R. Dull, *The French Navy and American Independence: A Study of Arms and Diplomacy, 1774–1787* (Princeton, NJ: Princeton University Press, 1975).
22. Aranda to Grimaldi, January 13, 1777, AHN, Estado, legajo 3884, no. 938 and no. 4.
23. Ibid.
24. Ibid., no. 939 and no. 6.
25. "Power" is capitalized in the original.
26. Attachment appended to the first letter, Aranda to Grimaldi, January 13, 1777, AHN, Estado, legajo 3884, no. 938 and no. 4.
27. For Bancroft's activities, see Van Doren, *Franklin*, 580–81.
28. Copy of a Memorial lately presented to the Minister of France by Lord Stormont, the English Ambassador at the Curt [*sic*] of Versailles, n.d., no. 501. This document was attached to Masserano to Floridablanca, April 22, 1777, AGS, legajo 1452, no. 47.

4. An Unofficial Alliance

1. An interesting firsthand account of that battle is given in Francisco de Saavedra, *Los decenios (Autobiografía de un sevillano de la ilustración)*, transcription, introduction, and notes by Francisco Morales Padrón (Seville: Servicio de Publicaciones, Excmo. Ayuntamiento de Sevilla, 1995), 83–92.
2. D. Antonio Ballesteros y Beretta, *Historia de España y su influencia en la Historia Universal*, vol. 5 (Barcelona: Salvat Editores, S.A., 1929), 197.
3. Grimaldi, May 4, 1776; and Resolution of the Spanish Council of the Indies, April 26, 1776, both in AGI, Santo Domingo, legajo 1059.
4. Aranda to Grimaldi, January 13, 1777, AHN, legajo 3884, no. 938 and no. 4.
5. Ibid., no. 939 and no. 6.
6. Ibid.
7. Ballesteros y Beretta, *Historia de España*, 5:203; and Chávez, *Spain and Independence*, 58.

8. Within three years, and after Spain declared war on Great Britain, Múzquiz would replace the Count of Ricla as secretary of war.
9. For a detailed overview of this subject, see Cummins, *Spanish Observers*.
10. Chávez, *Spain and Independence*, 25–30.
11. For example, Charles Lee to Luis de Unzaga, Williamsbourg, May 22, 1776 (two letters), and no date, all in AGI, Santo Domingo, legajo 2596.
12. Chávez, *Spain and Independence*, 30–31.
13. Masserano to Grimaldi, London, January 31, 1777, AGS, Estado, legajo 6996-16.
14. Ballesteros y Beretta, *Historia de España*, 5:58.
15. Dictum from the Count of Ricla, February 2, 1777, AHN, Estado, legajo 3884, exp. 3, folio 14.
16. Dictum from Grimaldi, February 1, 1777, AHN, Estado, legajo 3884, exp. 3, folio 15. He expressly wrote that the insurgents are "defending badly."
17. Dictum from José de Gálvez, February 2, 1777, AHN, Estado, legajo 3884, exp. 3, folio 16. Gálvez felt that "the just cause and Divine Providence" are "on our side."
18. Dictum of Múzquiz, February 2, 1777, published in Yela Utrilla, *España ante la independencia*, 603–4.
19. Dictum of Marquis González de Castejón, February 3, 1777, published in ibid., 606–9.
20. Grimaldi to Aranda (draft), February 4, 1777, El Pardo, AHN, Estado, legajo 3884, exp. 3, folio 18.
21. Grimaldi to Aranda, February 4, 1777, published in Yela Utrilla, *España ante la independencia*, 611–16.
22. Ibid.
23. Aranda's two long letters took at most eighteen days in transit from Paris to Madrid (or to El Pardo, outside of the Spanish capital). He wrote them on January 13, and Grimaldi wrote a reaction to them on February 1. That total does not account for the day they were mailed (probably January 14) and when Grimaldi received them (most likely before February 1). See Dictum of Grimaldi, February 1, 1777, AHN, Estado, legajo 3884, exp. 3, folio 15.
24. Calderón Cuadrado, *Empresarios españoles*, 238–39.
25. Vergennes to Marquis d'Ossun, February 14, 1777, AHN, Estado, legajo 3883, cited in Yela Utrilla, *España ante la independencia*, 617–18.
26. Grimaldi to Aranda, February 13, 1777, AHN, Estado, legajo 3883, cited in ibid., 617.
27. Luis M. Farías, *La América de Aranda* (Mexico, D.F.: Fondo de Cultura Económica, 2003), gives an interesting and favorable depiction of Aranda that completely omits any mention of Lee's trip to Spain and Aranda's involvement. For example, see pp. 205–10.
28. Calderón Cuadrado, "Spanish Financial Aid," 68–69.
29. Ibid., 68.

30. Diego Gardoqui to Arthur Lee, February 17, 1777, AHN, Estado, legajo 3883, cited in Yela Utrilla, *España ante la independencia,* 618–20, in original form; and in Calderón Cuadrado, *Empresarios españoles,* 239–40, in corrected English and with an important postscript telling Lee to meet in Burgos instead of the smaller town of Victoria.
31. As quoted in Calderón Cuadrado, "Spanish Financial Aid," 69.
32. Lee to the Committee of Secret Correspondence, Burgos, March 8, 1777, in Jared Sparks, ed., *The Diplomatic Correspondence of the American Revolution* (Boston: Hale and Gray, 1829), 2:40, quoted in Calderón Cuadrado, *Empresarios españoles,* 242. For Lee's suspicious nature, see Brands, *First American,* 546–47.
33. Chávez, *Spain and Independence,* 61.
34. Aranda to Floridablanca, Paris, April 13, 1777, AHN, Estado, legajo 3884, no. 1011 and no. 20.
35. Letter from Vergennes, April 8, 1777, note number 2, attached to Aranda to Floridablanca, Paris, April 13, 1777, AGS, Estado, legajo 4610-85, no. 2. This note in French was copied by Aranda or his secretary from the original. It is one of five numbered letters copied in unison and sent to Floridablanca as attachments. Aranda sent Floridablanca two letters on this date.
36. Congressional Commission to Vergennes, March 1777, AHN, Estado, legajo 3884, exp. 3, folio 35 in English and folio 19 in Spanish.
37. Ibid.
38. Franklin to Aranda, Paris, April 1, 1777, AHN, Estado, legajo 3884, exp. 3, folio 33. Also see Chávez, *Spain and Independence,* 62–63.
39. The words "united states" are not capitalized in the document.
40. John Hancock, "Congressional Commission," January 2, 1777, AHN, Estado, legajo 3884, exp. 3, folio 1, no. 21. Also published, with some differences, in Yela Utrilla, *España ante la independencia,* 578–79; and in total in the *Papers of Franklin* (Yale), 23:108–9. The document is reproduced in Carmen de Reparaz, *Yo solo: Bernardo de Gálvez y la Toma de Panzacola en 1781* (Madrid: Ediciones del Serbal, S.A., 1986), 232.
41. Franklin to Aranda, April 1, 1777, AHN, Estado, legajo 3884.
42. Publish in the *Papers of Franklin* (Yale), 22:634–35.
43. Regarding Arthur Lee's relationship with Franklin, see Brands, *First American,* 430, 437–38, 546–47.
44. Franklin to Aranda, April 7, 1777, AHN, Estado, 3884.
45. Aranda to Floridablanca, April 13, 1777, AGS, Estado, legajo 4610-85.
46. Ibid.
47. Aranda to Floridablanca, Paris, April 13, 1777, AHN, Estado, legajo 3884, exp. 3, folio 26.
48. Chávez, *Spain and Independence,* 63–64.
49. Calderón Cuadrado, "Spanish Financial Aid," 67.

Notes to Pages 60–65   143

5. An Interlude of Hope and Persistence

1. Bruce Lancaster, *The American Revolution* (New York: Houghton Mifflin, 1985), 199.
2. Floridablanca to Aranda, July 19, 1997, AGS, Estado, legajo 4011.
3. Dull, *The French Navy*, 83.
4. Floridablanca to Aranda (draft), n.d. (a handwritten short summary is dated September 27, 1777), AHN, legajo 3884. Apparently, the formal letter taken from this draft is Floridablanca to Aranda, June 3, 1777, published in Yela Utrilla, *España ante la independencia*, 671–72.
5. Van Doren, *Franklin*, 583.
6. Quoted in Brands, *First American*, 610–11.
7. Van Doren, *Franklin*, 580–82.
8. Copy of Stormont's memorial to Vergennes, n.d., attached to Masserano to Floridablanca, London, April 22, 1777, AGS, Estado, legajo 1492. Spain had its own spies in both London and Paris. Masserano, in London, does not explain how he came into possession of Stormont's memorial.
9. Aranda to Floridablanca, Paris, June 11, 1777, AGS, Estado, legajo 4611, no. 1055.
10. Franklin paper, June 1777, attached to ibid.
11. Floridablanca to Aranda, June 3, 1777, in Yela Utrilla, *España ante la independencia*, 671–72; and rough draft of the same in AHN, Estado, legajo 3884.
12. Aranda to Floridablanca, June 23, 1777, AGS, Estado, legajo 4611, no. 28 and no. 1067; Yela Utrilla, *España ante la independencia*, 673–74.
13. Franklin memorial, July 1777, AHN, Estado, legajo 3884, no. 29.
14. For example, Aranda came into possession of a copy of a letter that Vergennes wrote to Franklin and Deane in which the French minister warned Franklin about American corsairs in French ports. The French minister even specified Captain Wickes and the *Reprisal*, the very captain and ship that had transported Franklin to France. Vergennes to Franklin and Deane, July 16, 1777 (copy), AGS, Estado, legajo 4611-92.
15. Masserano to His Excellency, London, July 11, 1777, AGS, Estado, legajo 6997-35, no. 556.
16. Aranda to Floridablanca, Paris, September 27, 1777, AHN, Estado, legajo 3884.
17. Aranda to Floridablanca, Paris, July 20, 1777, AHN, Estado, legajo 3884, no. 1079 and no. 28.
18. Ibid.
19. Ibid.
20. Ibid.
21. Van Doren, *Franklin*, 584. Deane did not receive news of his congressional recall until March 1778.
22. Dull, *The French Navy*, 89.
23. Floridablanca to Aranda, July 19, 1777, AGS, Estado, legajo 4611.

24. Aranda to Floridablanca, July 20, 1777, AHN, Estado, legajo 3884.
25. Ibid.
26. For more on Franklin and privateers, see chapter 8.
27. Van Doren, *Franklin*, 584–85.
28. Rough draft to Aranda, December 9, 1777, attached to Aranda to Floridablanca, Paris, November 26, 1777, AGS, Estado, legajo 4612, no. 1178.
29. Dull, *The French Navy*, 127–28.
30. Aranda to Floridablanca, Paris, September 27, 1777, AHN, Estado, legajo 3884, no. 1139 and no. 33.
31. The Commissioners of the United States of America to the Count of Vergennes and the Count of Aranda, Passy, September 1777, AHN, Estado, legajo 2884, no. 24. Yela Utrilla published this letter in its original English with a Spanish translation: see *España ante la independencia*, 682–87. Yale also published the document in the *Papers of Franklin*, 24:555–63.
32. Yela Utrilla, *España ante la independencia*, 682–87.
33. Van Doren, *Franklin*, 586–87.
34. Ibid.
35. Ibid., 585; and Isaacson, *Franklin: An American Life*, 342.
36. Aranda to Floridablanca, Paris, September 27, 1777, AHN, Estado, legajo 3884, no. 1139 and no. 33.
37. Ibid.
38. Memorial from Spain to France, October 10, 1777, AHN, Estado, 3884; also in Yela Utrilla, *España ante la independencia*, 700–705.
39. Ibid., 703. For some reason Yela Utrilla dates this document October 17, while the document itself is dated October 10 and was signed off at San Lorenzo el Real on October 17.
40. Ibid. This sentiment is covered in points 5 and 6.
41. Lee to Aranda, December 9, 1777, AHN, Estado 3884; also published in Yela Utrilla, *España ante la independencia*, 712.
42. Memorial of the American Commission to Vergennes and Aranda, December 9, 1777, AHN, Estado 3884; also published in Yela Utrilla, *España ante la independencia*, 712.
43. Sagredo, "Personal Connections," 50.
44. Thomas A. Bailey, *A Diplomatic History of the American People* (Englewood Cliffs, NJ: Prentice-Hall, 1970), 28–29; and McCullough, *Adams*, 205.
45. Robert Morris and William Smith to B. Gálvez, York, PA, October 24, 1777; and Bernardo de Gálvez to Joseph de Gálvez, May 12, 1777, no. 41 and no. 27, both in AGI, Santo Domingo, legajo 2596. The agent was Oliver Pollock, a native of Ireland, a merchant, and an American patriot.
46. Patrick Henry to B. Gálvez, January 14, 1778, AGI, Santo Domingo, legajo 2596.

47. George Washington to Diego Joseph Navarro, Governor and Captain-General of Cuba, March 4, 1779, AGI, Santo Domingo, legajo 1233, no. 82.
48. Escarano to Floridablanca, October 30, 1777, AGS.
49. Escarano to Floridablanca, London, October 3, 1777, AGS, Estado, legajo 6998-9. The letter was sent through Bilbao on Spain's northern coast.
50. Chávez, *Spain and the Independence*, 69; Ballesteros y Beretta, *Historia de España*, 5:205; and letter directed to Franklin, Boston, October 24, 1777, AGS, libro 163, nos. 231–36.
51. Isaacson, *Franklin: An American Life*, 343.

6. Saratoga and a Diplomatic Gambit

1. For a very detailed and concise description of Burgoyne's failed attempt to split the colonies, see Lancaster, *American Revolution*, 199–225.
2. For example, Masserano to His Excellency, London, July 11, 1777, legajo 6997-35, no. 556; Escarano to Floridablanca, London, October 3, 1777, legajo 6998-9; and London, May 29, 1778, legajo 7001-13, all in AGS, Estado.
3. For an example of a historian's judgment about the significance of Saratoga, see Bailey, *Diplomatic History of the American People*, 32. Bailey claims that Saratoga "must be regarded as one of the decisive battles of world history." Jonathon Dull, who used the French archives, argues the opposite. See Dull, *A Diplomatic History*, 89–92; and *The French Navy*, 90.
4. Isaacson, *Franklin: An American Life*, 343.
5. Chávez, *Spain and Independence*, 69.
6. Dull, *The French Navy*, 86–87.
7. Ibid., 90.
8. Floridablanca to Aranda, December 23, 1777, AHN, Estado, legajo 4072, no. 1; also in Yela Utrilla, *España ante la independencia*, 717–22.
9. Ibid.
10. Ibid.
11. Aranda to Floridablanca, December 28, 1777, AHN, Estado 3884, no. 1201. Published in Spanish in Yela Utrilla, *España ante la independencia*, 723–25.
12. Ibid.
13. Draft of Floridablanca to Aranda, El Pardo, January 13, 1778, AHN, Estado, legajo 3884, no. 69. The draft is in the handwriting of two people. The draft in final form apparently was sent to Aranda under the same date. See Dispatch, Floridablanca to Aranda, January 13, 1778 (No. 1. Minuta), in Yela Utrilla, *España ante la independencia*, 736–40.
14. Floridablanca to Aranda, January 13, 1778 (no. 2. Reservado Minuta), in ibid., 740–47.
15. Ibid.

16. Genoveva Enríquez Macias, "Guillermo Terry, armador en Cádiz, y su navio 'Soberbio': Guerra y comercio en la primera mitad del siglo XVIII" (PhD diss., Universidad de Sevilla, Spain, 2023), 195.
17. In anticipation of a conflict, two months before the battles at Saratoga, Spain followed France's lead and sent two observers to the colonies. These men were Juan Miralles y Trajan (to be Spain's unofficial liaison to Congress) and his brother-in-law, Juan Elegio de la Puente (to observe American military activity). Both were known to colonial leaders. Royal Order, August 26, 1777, AGI, Santo Domingo, legajo 1598; see also Chávez, *Spain and the Independence*, 71–74; and Cummins, *Spanish Observers*, 108–9.
18. Draft, Floridablanca to Aranda, January 13, 1778, AHN, Estado, legajo 3884, no. 69.
19. Ibid.
20. Extract of a letter, Vergennes to Montmorin, January 2, 1778, AGS, Estado, legajo 4612, no. 199.
21. Hutton to Franklin, January 21, 1778, PBF.
22. Draft, Floridablanca to Aranda, January 13, 1778, AHN, Estado, legajo 3884, no. 69.
23. As quoted in Chávez, *Spain and Independence*, 75.
24. Floridablanca to Aranda, January 13, 1778, El Pardo, AHN, Estado, legajo 3884, folio 69.
25. Aranda to Floridablanca, January 31, 1778, AHN, Estado, legajo 3884, exp. 7, no. 1222; quoted in Ruigómez de Hernández, *El gobierno español*, 127.
26. Floridablanca to Aranda, February 2, 1778, El Pardo, AHN, Estado, legajo 3884.
27. Quoted in Isaacson, *Franklin: An American Life*, 346. Also see Dull, *A Diplomatic History*, 92–93.
28. Dull, *A Diplomatic History*, 92.
29. Chávez, *Spain and Independence*, 79.
30. Yale historian Edmund Morgan is quoted in Isaacson, *Franklin: An American Life*, 349.
31. Aranda to Floridablanca, Paris, March 19, 1778, AGS, Estado, legajo 4616-87-I.
32. Dull, *The French Navy*, 103.
33. Ibid., 118–19.
34. For a detailed description of France's strategy upon signing the treaties, see Dull, *The French Navy*, 112–26.
35. Escarano to Floridablanca, London, April 14, 1778, AGS, Estado, legajo 7000-71. Escarano had replaced Masserano, who died on October 26, 1777. King George III openly recommended that Escarano succeed Masserano. Floridablanca to Aranda, December 23, 1777, AHN, Estado, legajo 4072, no. 1; also in Yela Utrilla, *España ante la independencia*, 717–22.

36. The first of the six volumes of *The History of the Decline and Fall of the Roman Empire* was published in February 1777. Volumes two and three came out in March 1781. Gibbon quoted in Bailey, *Diplomatic History of the American People*, 35.
37. Ferreiro, *Brothers at Arms*, 138, 141.
38. Quoted in Dull, *The French Navy*, 133.
39. Montmorin to Vergennes, quoted in Lancaster, *The American Revolution*, 235.

7. A Declaration of War and a New Focus

1. Cummins, *Spanish Observers*, 105–10, 151.
2. Samuel Adams to Caleb Davis, December 5, 1778, p. 287; Henry Laurens to Patrick Henry, December 6, 1778, pp. 114–20; both published in Smith, *Letters of Delegates*, vol. 12.
3. Dull, *A Diplomatic History*, 102.
4. Escarano to Floridablanca, London, May 29, 1778, AGS, Estado, legajo 7001-12.
5. Ibid.
6. Chávez, *Spain and Independence*, 128.
7. For the influence of the *peso fuerte*, see ibid., 216. The English word "dollar" comes from the German "*thaler.*" Massachusetts, Connecticut, and Virginia used Spanish coins as legal tender.
8. Dull, *The French Navy*, 117.
9. Van Doren, *Franklin*, 583–84.
10. Congressional Credential of Arthur Lee, June 5, 1777, in Yela Utrilla, *España ante la independencia*, 672–73; Van Doren, *Franklin*, 583.
11. Yela Utrilla, *España ante la independencia*, 84, 607–8; Dull, *A Diplomatic History*, 100–101.
12. Brands, *First American*, 582.
13. Franklin to Richard Bache, quoted in Van Doren, *Franklin*, 608.
14. Ibid., 609.
15. Franklin to Joseph Reed, quoted in ibid., 609.
16. Dull, *The French Navy*, 127.
17. Aranda to Floridablanca, February 23, 1778, AHN, Estado, exp. 8, folio 90; and Chávez, *Spain and Independence*, 82–83.
18. For example, Patrick Henry to Bernardo de Gálvez, January 14, 1778, AGI, Santo Domingo, legajo 2596, wherein Henry is requesting "woolens, especially blankets and tarps, and munitions" and 150,000 pistols.
19. Chávez, *Spain and Independence*, 85.
20. Ibid.
21. Ibid.
22. Marcos Marreno Valenzuela, "Sobre la rebellion de las colonias Ynglesas de América," 1778, AGI, Indiferente General, folio 17, 1791; and cover letter

Valenzuela to J. Gálvez, November 20, 1778, AGI, Indiferente General. The report is bound with green thread.
23. Dull, *The French Navy*, 128–29.
24. Gouverneur Morris to the *Pennsylvania Packet*, February 27, 1779, in Smith, *Letters of Delegates*, 12:114–20; and as quoted in Chávez, *Spain and Independence*, 126. For an overview of Spain's relationship with the colonies and its negotiations with Britain, see ibid., 126–32.
25. Chávez, *Spain and Independence*, 128; and Conrad-Alexandre Gérard to the President of Congress, February 9, 1779, in Francis Wharton, ed., *The Revolutionary Diplomatic Correspondence of the United States*, vol. 3 (Washington, DC: Government Printing Office, 1889), 39–40; and William Henry Drayton's Notes to the Proceedings of the Committee of the Whole of Congress, February 9, 1779, in Smith, *Letters of Delegates*, 12:71–72.
26. William Henry Drayton to King George III, February 13, 1779, in Smith, *Letters of Delegates*, 12:61–69. The all-caps emphasis is in the original.
27. Franklin to the Committee of Foreign Affairs, Paris, May 26, 1779, "Proceedings of Congress . . . , Report of the Committee Assigned to Deal with Letters of Lee and Gerard," February 23, 1779; Franklin to Patrick Henry, Paris, February 26, 1779, both in Wharton, *Diplomatic Correspondence*, 3:193 and 67–68, respectively.
28. Ultimatum proposed by the court of Madrid to the courts of France and England, April 3, 1779, *Diplomatic Correspondence*, 3:466, 481–82. This is an English translation. A version in Spanish may be found in Almodóvar to Floridablanca, London, April 16, 1779, AGS, Secretaría de Estado: Inglaterra (años 1750–1820), legajo 7021, atado 2, no. 13. The document includes the acknowledgement of Almodóvar, Spain's new ambassador to England, that he received it thirteen days after its date, which is to say April 16, 1779.
29. Almodóvar to Floridablanca, April 16, 1779, AGS, Secretaría de Estado: Inglaterra (años 1750–1820), legajo 7021, atado 2, no. 14.
30. Extract of an answer from the Court of London to the proposition contained in the ultimatum of Spain, May 4, 1779, in Wharton, *Diplomatic Correspondence*, 3:483.
31. Washington to Jay, August 16, 1779, West Point, in George Washington, *The Writings of Washington from the Original Manuscript Sources, 1745–1799*, vol. 16, ed. John C. Fitzpatrick (Washington, DC: Government Printing Office, 1904), 115.
32. Dull, *A Diplomatic History*, 109.
33. Chávez, *Spain and Independence*, 133; Dull, *The French Navy*, 90–91; and Enrique Fernández y Fernández, *Spain's Contribution to the Independence of the United States* (Washington, DC: Embassy of Spain, 1985), 9.
34. Arthur Lee, Memorial to the court of Spain, Paris, June 6, 1779, in Wharton, *Diplomatic Correspondence*, 3:209. There is an English document titled "The

Way to Bring England to Her Sense," with no date or name, but it appears to be one of Lee's letters. It is located in AGS, Estado, legajo 8162, signatura 5.
35. Chávez, *Spain and Independence,* 136; and Floridablanca to Arthur Lee, Madrid, August 6, 1779, in Wharton, *Diplomatic Correspondence,* 3:290. Floridablanca notes the two letters, dated June 7 and 25, 1778. The second letter has not been located.
36. George Washington to Lord Stirling, West Point, August 28 and 29, 1779, both in Washington, *Writings,* 16:198–200.
37. Jay to Franklin, Martinique, December 27, 1779, *Franklin Papers* online.
38. As quoted in Chávez, *Franklin and Spain,* 49. Also see Franklin to Jay, Passy, October 2, 1780, *Papers of Franklin* (Yale), 26:466.
39. Quoted in Van Doren, *Franklin,* 676; and Wood, *Americanization of Franklin,* 198.
40. Sagredo, "Personal Connections," 62.

8. Corsairs and Intrigue

1. Carlos Cólogan Soriano, *Un corsario al servicio de Benjamin Franklin* (Islas Canarias: Gaviño de Franchy Editores, 2013), 13.
2. John Paul Jones quoted in Richard J. Werther, "Captain Lambert Wickes and 'Gunboat Diplomacy,' American Revolution Style," *Journal of the American Revolution* (January 3, 2019), allthingsliberty.com.
3. John Frayler, "Privateers in the American Revolution," National Park Service, Salem Maritime National Park, https://www.nps.gov/articles/privateers-in-the-american-revolution.htm/.
4. Lancaster, *American Revolution,* 251.
5. Harry Kelsey, *Sir Francis Drake: The Queen's Pirate* (New Haven, CT: Yale University Press, 1998), 136.
6. Brands, *First American,* 180, 533.
7. Kenneth J. Hagan, "The Birth of American Naval Strategy," in Donald Stoker, Kenneth J. Hagan, and Michael T. McMaster, *Strategy in the American War of Independence: A Global Approach* (London: Routledge, 2010), 47.
8. Brands, *First American,* 503–4.
9. Franklin to Jay, Passy, October 4, 1779, *Franklin Papers* online.
10. Cólogan Soriano, *Un corsario,* 14.
11. Brands, *First American,* 539; Van Doren, *Franklin,* 617; quote is from Franklin to Richard Oswald, Passy, January 14, 1783, *Franklin Papers* online.
12. Franklin to Oswald, January 14, 1783, *Franklin Papers* online; and Brands, *First American,* 583–85.
13. Van Doren, *Franklin,* 541, 565.
14. Dull, *The French Navy,* 88.
15. Isaacson, *Franklin: An American Life,* 387.

16. For example, see Eleanor S. Coleman, *Gustavus Conyngham, USN: Pirate or Privateer, 1747–1819* (Washington, DC: University Press of America, 1982).
17. Morris's company, along with at least twenty-five other American merchants, did business with Gardoqui e hijos. See Calderón Cuadrado, *Empresarios españoles*, 198–99.
18. Dull, *The French Navy*, 88.
19. Cummins, *Spanish Observers*, 101.
20. See Werther, "Captain Lambert Wickes."
21. Carlos Cólogan Soriano, *Tenerife Wine: Historias del comercio de vinos, siglo XVIII (1760–1797)* (Islas Canarias: Self-published, 2017), 17, 140–43; Cólogan Soriano, *Un corsario*, 12; and Van Doren, *Franklin*, 564.
22. Dull, *A Diplomatic History*, 86–87.
23. Van Doren, *Franklin*, 572.
24. Werther, "Captain Lambert Wickes."
25. Cólogan Soriano, *Tenerife Wine*, 206.
26. There are many accounts of this episode. For a succinct description see Dull, *The French Navy*, 76–81. Vergennes ordered Wickes's small fleet sequestered and then ordered him to sea without French protection. He also sent orders to all the French ports prohibiting the arming of privateers and restricting the entrance of privateers with their prizes. Franklin did not object. On the other hand, he did not comply with the British demand to return the prizes. To do so would label the Americans pirates rather than belligerents.
27. Aranda to Floridablanca, July 20, 1777, AHN, Estado, legajo 3884.
28. American Commissioners to Vergennes and Aranda, Passy, September 25, 1777, *Franklin Papers* online.
29. Franklin to Jay, Passy, October 4, 1779, ibid.
30. Ibid.
31. Van Doren, *Franklin*, 616–18.
32. Cummins, *Spanish Observers*, 177–78.
33. Jonathon Williams to Franklin, Nantes, July 13, 1779, AGS, Estado, legajo 4620-129, attachment B to Aranda to Floridablanca, Paris, July 19, 1779, ibid., 126. After the war, Williams returned to America with Franklin. He became the first superintendent of West Point. Van Doren, *Franklin*, 576, 601, 727.
34. Aranda to Floridablanca, AGS, Estado, legajo 4620-129, with two attached letters, A and B.
35. Summary note from El Escorial to Aranda, October 23, 1777, written on Aranda to Floridablanca, Paris, November 26, 1777, AGS, Estado, legajo 4612, no. 1178.
36. Memorial of Franklin, Deane, and Lee, Paris, November 26, 1777 (in French), attached to Aranda to Floridablanca, ibid.
37. Marginal note and attachment, Aranda to Floridablanca, ibid.
38. Graciano Sieulanne to Franklin, Santa Cruz de Tenerife, July 30, 1778, Archivo Historical Provincial de Santa Cruz, Tenerife/Archivo Zárate-Cólogan

(AHPTF/AZC), signature 121. Reproduced in Spanish in Cólogan Soriano, *Tenerife Wine,* 306–7.
39. Franklin to M. Grand (copy sent to Floridablanca), Paris, November 3, 1778, AGS, Estado, legajo 4618-52.
40. Cólogan Soriano, *Tenerife Wine,* 307.
41. Cólogan Soriano, *Un corsario,* 195.
42. Quoted in ibid., 213.
43. Ibid., 169–75.
44. Gustavus Conyngham, "Narrative of Captain Gustavus Conyngham, U.S.N., While in Command of the 'Surprise' and 'Revenge,' 1779," *Pennsylvania Magazine of History and Biography* 22, no. 4 (1898): 483.
45. Henry Laurens, A Proclamation, York, PA, May 9, 1778, AGS, legajo 4618, no. 5354; and Charles Thompson, Extract from the Minutes, May 11, 1778, ibid., no. 5556. Both documents are written in English in the same hand (apparently Franklin's). Each document has with it a French translation written in a different hand.
46. Laurens, Proclamation, May 9, 1778, AGS, legajo 4618-5354.
47. Thompson, Extract from the Minutes, May 11, 1778, ibid., no. 5556.
48. Aranda to Floridablanca, Paris, September 9, 1778, AGS, Estado, legajo 4618-51.
49. Franklin to M. Grand (copy sent to Floridablanca), Paris, November 3, 1778, AGS, Estado, legajo 4618-52. Franklin's apologies for Conyngham's misconduct can be found in *Papers of Franklin* (Yale), 28:9–20, 66–67.
50. *Papers of Franklin* (Yale), 28:9–20, 66–67.
51. Cólogan Soriano, *Un corsario.*
52. For a succinct explanation of this episode, see Cólogan Soriano, *Tenerife Wine,* 320, 323–25, 342–48.
53. A *fanega* was roughly equal to a bushel.
54. Juan Cólogan to Tomás Cólogan, Ostend, December 27 and 31, 1780, Signatura 779-75-1R, AHPTF/AZC. Juan also bemoaned how the Netherland's entry into the war was making trade very difficult.
55. Tomás Cólogan to Juan Cólogan, Tenerife, June 6, 1781, Signatura 121, AHPTF/AZC. Published in Spanish, and in part, in Cólogan Soriano, *Tenerife Wine,* 244.
56. Ibid. Tomás Cólogan never names the *Golden Rose,* instead calling the ship the "*Good Boors.*" The context of this and subsequent letters points to the *Golden Rose.*
57. Tomás Cólogan to Juan Cólogan (of Cólogan, Pollard & Co.), Tenerife, August 2, 1781, Signatura 121, AHPTF/AZC. Published in abbreviated form in Cólogan Soriano, *Tenerife Wine,* 346.
58. Tomás Cólogan to Robert Morris, Tenerife, June 7, 1781, Signatura 121, AHPTF/AZC. Published in Spanish in Cólogan Soriano, *Tenerife Wine,* 344–46.

59. Cólogan Soriano, *Tenerife Wine*, 342, 344.
60. Tomás Cólogan to Juan Cólogan, August 2, 1781, Signatura 121, AHPTF/AZC.
61. Peter Whiteside to John Cólogan & Sons, Philadelphia, August 4, 1781; reproduced in Spanish in Cólogan Soriano, *Tenerife Wine*, 347–48.
62. Conyngham had been captured and imprisoned, eventually to successfully escape at the end of the war.
63. Aranda to Floridablanca, Paris, May 18, 1782, AGS, Estado, legajo 4626-179, no. 2191.

9. Betrayal and the Making of Peace

1. Chávez, *Spain and Independence*, 198–203.
2. John Adams to the President of Congress, August 3, 1779, in Wharton, *Diplomatic Correspondence*, 3:282–83; Samuel Adams to Samuel Cooper, February 21, 1779, in Smith, *Letters of Delegates*, 12:102–3. Also see Chávez, *Spain and Independence*, 132, 135.
3. Martha Gutiérrez-Steinkamp, "Spain and the Independence of the Thirteen American Colonies," in *Recovered Memories: Spain, New Orleans and the Support for the American Revolution*, ed. José Manuel Cuerro Acosta (New Orleans: Louisiana State History Museum/Edición Iberdrola, 2018), 48.
4. Calderón Cuadrado, *Empresarios españoles*, 237–38. Note that 1777 was before Spain entered the war.
5. Ibid. Here she details that by the end of 1776, Spain had sent 12,826 bombs, 51,134 balls, 30,000 rifles with bayonets, 30,000 complete suits (uniforms), 27 mortars, and 4,000 tents.
6. Richard B. Morris, *The Peacemakers: The Great Powers and American Independence* (New York: Harper Torchbooks, 1965), 241. Morris cites John Jay's complaint to Floridablanca without any contextual comment. Eric Beerman, *España y la independencia de Estados Unidos* (Madrid: Editorial MAFRE, S.A., 1992), 169; Chávez, *Spain and Independence*, 197; and Saavedra, *Journal... from 25 June 1780 until the 20th of the Same Month of 1783*, 172–73, in which Spain's observer, Francisco Rendón, relates the negative reaction in the Continental Congress and letters to the *New York Gazette*, October 15, 1781. For an overview of the prisoners sent to New York, see Cummins, *Spanish Observers*, 176–77.
7. For example, Van Doren, *Franklin*, 685: "Spain, little help as she had given France in the war..."
8. Wood, *Americanization of Franklin*.
9. Dull, *A Diplomatic History*, 149; and Ferreiro, *Brothers at Arms*, 123.
10. Franklin to Gardoqui, October 9, 1780, *Franklin Papers* (Yale), 33:386–87.
11. For example, the diary of the Battle of Pensacola was published in *La Gazeta de Madrid* in August 1781. Beerman, *España y la independencia de Estados*

Unidos, 166, gives the publication dates as August 7 and 21. Carmen de Reparaz, *Yo solo,* 221, reproduces the page of *La Gazeta de Madrid* with the date August 10, 1781, which is months before Yorktown. At Franklin's request, Jay inquired of the Spanish officials an accounting of Spain's aid. He never received a complete answer; nor, apparently, did they bother to appraise him of Spain's financial support of the battle at Yorktown. See Franklin to Jay, Passy, October 2, 1780; and Jay to Franklin, Madrid, October 5, 1780, *Franklin Papers* online.

12. Chávez, *Spain and Independence,* 209–10. For clarity, Jay arrived in Madrid on April 4, 1780; the British convoy was captured August 8 and 9, 1780. Spanish victories in Nicaragua were in January 1781; at St. Joseph on February 12, 1781; and at Pensacola on May 10, 1781. The British surrendered at Yorktown on October 18, 1781. The Spanish won at Menorca on February 2, 1781. Jay was in Madrid during all this time and a little while afterward.
13. Van Doren, *Franklin,* 676.
14. Franklin's perplexity over the "storm" of bills is evident throughout his and Jay's correspondence. Jay started requesting payment of bills while in transit to Spain and kept at it throughout his stay in Madrid. See the correspondence between Jay and Franklin ranging from January 26, 1779, through April 1782, *Franklin Papers* online.
15. Jay to Franklin, Madrid, March 28, 1781. Jay gives the date of Gardoqui's letter as March 15, 1781, *Franklin Papers* online.
16. For "storm of bills," see Franklin to Jay, Passy, October 2, 1780, ibid.
17. Franklin to Jay, Passy, June 13, 1780, ibid.
18. Franklin to Jay, Passy, April 22, 1782, ibid.
19. Jay to Franklin, Madrid, January 11, 1782, ibid.
20. Franklin to Jay, Passy, March 16, 1782, ibid.
21. Franklin to Jay, Passy, April 22, 1782, ibid.: "As your residence in Madrid is no longer necessary..."
22. Jay to Franklin, Madrid, October 5, 1780, ibid.
23. Jay to Franklin, Madrid, November 21, 1781, in which Elbridge Gerry wrote to Jay about the expectation of victory; and November 22, 1781, in which news of the victory is certain and the details given. Both in PBF.
24. Saavedra, *Journal,* 200–203; and *Los decenios,* 164.
25. In *Los decenios,* Saavedra wrote that they needed 500,000 *pesos fuertes* and that "the necessary amount" was raised (*se junto el dinero necesario*). In "Diario inédito," quoted in Reparaz, *Yo solo,* 250, Saavedra writes that the money raised in Havana amounted to 500,000 *pesos fuertes.* The list of donor totals gives the amount at 4,526,000 *reales,* or at a rate of eight *reales* to one peso, 565,000 *pesos fuertes.* For the list, see appendix 4 in Chávez, *Spain and Independence,* 235. Upon his arrival in the Chesapeake Bay, de Grasse reported to General Washington that he had 1.2 million *pesos* to give to Washington and Rochambeau. Rochambeau to George Washington, Rochambeau Papers and Rochambeau

Family Archive, General Collection, Beinecke Rare Book and Manuscript Library, Yale. Also see Saavedra, *Los decenios,* 185 and 192, and Saavedra, *Journal,* 220–23, 266, 297–98, for additional money given to aid the French.
26. Chávez, *Spain and Independence,* 202–3. In a compiled autobiography written a few years later, Saavedra wrote that he and the "intendent," Ignacio Peñalver, were the key persons in raising the money in Havana. He also noted that de Grasse sent him a letter to thank the merchants of Havana as well as Peñalver. Francisco de Saavedra, June 1, 1783, Biblioteca de Francisco de Saavedra, Archivo Histórico Facultad Teología, Fondo Saavedra, Universidad de Granada (hereafter BS AHFT).
27. Saavedra, "Diario inédito," quoted in Reparaz, *Yo solo,* 248: "*Para que no se malograse el golpe más decisive de toda la Guerra.*"
28. De Grasse to Washington, n.d., Rochambeau Papers, General Collection, Beinecke Library, Yale.
29. Quoted in Lancaster, *American Revolution,* 316.
30. Quoted in Stephen Bonsal, *When the French Were Here* (Garden City, NY: Doubleday, 1945), 119–20.
31. Franklin to Jay, Passy, March 16, 1782, PBF.
32. Franklin to Jay, Passy, April 22, 1782, ibid. Laurens was captured at sea while on his way to France. Franklin arranged his release through a prisoner exchange for General Burgoyne. Interestingly, Richard Oswald, as an act of good faith, paid a good part of Laurens's bail. At the same time, Oswald represented Great Britain in its negotiations with Franklin. See Van Doren, *Franklin,* 669.
33. Franklin to Jay, Passy, April 23, 1782, *Franklin Papers* online.
34. Bemis, *Diplomacy of the American Revolution,* 207–8, and 680–81.
35. Van Doren, *Franklin,* 673.
36. Oltra and Pérez Samper, *Aranda,* 203; and Sagredo, "Personal Connections," 51.
37. Quoted in Morris, *The Peacemakers,* 305. There is some confusion between sources as to whether the first meeting took place the day after Jay's arrival or two days after.
38. Aranda to Franklin, Paris, September 20, 1784, PBF: "*Ministre Plenipotentiare des Etats de l'Ameriqe Septentrionale.*"
39. Oltra and Pérez Samper, *Aranda,* 208–9.
40. Van Doren, *Franklin,* 677.
41. Jay to Franklin, San Ildefonso, August 20, 1781, PBF.
42. Dull, *The French Navy,* 249.
43. Aranda's diary can be found in AHN, Estado, Francia, legajo 3885. Oltra and Pérez Samper, *Aranda,* 204–8, base their account on Aranda's diary. Jay's notes are found in Jay, *The Diary of John Jay during the Peace Negotiations of 1782,* ed. Frank Monaghan (New Haven, CT: Yale University Press, 1934). Morris, *The Peacemakers,* bases his account on Jay's diary. These are two examples.
44. Oltra and Pérez Samper, *Aranda,* 222, 225.

45. Morris, *The Peacemakers*, 404.
46. Ibid., 306.
47. Ibid., 307.
48. Dull, *A Diplomatic History*, 149.
49. Morris, *The Peacemakers*, 344.
50. Quoted in Chávez, *Franklin and Spain*, 51; original at *Franklin Papers* online.
51. Isaacson, *Franklin: An American Life*, 415.
52. Ibid., 415–16.
53. Quoted in Van Doren, *Franklin*, 697. Also published in Franklin, *Writings*, 8:644–45.
54. For more on the plan to attack Jamaica, see Chávez, *Spain and Independence*, 183, 204–7. For Saavedra's mission to France, see Saavedra, *Journal*, 324, 331–38, and *Los decenios*, 198–206.
55. Bailey, *Diplomatic History of the American People*; and Morris, *The Peacemakers*.
56. Dull, *The French Navy*, 249.
57. Ibid., 283–85, 287–88, 300–301.
58. Saavedra, *Journal*, 332–38, 375–78. Morales Padrón notes in a footnote that over twelve thousand French troops, including the Marquis de Lafayette, had gathered at Cádiz (375). While in Paris those two weeks, Saavedra visited museums, surveyed historic structures, and listed in his journal six operas that he enjoyed. The well-read and educated Saavedra had translated English into Spanish and could speak French and read Latin. It is almost inconceivable that he and Franklin did not meet rather than miss each other like two ships at sea passing in opposite directions. Saavedra certainly knew of Franklin, for he collected the American's published works. See BS AHFT.
59. Dull, *French Navy*, 319.
60. Dull, *A Diplomatic History*, 156, 317–18; and Isaacson, *Franklin: An American Life*, 404.
61. Aranda quoted in Oltra and Pérez Samper, *Aranda*, 220–22.
62. Ibid., 221.
63. Quoted in Dull, *The French Navy*, 332.
64. Ibid., 331–32.
65. Quoted in Morris, *The Peacemakers*, 404–5.
66. Van Doren, *Franklin*, 698.
67. Quoted in Sagredo, "Personal Connections," 51.
68. Beerman, *España y la independencia de Estados Unidos*, 64–67. Also see Rafael Sánchez Mantero, *La mission de John Jay en España (1779–1782)*, an extract from *Anuario de Estudios Americanos*, vol. 23, 1411.
69. See McCullough, *Adams*, 239–42; and Isaacson, *Franklin: An American Life*, 392–98.
70. The episode of the American, whose name comes to us as "Mister Montgomery," is in Aranda to Floridablanca, Paris, July 19, 1779, AGS, Estado, legajo

4620-126; attachment, notes of Aranda, July 19, 1779, includes a copy of Montgomery to Franklin, Alicante, June 26, 1779, no. 127.
71. Franklin to don Gabriel de Bourbon y Sajonia, Philadelphia, December 12, 1775, AGP, legajo 501.

Epilogue

1. For Adams, see Morris, *The Peacemakers*, 409; for Madison, see Dull, *A Diplomatic History*, 112–13.
2. Floridablanca's attached answer, Aranda to Floridablanca, Paris, July 23, 1783, AGS, Estado, legajo 4630-187 (letter 2487). Carmichael remained the United States' commercial agent in Spain until 1792, when George Washington finally named him the full minister plenipotentiary. He left his post in 1794 because of ill health and returned to America with a Spanish wife and one child.
3. Instructions included in American Deputies to Aranda, October 28, 1784, in Yela Utrilla, *España ante la independencia*, 919–20; and Francisco Rendón to José de Gálvez, June 20, 1784, AGI, Indiferente General, legajo 1606, no. 102, folio 132/4.
4. Bailey, *Diplomatic History of the American People*, 52.
5. The American Diplomats to Aranda, September 22, 1784, in Yela Utrilla, *España ante la independencia*, 917–19; and *Franklin Papers* online.
6. Despacho de Aranda a los Diputados Americanos, September 27, 1784, in Yela Utrilla, *España ante la independencia*, 918–19; and Aranda to the American Commissioners, September 27, 1784, *Franklin Papers* online.
7. American Deputies to Aranda, October 28, 1784, in Yela Utrilla, *España ante la independencia*, 919–20; and American Commissioners to Aranda, October 28, 1784, *Franklin Papers* online.
8. Carmichael to Franklin, Madrid, September 25, 1784, quoted in Calderón, "Spanish Financial Aid," 71. In 1788, or four years later, Gardoqui was nominated and admitted into the American Philosophical Society.
9. Floridablanca to Aranda, October 1784, in Calderón, "Spanish Financial Aid," 920–21.
10. Bailey, *Diplomatic History of the American People*, 60–62.
11. Aranda to Franklin, Paris, March 6, 1783 (listed as unpublished), *Franklin Papers* online. Aranda wrote, "He would like to participate with the greatest satisfaction."
12. Aranda to Floridablanca, Paris, July 23, 1783, legajo 4630-187 (letter number 2487) with Floridablanca's answer attached; and Aranda to Floridablanca, legajo 4639-234 (letter number 2523), both in AGS, Estado.
13. Campomanes advocated the idea that the state had supremacy over the church, which was a position sometimes referred to as Erastianism, after the Swiss theologian and physician Thomas Erastus.

14. Sagredo, "Personal Connections," 58.
15. Franklin to Pedro de Campomanes, Passy, June 5, 1784, *Franklin Papers* online.
16. Mercedes Agueda Villar, *Legacy: Spain and the United States*, 182.
17. *Franklin Papers* online contains a short Gardoqui biographical sketch.
18. Minutes of the Board of Directors of the Real Academia de la Historia, Madrid, July 9, 1784, Records of the Real Academia de la Historia. The minutes are kept in a series of books housed in the office of the Academy's secretario perpetuo.
19. Campomanes to Franklin, Madrid, July 26, 1784, PBF. The Campomanes and Franklin correspondence is also in *Papers of Franklin* (Yale), 34:353, 406, 531, 565; 35:399, 641; 36:465, 604, 643.
20. Brands, *First American*, 645–46, 649–50.
21. Franklin to Campomanes, Philadelphia, December 4, 1786, Archivo Privado de la Familia Gasset, Papers of the Count of Campomanes, Library of the Fundación Universitaria, Madrid. The certificate is framed and hangs on a wall in a private Madrid residence of one of Campomanes's descendants. It and Franklin's accompanying letter is reproduced in Agueda Villar, *Legacy: Spain and the United States*, 182.
22. Campomanes to Franklin, Madrid, May 24, 1787 (draft), Papers of the Count of Campomanes, Library of the Fundación Universitaria, Madrid. This is a very rough draft of this letter. The final version is in *Franklin Papers* online.
23. Diego de Gardoqui to Duke of La Aleudia, San Lorenzo del Escorial, October 16, 1794, AHN, Estado, legajo 3898; and Fernández y Fernández, *Spain's Contribution*, 16.
24. Oltra and Pérez Samper, *Aranda*, 237.
25. Isaacson, *Franklin: An American Life*, 416–17.
26. Pantaleón Aznar, *Vida del Dr. Franklin sacada de documentos auténticos* (Madrid, 1798): "Ofrezco la vida de Benjamin Franklin, quien no se debe olvidar entre los genios de Europa que se han distinguido en este siglo."
27. "Lista" (List of books in Saavedra's Library at the time of his death), BS AHFT.
28. For an excellent overview of the Black Legend and its effect on the United States, see Philip Wayne Powell, *The Tree of Hate: Propaganda and Prejudices Affecting United States Relations with the Hispanic World* (Albuquerque: University of New Mexico Press, 1971).
29. Manuel Lucena Salmoral, "La junta central suprema de España e el comercio americano," *Estudios de Historia y Económica de América*, no. 1 (1985): 65, 67. Lucena Salmoral lists some of the ships that arrived in the Spanish port of Cádiz: *Vigilante, Silens*, and *Océano*, delivering sugar, coffee, and tobacco.
30. Beerman, *España y la independencia de Estados Unidos*.
31. Van Doren, *Franklin*, 685 and 621, respectively.

Bibliography

Agueda Villar, Mercedes, et al. *Legacy: Spain and the United States in the Age of Independence, 1763–1848.* Washington, DC: Smithsonian Institution, 2007.
Alvord, Clarence W. "The Conquest of St. Joseph, Michigan, by the Spaniards in 1781." *Michigan History Magazine* (1930): 398–414. Originally published in *Missouri Historical Review* 2 (1908): 195–210.
Anes Álvarez, Gonzalo, and Eduardo Garrigues, eds. *La ilustración española en la independencia de los Estados Unidos: Benjamin Franklin.* Madrid: Marcial Pones, 2004.
Aznar, Pantaleón. *Vida del Dr. Franklin sacada de documentos auténticos.* Madrid: 1798.
Bailey, Thomas A. *A Diplomatic History of the American People.* Englewood Cliffs, NJ: Prentice-Hall, 1970.
Ballesteros y Beretta, Antonio. *Historia de España y su influencia en la Historia Universal.* Vol. 5. Barcelona: Salvat Editores, S.A., 1929.
Beerman, Eric. *España y la independencia de Estados Unidos.* Madrid: Editorial MAFRE, S.A., 1992.
Bemis, Samuel Flagg. *The Diplomacy of the American Revolution: The Foundations of American Diplomacy.* Bloomington: Indiana University Press, 1957.
Bonsal, Stephen. *When the French Were Here.* Garden City, NY: Doubleday, 1945.
Bowen-Hessel, E. Gordon, Dennis M. Comal, and Mark L. Hayes. *Sea Raiders of the American Revolution: The Continental Navy in European Waters.* Washington, DC: Naval Historical Center, 2003.
Brands, H. W. *The First American: The Life and Times of Benjamin Franklin.* New York: Doubleday, 2000.
Calderón Cuadrado, Reyes. *Empresarios españoles en el proceso de independencia norteamericana: La Casa Gardoqui e hijos de Bilbao.* Madrid: Unión Editorial, 2004.
———. "Spanish Financial Aid for the Process of Independence of the United States of America: Facts and Figures." In *Legacy: Spain and the United States in the Age of Independence, 1763–1848,* by Mercedes Agueda Villar et al. Washington, DC: Smithsonian Institution, 2007.
Chávez, Thomas E. *Doctor Franklin and Spain: The Unknown History.* Santa Fe: Press of the Palace of the Governors, 2016.
———. *La diplomacia de la independencia: Documentos de Benjamin Franklin en España.* Henares de Alcalá, Spain: Instituto Franklin–Universidad de Alcalá, 2019.

———, ed. *The Diplomacy of Independence: Benjamin Franklin Documents in the Archives of Spain*. Philadelphia: American Philosophical Society, 2024.

———. *Spain and the Independence of the United States: An Intrinsic Gift*. Albuquerque: University of New Mexico Press, 2002.

Chidsey, Donald Barr. *The American Privateers*. New York: Dodd, Mead, 1962.

Coleman, Eleanor S. *Gustavus Conyngham, USN: Pirate or Privateer, 1747–1819*. Washington, DC: University Press of America, 1982.

Cólogan Soriano, Carlos. *Tenerife Wine: Historias del comercio de vinos, siglo XVIII (1760–1797)*. Islas Canarias: Self-published, 2017.

———. *Un corsario al servicio de Benjamin Franklin*. Islas Canarias: Gaviño de Franchy Editores, 2013.

Conyngham, Gustavus. "Narrative of Captain Gustavus Conyngham, U.S.N., While in Command of the *Surprise* and *Revenge*, 1779." *Pennsylvania Magazine of History and Biography* 22, no. 4 (1898): 479–88.

Cuerro Acosta, José Manuel, ed. *Recovered Memories: Spain, New Orleans and the Support for the American Revolution*. New Orleans: Louisiana State Museum, 2018.

Cummins, Light Townsend. *Spanish Observers and the American Revolution, 1775–1783*. Baton Rouge: Louisiana State University Press, 1991.

Dull, Jonathon R. *A Diplomatic History of the American Revolution*. New Haven, CT: Yale University Press, 1985.

———. *The French Navy and American Independence: A Study of Arms and Diplomacy, 1774–1787*. Princeton, NJ: Princeton University Press, 1975.

Enríquez Macias, Genoveva. "Guillermo Terry, armador en Cádiz y su navío 'Soberbio': Guerra y comercio en la primera mitad del siglo XVIII." PhD diss., University of Seville, Spain, 2023.

Farías, Luis M. *La América de Aranda*. Mexico City, D.F.: Fondo de Cultura Económica, 2003.

Ferling, John. *Independence: The Struggle to Set America Free*. New York: Bloomsbury Press, 2011.

Fernández y Fernández, Enrique. *Spain's Contribution to the Independence of the United States*. Washington, DC: Embassy of Spain, 1985. (Originally published in *Revista/Review Interamericana* 10, no. 3 [1980]).

Ferreiro, Larrie D. *Brothers at Arms: American Independence and the Men of France and Spain Who Saved It*. New York: Knopf, 2016.

———. "El legado de Gálvez en los Estados Unidos." *Desperta Ferro: Historia Moderna* 59 (2022): 56–71.

Floyd, Troy S. "Bourbon Palliatives and the Central American Mining Industry, 1765–1800." *The Americas* 18, no. 2 (October 1961).

Franklin, Benjamin. *The Papers of Benjamin Franklin*. Digital edition by the Packard Humanities Institute. https://franklinpapers.org.

———. *The Papers of Benjamin Franklin*. 44 vols. Edited by Leonard W. Larabee et al. New Haven, CT: Yale University Press, 1959–.

Frayler, John. "Privateers in the American Revolution." National Park Service, Salem Maritime National Park. https://www.nps.gov/articles/privateers-in-the-american-revolution.htm/.

Gutiérrez-Steinkamp, Martha. "Spain and the Independence of the Thirteen American Colonies." In *Recovered Memories: Spain, New Orleans and the Support for the American Revolution,* edited by José Manuel Cuerro Acosta. New Orleans: Louisiana State History Museum/Edición Iberdrola, 2018.

Hagan, Kenneth J. "The Birth of American Naval Strategy." In *Strategy in the American War of Independence: A Global Approach,* by Donald J. Stoker, Kenneth J. Hagan, and Michael T. McMaster. London: Routledge, 2010.

Isaacson, Walter. *Benjamin Franklin: An American Life.* New York: Simon and Schuster, 2003.

Jay, John. *The Diary of John Jay during the Peace Negotiations of 1782.* Edited by Frank Monaghan. New Haven, CT: Yale University Press, 1934.

Jones, Charles Henry. *Captain Gustavus Conyngham: A Sketch of the Services He Rendered to the Cause of American Independence.* Philadelphia: Pennsylvania Society of Sons of the Revolution, 1903. Reprint, Forgotten Books, 2018.

Kelsey, Harry. *Sir Francis Drake: The Queen's Pirate.* New Haven, CT: Yale University Press, 1998.

Lancaster, Bruce. *The American Revolution.* New York: Houghton Mifflin, 1985.

Leech, Thomas. "Colophon." In *Doctor Franklin and Spain: The Unknown History,* by Thomas E. Chávez. Santa Fe: Press of the Palace of the Governors, 2016.

Lizalde, José Ignacio Lorenzo. "Hallazgo de la tumba del conde de Aranda: Su identificación y reconstrucción fislognómica." In *El conde de Aranda y su tiempo,* vol. 2, edited by Eliseo Serrano Martín. Zaragoza, Spain: Instituto Fernando de Católica, 2000.

López-Chávez, Celia. "Benjamin Franklin, España y la diplomacia de una armónica." *Espacio, Tiempo y Forma: Revista de la Facultad de Geografía e Historia* 4, no. 13 (2000): 319–27.

Lucena Salmoral, Manuel. "La junta central suprema de España e Indias y el comercio americano." *Estudios de Historia y Económica de América* 1 (1985): 55–70.

Lydon, James G. Review of *Captain Gustavus Conyngham, USN: Pirate or Privateer, 1747–1819,* by Eleanor S. Coleman. *Journal of American History* 70, no. 3 (December 1983): 655–56.

Maclay, Edgar Stanton. *A History of American Privateers.* New York: D. Appleton, 1889.

McCullough, David. *John Adams.* New York: Simon and Schuster, 2001.

Morris, Richard B. *The Peacemakers: The Great Powers and American Independence.* New York: Harper Torchbooks, 1965.

Norton, Louis Arthur. "Captain Gustavus Conyngham: America's Successful Naval Captain or Accidental Pirate?" *Journal of the American Revolution* (April 15, 2015). allthingsliberty.com.

Nesser, Robert W., ed. *Letters and Papers Relating to the Cruises of Gustavus Conyngham, A Captain of the Continental Navy, 1777–1779*. New York: Naval History Society/De Vine Press, 1915.

Ochoa Brun, Miguel-Ángel. "La misión diplomática de Benjamin Franklin a Europa y las relaciones internacionales." In *La ilustración española en la independencia de los Estados Unidos: Benjamin Franklin,* edited by Gonzalo Anes Álvarez and Eduardo Garrigues, 67–123. Madrid: Marcial Pons, 2007.

Oltra, Joaquín, and María Ángeles Pérez Samper. *El conde de Aranda y los Estados Unidos.* Barcelona: Promociones y Publicaciones Universitarias, 1987.

O'Shaughnessy, Andrew, John A. Ragosta, and Marie-Jeanne Rossignor, eds. *European Friends of the American Revolution.* Charlottesville: University of Virginia Press, 2023.

Paquette, Gabriel, and Gonzalo M. Quintero, eds. *Spain and the American Revolution: New Approaches and Perspectives.* New York: Routledge, 2019.

Payne, Stanley G. *A History of Spain and Portugal.* Madison: University of Wisconsin Press, 1973.

Pérez Samper, María Ángeles. *El conde de Aranda.* Barcelona: Promociones Universitarias, S.A., 1951.

Perkins, James Breck. *France in the American Revolution.* Boston: Houghton Mifflin, 1911.

Powell, Philip Wayne. *The Tree of Hate: Propaganda and Prejudices Affecting United States Relations with the Hispanic World.* Albuquerque: University of New Mexico Press, 1971.

Reparaz, Carmen de. *Yo solo: Bernardo de Gálvez y la Toma de Panzacola en 1781.* Barcelona: Ediciones del Serbal, S.A.

Ruigómez de Hernández, María Pilar. *El gobierno español del despotismo ilustrado ante la independencia de los Estados Unidos de América: Una nueva estructura de la política internacional (1773–1783).* Madrid: Ministro de Asuntos Exteriores, 1978.

Saavedra [de Sangronis], Francisco de. *Los decenios (Autobiografía de un sevillano de la ilustración).* Sevilla: Ayuntamiento de Sevilla, 1995.

Saavedra de Sangronis, Francisco. *The Journal of Francisco Saavedra de Sangronis, 1780–1783.* Translated and edited by Francisco Morales Padrón. Gainesville: University of Florida Press, 1989.

Sagredo, Antonia. "Personal Connections between Spaniards and Americans in the Revolutionary Era: Pioneers in Spanish-American Diplomacy." In *Legacy: Spain and the United States in the Age of Independence, 1763–1848,* edited by Mercedes Agueda Villar et al., 45–63. Washington, DC: Smithsonian Institution, 2007.

Sánchez Mantero, Rafael. *La mission de John Jay en España (1779–1782).* Sevilla: G.E.H.A.-Alfonso XII. 1966.

Shomette, Donald Grady. *Privateers of the Revolution: War on the New Jersey Coast, 1775–1783.* Atglen, PA: Schiffer Military, 2016.

Sjostrom, Kristine L. *Fernando de Leyba (1734–1780): A Life of Service and Sacrifice in Spanish Louisiana.* Seville: Privately published, 2022.
Smith, Paul H., ed. *Letters of Delegates to Congress, 1774–1789.* 25 vols. Washington, DC: Library of Congress, 1976–91.
Sparks, Jared, ed. *The Diplomatic Correspondence of the American Revolution.* Vol. 2. Boston: Hale and Gray, 1829.
Stoker, Donald, Kenneth J. Hagan, and Michael T. McMaster. *Strategy in the American War of Independence: A Global Approach.* London: Routledge, 2010.
Tusell, Javier, ed. *Historia de España.* Madrid: Taurus, 1998.
Van Doren, Carl. *Benjamin Franklin.* 1938. Reprint, New York: Garden City Publishing, 1941.
Washington, George. *The Writings of George Washington from the Original Manuscript Sources, 1745–1799.* Edited by John C. Fitzpatrick. Washington, DC: Government Printing Office, 1904.
Werther, Richard J., "Captain Lambert Wickes and 'Gunboat Diplomacy,' American Revolution Style." *Journal of the American Revolution* (January 3, 2019). allthingsliberty.com.
Wharton, Francis, ed. *The Revolutionary Diplomatic Correspondence of the United States.* Washington, DC: Government Printing Office, 1889.
Wood, Gordon S. *The Americanization of Benjamin Franklin.* New York: Penguin Books, 2004.
Yela Utrilla, Juan Francisco. *España ante la independencia de los Estados Unidos.* Lérida: Gráficos Academia Mariana, 1925. Reprint, Madrid: Ediciones Istmo, S.A., 1988.

INDEX

Page numbers in italics indicate illustrations.

Abarca de Bolea, Pedro Pablo. *See* Aranda, Count of
Adams, Abigail, 34
Adams, John, 130; as American commissioner, 82, 85, 116; Arthur Lee's letters to, 56; Declaration of Independence and, 17; meets with Admiral Howe, 18; as minister plenipotentiary, 125–26; negotiates peace treaty, 93, 116, 120, 123; on Spanish assistance, 112, 116
Adams, Samuel, 56, 85, 88, 112
Almodóvar, Marqués de, 91, 128
American Commission: and American corsairs, 73; contact with Spain, 30; internal struggles of, 61, 87–88; led by Franklin, 55–59, 74, 88, 117; mission to Paris, 5, 26–29, *32*, 33–42, 47–59; privateering and, 100–101, 104–5; seeks aid for rebellion, 65–72, 89; seeks alliances abroad, 26, 99; success of, 56–61, 82, 131; treaties and, 18, 26, 52, 71, 81–83, 85, 116; and victory at Saratoga, 74; and victory at Yorktown, 112. *See also* Deane, Silas; Franklin, Benjamin; Lee, Arthur
American Constitution, 18, 125–27
American independence: Count of Aranda on, 33, 35, 38–41, 130; Count of Floridablanca on, 59, 85; Count of Vergennes on, 130; France's role in, 39–40, 47; Franklin's role in, 12–14; Franklin's views on, 7, 14, 35–36, 81, 87; and problem of governance, 125–26; Spain's key role in, 1–5, 30, 87, 90–94, 112–13, 126, 129–31; Spain's views of, 12–13, 39–40, 75–79; thirteen colonies and, 125–27
Americanization of Benjamin Franklin, The (Wood), 113
American Philosophical Society, 3, 128–29
American Revolution: colonists' victories in, 73–76, 80, 112; Count of Vergennes on, 113; financial aid for, 15–16; France's role in, 115, 117, 124, 131; Franklin's role in, 129; Franklin's views on, 14, 35–36, 68; funded by privateering, 95, 97–99; Intolerable Acts and, 131; news delays during, 72; and peace negotiations, 76–77, 116–24; Spain's financial aid for, 89–90, 112–16; Spain's key role in, 1–5, 112–18, 129–31; Spain's views of, 41–42, 46–47, 49; and Spanish ports, 112. *See also* Saratoga; Yorktown
Amphitrate (ship), 36–39, 51
anti-Catholic sentiment, 130–31
Aranda, Count of, 43, 74, 125; on aid for colonists, 39–41, 49, 89, 112; as ambassador to France, 23, *24*; and American Commission, 29–30, 33–40, 49, 71–72, 89; complains about Americans, 112, 121; descriptions of, 118; Franklin gives constitution to, 127; Franklin sends requests for aid, 38–39, 66, 68–69; Franklin's letters to, 53–55, 63–65, 113; on Franklin's mission, 25–30, 34–35; on Arthur Lee, 57, 66; meets with commissioners, 35, 52, 57–58; meets with Franklin, 29–30, 34–40, 105, 117; meets with Vergennes, 25–28, 34, 38–39; peace negotiations of, 76–77, 117–23; on Portugal, 45; and privateering, 101–9, 111; reports to Floridablanca, 57–58, 62–66, 72; reports to Grimaldi, 45–50, 63; reports to King Carlos III, 39–41, 45; supportive of Franklin, 87–88, 122; supports war against Britain, 39–42, 75; on treaties of alliance, 82–83; and treaties with America, 40–41, 47–48, 71, 126; works with John Jay, 117–19, 121–22. *See also* American independence: Count of Aranda on

165

arms/ammunition, 16, 18–19, 24, 34, 36, 52, 63, 67, 69, 72, 98
Arnold, Benedict, 17, 74
Autobiography (Franklin), 130
Aznar, Pantaleón, 130

Bache, Benny, 18, 22
Bahamas, 22, 53, 118, 122–23
Bailey, Thomas A., 121, 125
Bancroft, Edward, 37, 42, 61–62, 77, 83
Barbeu-Dubourg, Jacques, 23–25, 27
Battle of Toulon, 78
Beaumarchais, Pierre-Augustin Caron de, 19, 24, 27, 36, 56–57
Beerman, Eric, 123, 131
Bilbao (port), 11, 34, 51–52, 59, 61–63, 70, 89
Black Prince (ship), 101
Bodoni, Giambattista, 14
Borbón, Gabriel de, 10–11, 13–16
Boston, Massachusetts, 11, 15, 63, 103–4, 107
Boston Tea Party, 8–9, 12
Bourbon, House of, 25, 48–49, 75, 77
Bourbon Compact, 15–16, 25, 34, 66. *See also* Third Bourbon Family Compact
Brands, H. W., 95
Brazil, 16, 40, 45, 108
British: blockade, 16, 95–96; colonies, 12, 16, 39, 42, 45, 130–31; custom duties, 116; government, 7–13, 44, 64, 79, 86–87, 89, 91–92, 101; merchants, 37–38, 98–99; press, 11–12; prisons, 97, 109; warships, 63, 72
British Army, 15, 18, 64, 74, 111
British Navy, 15, 18, 37, 64, 83
British Parliament, 7, 11–12, 16, 60, 75, 79, 84, 86, 120
Brothers at Arms (Ferreiro), 2
Buick and Company, 37–38
Burgoyne, John, 60, 65, 68, 72–76, 86
Burke, Edmund, 12

Cabarrús, Francisco, 114–15
Cádiz, 20, 37, 69, 99, 103, 106, 121
Campomanes, Count of, 127–30
Canada, 17–18, 40, 53, 60, 72, 116, 130
Caribbean, 21, 64, 98, 102, 113, 118, 120
Carlos III, King, 50; and aid for colonists, 49, 60, 89; ambassadors of, 23, 43; and American independence, 70, 75–76, 87, 90–91; Aranda's reports to, 39–40, 72; ascends to throne, 10; and Bourbon alliances, 15–16, 20; and Franklin's mission, 26, 35, 37, 39–40; ministers of, 42, 45–48, 126; portrait of, *21;* praises Aranda, 123; and privateering cases, 105; reforms of, 43; Seven Years' War and, 20, 46; sons of, 4, 10–11; stance towards Great Britain, 48; treaties of alliance and, 82, 92–93
Carmichael, William, 114, 116, 122, 125–28
Carvalho Mello, Sabastião José de, 16, 44
Castejón, Pedro González de, 46, 48
Catherine II, Empress, 96
Catholic Church, 130–31
Central America, 4, 16, 21–22, 89, 113–14, 118
Cevallos, Pedro de, 44–45, 47
Cólogan, Juan, 109–12
Cólogan, Tomás, 99, 106–12
Colonial Army, 17
Colonial Navy, 24, 37
Committee of Secret Correspondence, 16, 18, 26, 52, 55, 99
Common Sense (Paine), 16–17
conjuración de Calatina y la Guerra de Jugurta, La (Crispo), 13–14
Contesse de Monton, La (ship), 107
Continental Army, 14, 63, 72, 97–98, 115, 124
Continental Congress: American Commission and, 66–68, 88; on America's victory, 124; appoints Committee of Secret Correspondence, 16, 18, 26; and arms for rebellion, 72; Bourbon courts and, 68, 77; cedes West Florida to Spain, 89; complaints of privateering and, 102–8; and European allies, 52–56, 62, 67–68; foreign representatives and, 46, 85–86; Franklin represents/works with, 13–18, 25, 29–30, 33–35, 126; needs financial aid, 15; official documents/papers of, 3, 14, 34, 36; prepares Declaration of Independence, 17–18; president of, 90, 93, 107; and problem of governance, 18, 125–26; Spain's ultimatum read to, 90; and treaties with Europe, 68, 81, 126–27; votes for independence, 17–18. *See also* Second Continental Congress
Continental Convention, 11–12

Continental Navy, 89, 98–100
Conyngham, Gustavus, 98, *100*, 101–2, 105–9, 111, 124
corsairs, 118; British, 109; cease wartime activities, 124; explanation of, 95–96; Franklin and, 97, 100, 108, 110; in French ports, 64–66, 102; Letter of Marque for, 95–97, 109, 111; prey on British ships, 96, 100–102; Spain's complaints about, 106, 108; in Spanish ports, 29–30; violate French neutrality, 63. *See also* privateering
Crispo, Cayo Salusio, 13
Cuadrado, Reyes Calderón, 36, 112
Cuba, 4, 46, 85, 98, 112, 115. *See also* Havana
Cummins, Light Townsend, 15
currency, 14, 87, 90, 96, 109–10

Davis, Marianne, 8
Deane, Silas, 37; contracts malaria, 34–35; Lee's complaints against, 52, 58, 61, 73; mission to France, 18, 26–30, 33–34, 42, 52, 57, 62, 65; portrait of, *19;* and privateering, 98, 105; recalled by Congress, 19, 56–57, 73, 77, 82, 88; at Versailles, *32*
Declaration of Independence, 17–18, 24–25, 33, 56
de Grasse, Admiral, 115–16, 120–21
d'Estaing, Count, 83, 85, 121
Diplomacy of Independence: Benjamin Franklin Documents in the Archives of Spain, 3
Doctor Franklin and Spain: The Unknown History, 2
d'Ossun, Marquis, 70
Drake, Francis, 96
Drayton, William Henry, 90–91
Dull, Jonathon, 2, 75, 113, 121
Dunkirk, 34, 65, 101, 117

East Florida, 16, 53, 122
England. *See* British; Great Britain; London
Escarano, Francisco, 8–13, 72–74, 77, 83–84, 86
Esquilache, Marquis, 43, 46
European Friends of the American Revolution, 2

Ferreiro, Larrie D., 2, 113
fishing rights, 41, 116–17

Florida, 16, 21–22, 41, 53, 98. *See also* East Florida; Floridas; West Florida
Floridablanca, Count of, 121; on aid for Americans, 60–61; on alliance with France, 91–92; and American Commission, 58–59, 61–62, 71–72; Aranda's reports to, 57, 62–66, 72, 121; on Arthur Lee, 66, 92–93; as chief minister to King Carlos, 42, 45–46, 53; description of, 58–59; drafts plan for war, 77–80; Franklin's letters to, 107–8, 113; letters to Aranda, 61, 65, 125; meets with John Jay, 114; negotiates peace with Great Britain, 85–87, 89–92; portrait of, *58;* and privateering, 103–8; "wait and see" policy of, 65–66; and war in America, 72, 75–76
Floridas, 53, 119–20, 122–23, 130. *See also* East Florida; West Florida
Fort Ticonderoga, 15, 60, 73–74
Fortunée, La (ship), 104–5
Fox, Charles, 60, 74
France, 55; alliance with America, 81–82, 99; alliance with Spain, 84, 88–89, 91–93; avoids rebellion, 60–63, 65; colonists seek aid from, 15–16, 18; declares war on Great Britain, 102–3; forces in Caribbean, 63–64; Franklin requests aid from, 66–69; Franklin's mission to, 15–20, 22–30, *32,* 33–42, 44, 49; Franklin's voyage to, 4–5, 20, 95, 100; and plans for war, 5, 34–35, 41, 74–84; recognizes the colonies, 81, 88; responds to new request for aid, 69–71; sends aid to colonists, 18–19, 23–24, 26–28, 34, 36–37, 47–49, 57–58, 61–63, 113; signs treaties of alliance, 87, 105; war against Great Britain, 41, 83–84, 89, 115. *See also* Paris
Franklin, Benjamin, 3, 50; admitted to Royal Academy of History, 128–29; Aranda's support of, 122; Articles of Confederation of, 14; on Boston Tea Party, 8–9; chairs constitutional convention, 18; chairs Pennsylvania's "Defense Committee," 14; on Committee of Secret Correspondence, 99; and congressional instructions, 53, 55, 126; criticism of, 7, 58, 88; crowning diplomatic achievement of, 82; on Declaration of Independence committee, 17; descriptions of, 9, 28, 73; diplomatic role with Spain, 1–4, 15,

Franklin, Benjamin (*continued*)
117, 124; as director of naval affairs, 100; Escarano's views of, 8, 10; exchanges publications with Campomanes, 127–29; health of, 17–18, 33, 119, 123; Hutchinson's letters and, 7–9; on John Jay, 93–94, 114–17, 119–20; John Paul Jones and, 96–97; last months in Europe, 125–30; Lee's complaints against, 52, 58, 61, 88, 105; letters to allies, 53–56, 59; letters to Aranda, 63–65; letters to don Gabriel, 14–16; meets with Aranda, 47, 49, 52–53, 62–63; meets with British emissaries, 75; meets with James Hutton, 79; meets with Vergennes, 81–82; as minister plenipotentiary, 88, 117, 125; mission to Canada, 17–18; paper currency of, 14; political works by, 128; popularity of, 1, 33, 55–56, 88, 129–30; as postmaster, 9, 13; praise of, 128–30; printing interests of, 14; seeks aid from allies, 26–30, 33–38; seeks alliances abroad, 14–16, 30, 99; sends paper to Vergennes, 62; Spain responds to memorial, 69–71; and Spain's peace negotiations, 112; on Spain's support, 29, 87, 113, 129; on Spaniards, 15; on spies, 42, 61–62, 77; and treaties of alliance, 81–82, 85; at Versailles, 22, *32*, 33, 82; writes memorial for more aid, 66–69; writes news release on victory, 75. *See also specific places; specific topics*
Franklin, William Temple, 16–17, 129
Franklin, William Temple Jr., 18, 22
French Army, 60, 115, 124
French Navy, 38–39, 49, 60, 69, 82–83, 113
French Navy and American Independence, The (Dull), 75
French ports, 34, 57, 65, 67, 69, 98–102, 105. *See also* Cádiz
frigates. *See* warships
Fuentes y Villapando, Ambrosio de. *See* Ricla, Count of

Gage, Thomas, 15
Gálvez, Bernardo de, 52, 72, 89, 115
Gálvez, José de, 45–47, 89–90, 103
Gardoqui, Diego de, 112–14; admitted to American Philosophical Society, 128; oversees aid to colonists, 50–52, 69; portrait of, *51;* as Spain's first minister to America, 126–28; on Spain's key role, 129–30; works with American Commissioners, 34, 51–52, 89, 106
Gardoqui e hijos, 50–52, 59, 89, 99
Gates, Horatio, 74
Geddes, George, 109
George III, King, 13, 16, 27, 79, 83, 90–92
Gérard, Conrad-Alexandre, 81, 85–86, 90, 103
Gibbon, Edward, 84, 130
Gibraltar, 22, 41, 79, 85, 87, 91, 113, 118, 120–23
Gibson, George, 16, 19
glass armonica, 8–11, 13, 73
Golden Rose (ship), 109–10
Grand, Rodolphe-Ferdinand, 66–69, 103–5, 107, 109–10
Great Britain: acts against colonies, 16; and American independence, 79, 84, 91, 116; Burgoyne's plan for, 60; convoys of, 83, 114; declares war on France, 83–84; defeat of, 64, 115–16; economic burdens of, 39, 41; and French merchantmen, 63; naval power of, 41, 46, 64, 82–84, 96; opposed by France/Spain, 45; possessions of, 53; refuses Spain's ultimatum, 91–92; separated from Portugal, 43–45; signs preliminary peace treaty, 120, 122–23; Spain's actions against, 19–21, 30, 38–39, 113; Spain sends ultimatum to, 90–92; suspicious of the French, 61; weak maritime fleet of, 41; West Florida ceded to, 119–20. *See also* British; London; peace negotiations: with Great Britain
Grimaldi, Marquis of, 15, 18, 23, 30, 43, *44,* 45–54, 58–59, 63
"gunboat diplomacy," 99

Hancock, John, 55–56
Hartley, Mister, 86
Havana, 19, 34, 52, 61, 89, 115
Hector, Charles Henri. *See* d'Estaing, Count
Henrica Sofia (ship), 106–8
Henry, Patrick, 72, 89, 91
Heredia, Ignacio, 104
Holker (ship), 109
Holland, 52–53, 57–58, 61–62, 80, 82, 99, 109, 116–17
Howe, Richard, 18

Howe, William, 60, 65, 68, 73–76
Hutchinson, Thomas, 7–9
Hutton, James, 79

India, 83, 98, 117
Infante. See Borbón, Gabriel de
"Information to those who would remove to America" (Franklin), 128
Intolerable Acts, 11–12, 131
Intrinsic Gift: Spain and the Independence of the United States, An, 1–2
Izard, Ralph, 88

Jamaica, 22, 98, 118, 120–21
Jay, John, 3–4, 90, 92, *93*, 94, 101, 113–23, 125, 127
Jefferson, Thomas, 17–18, 125, 131
Jesuits, 43, 59, 127
Jones, John Paul, 95–97, 101
Joseph, Maximilian, 81
Jovellanes, Gaspar Melchor de, 128

Lacy, Count of, 35, 47
Lafayette, Marquis de, 88, 121
Lángara, Juan de, 113
Laurens, Henry, 85, 107, 116
League of Armed Neutrality, 96, 102
Lee, Arthur, 105; as American commissioner, 16, 18, *20*, 26, 28–30, 33–35, 37–38; as commissioner to Spain, 66, 92–93, 106; on Franklin and revolution, 68; as Franklin's rival, 56–58, 87–88; meets with Aranda, 29–30, 35, 38, 89; meets with Grimaldi, 50–52; recalled by Congress, 88, 92–93; sows dissent, 56–58, 61, 73, 87–88; and treaties of alliance, 71, 85; at Versailles, *32*, 82; at Vienna, 65
Lee, Charles, 16, 47
Lee, Richard Henry, 17, 88
Leyenda negra (Black Legend), 130
London: Arthur Lee in, 18; Burgoyne imprisoned in, 73–74; Franklin in, 7–13, 33, 56, 97; Franklin's backers in, 18; placard on corsairs in, 64; Spain's ambassadors in, 42, 47, 63, 72, 74, 83, 86, 89–90; spy Bancroft in, 77, 83; trade goods/trade merchants in, 103, 106–7
Louisiana, 16, 19, 22, 34, 40, 47, 72. *See also* New Orleans
Louis XIV, King, 33

Louis XVI, King, 57, 77; and invasion of Jamaica, 120–21; minister of state to, 23, 28; and plans for war, 35, 65, 75; portrait of, *70;* ratifies treaties with colonies, 81–83; receives American commissioners, *32,* 82; writes to King Carlos III, 82

Madison, James, 125
Madrid: American representatives accepted in, 93–94, 121, 125; American representatives refused by, 50–51, 55–56, 66, 72–73; Arthur Lee sent to, 50–51, 56, 66; Carmichael replaces Jay in, 116, 125; Franklin's appointment to, 55–56, 72–73; French ambassadors in, 60, 70, 79, 84, 90, 114, 117; Gardoqui called to, 50–51; John Jay's failed efforts in, 4, 93–94, 114–15; mail system and, 37, 50; ministers in, 46–47; press of, 12; Saavedra sent to, 120; treaty negotiations in, 126
Malvinas Islands, 64
Manchester, Duke of, 123
Manifest Destiny, 119
Mansfield, Lord, 72–73
Massachusetts legislature, 7, 9, 56
Masserano, Prince of, 13, 18, 42, 47, 63, 74
Maurepas, Count of, 57, 82
McClenachan, Blair, 109
Memories of His Private Life Written by Him (Franklin), 130
Menorca, 22, 85, 91, 113–14, 118, 122–23
Mexico, 4, 22, 34, 61, 76, 89, 112, 115
Miralles y Trajan, Juan de, 85–86, 90, 103, 109, 125
Mississippi River, 16, 21–22, 41, 117–19, 123, 127
Moravians, 79
Morris, Gouverneur, 90
Morris, Richard B., 121
Morris, Robert, 18, 89, 97–100, 109–11, 124
Morris, Thomas, 104
Múzquiz y Goyeneche, Miguel, 46–48

Nantes, 22, 24, 65, 98, 103–4
Napoleon, 131
neutrality: of European nations, 48; of France, 57, 63, 99; and privateering, 57, 96, 99, 101–3, 105, 108; of Spain, 38, 50, 86, 89, 99, 102–3, 105. *See also* League of Armed Neutrality

New England, 22, 51, 127
Newfoundland, 41, 53, 116
New Orleans, 16, 19, 34, 46–47, 52, 72, 118
New Spain, 4, 40, 46

Ochoa Brun, Miguel Ángel, 12

Paine, Thomas, 16–17
Paris, 47; American Commission in, 18, 26–28, 33, 37, 39, 49–50, 52, 55–58, 61, 82, 89; American ministers plenipotentiary in, 125; description of, 31, 33; Franklin orders John Jay to, 114–17; Franklin represents Congress in, 4–5, 25, 116; Franklin's arrival in, 4, 22–23, 26, 39; Franklin's life in, 33, 127; Spain's ambassador in, 23, 48; treaties signed in, 82. *See also* Treaty of Paris
Patty (ship), 103
peace negotiations: and American corsairs, 124; boundaries and, 116–20; by Count of Floridablanca, 122–23; by Count of Vergennes, 116–23; fishing rights and, 116–17; and France, 117, 120, 123; by Franklin, 116–19, 123–24; with Great Britain, 75–81, 85–93, 112, 116–24; and invasion of Jamaica, 120–21; John Jay's role in, 116–24; preliminary treaty for, 120–23; by Spain, 75–77, 85–87, 112; Spain's expectations for, 117–20, 122–23; and trade agreements, 117
Penet, Pierre, 22, 97–98
Pensacola, 16, 22, 47, 53, 103, 112–13
Phélypeaux, Jean Frédéric. *See* Maurepas, Count of
Philadelphia: continental conventions in, 11–14; corsairs sell prizes in, 107, 109; Franklin returns to, 12–13, 125, 129; threatened by Howe, 65, 68, 73, 75
pirates/piracy, 4, 95–98, *100*, 102, 104–8, 111
Pollock, Oliver, 47
Pombal, Marquis of, 16, 44
Portugal, 108; and American colonies, 53–54, 111; settlements with Britain, 16, 19–20; Spain's attack against, 20, 43–45, 54–55; Spain's relationship with, 25–26; usurps Spanish territory, 40
Pringle, John, 12
prisoner exchanges, 73, 97, 101, 103, 113

privateering, 92; by Americans, 57, 66, 73, 97–102, 109; and British ships, 100–102, 107–9; commissions for, 98, 102–3; Continental Navy and, 98; explanation of, 95–96; and flying false flags, 99, 102, 104; Franklin and, 57, 66, 73, 95, 97–111; French ports and, 57, 65–66, 99–105; and French ships, 104–5; funds colonists' revolution, 97–99; by Great Britain, 96, 104, 109–10; prizes/ships sold in Boston, 103–5, 107; restitution for, 104–5, 107; and Spain, 98, 102–3, 105–7. *See also* corsairs
Privy Council (England), 7, 9

Quakers, 40
Quebec Act, 130

Real Academia de la Historia, 3–4
Rendón, Francisco, 125
Reprisal (ship), 18–19, 22, 100–101
Revenge (ship), 107
Ricla, Count of, 45–47
Rochambeau, Comte de, 115
Roderique Hortalez et Cie, 19, 26–27, 36, 69
Rodney, George, 113
Royal Academy of History (Spain), 127–29
Royal Navy, 96, 98. *See also* British Navy
Russia, 35, 45, 78, 80, 82, 96

Saavedra de Sangronis, Francisco, 115, 120–21, 130
San Julian (ship), 76
Saratoga, 65, 68, 72–75, 80, 82, 86, 88
Second Continental Congress, 12–14. *See also* Continental Congress
Seven Years' War, 15–16, 20–21, 40, 43, 46, 54
Sieulanne, Graciano, 105–8, 124
Smith, William, 89
smuggling, 20–21, 79, 98, 101
Soriano, Carlos Cólogan, 95
South America, 16, 19–20, 44–47, 54–55, 61, 76, 80, 89–90
Spain: actions against Great Britain, 19–21, 30, 43–45; alliance with America, 102–3; alliance with France, 5, 24, 45, 63, 89, 91–93, 118, 120–21; ambassador to Great Britain, 13; American ambassador to, 125;

American ports of, 15; America sends aid to, 131; avoids joining rebellion, 60–63, 65; Bourbon kings of, 15–16; currency of, 87; expenses during war, 113; fleets in South America, 44–45, 54–55, 61, 76, 80; Franklin requests more aid from, 66–69; Franklin seeks as ally, 14–16, 30, 99; grants asylum to ships, 29; John Jay minister to, 93–94; maritime fleet of, 44–45; military prowess of, 113, 118; and plans for war, 74–85, 89–90, 93; possessions in America, 4, 16, 20–22, 30, 34, 39–40, 46, 70, 118, 123; responds to new request for aid, 69–71; sends aid to colonists, 5, 16, 18–20, 23–30, 34–37, 43, 47–52, 57–63, 76, 89, 112–16, 131; sends representative to America, 126–27; sends ultimatum to Great Britain, 90–92; separates Great Britain and Portugal, 43–45; victories of, 113–14, 118–19; war against Great Britain, 22, 90–94, 103, 112; West Florida ceded to, 89. *See also* Madrid

Spain and the American Revolution: New Approaches and Perspectives, 2
Spanish archives, 1–3, 37, 54, 131
Spanish Army, 60
Spanish Navy, 38, 46, 49, 60–61, 69, 82, 84, 93, 115
Spanish ports, 34, 45, 52, 112
Spanish press, 12, 114
spies, 37, 42, 45, 61–62, 77
Staten Island, New York, 18
Stormont, Lord, 41–42, 62, 82–83
Suffolk, Lord, 12–13

Tenerife, 99, 103, 105–7, 109–10
Third Bourbon Family Compact, 16, 25, 43, 82. *See also* Bourbon Compact
Thompson, Charles, 107
trade: and British blockade, 16; and British custom duties, 116; with the colonies, 16, 50–51, 81, 117; disrupted by corsairs, 96, 98–99, 102–3, 110; of France, 45, 78, 81; Franklin on, 28–29; with Great Britain, 21, 41, 78–79, 96, 98–99, 120; merchant houses of, 99; negotiations over, 127; of Spain, 21–22, 37–38, 40, 45, 50–52, 67, 78–79, 99, 111; treaties for, 34–35, 67–68; with West Indies, 22

treaties: of alliance, 80, 85, 87, 105; of alliance and trade, 34–35, 67–68, 81–83; between America and Great Britain, 120, 123; and American independence, 125; of amity and commerce, 81, 126–27; Franklin's role in, 18, 26, 34–35, 81; to outlaw privateering, 97; for peace, 116–17, 120–23; Spain's response to, 40–41, 47–49, 52, 69, 76, 78. *See also* American Commission: treaties and; peace negotiations
Treaty of Paris, 21, 43, 111

University of New Mexico, 2
Unzaga y Amézaga, Luis de, 16, 19, 34, 47
Uruguay, 20, 43
Utrilla, Francisco Yela, 131

Van Doren, Carl, 1, 68, 113, 131
Vergennes, Count of, 41, 49; on alliance with Spain, 84, 90; and American Commission, 25–30, 33–35, 38–39, 50, 57, 62, 65, 71–72, 74–75; Aranda corresponds with, 23, 70; Aranda meets with, 25–27, 34, 38, 77; assesses military strength, 60; congressional instructions and, 53; on Franklin, 25–29, 34; Franklin corresponds with, 53–54, 62; Franklin meets with, 28, 81–82; Franklin sends aid request to, 66; as minister of state, 23; and plans for war/peace, 34–35, 79–83; portrait of, *28;* and privateering, 101–2, 104–5; recognizes the colonies, 81; and treaties of alliance, 82–83; "wait and see" policy of, 65–66
Versailles, 25–27, 31, *32*, 33, 38–39, 82, 90, 92, 123

War of Spanish Succession, 16
warships, 20, 24, 37–38, 53, 63, 69, 72, 77, 83, 95–96
Washington, George, 3, 16, 93, 125; de Grasse offers aid to, 115; Franklin and, 14, 97; on Great Britain, 92; needs support, 17; papers of, 3, 36; privateering and, 97; thanks Spain for "friendship," 72, 89; on victory, 112
Wedderburn, Alexander, 9
West Florida, 16, 22, 53, 89, 119–20, 122

West Indies, 18, 21–22, 49, 53, 114–15, 118, 120–21
Weymouth, Lord, 87
Wickes, Lambert, 22, 98–101
Williams, Jonathon, Jr., 13, 104

Willing, Morris, & Swanwick, 99
Wood, Gordon, 113

Yorktown, 64, 111–12, 114–16, 120

The Revolutionary Age

Declarations of Independence: Indigenous Resilience, Colonial Rivalries, and the Cost of Revolution
  Christopher R. Pearl

Dishonored Americans: The Political Death of Loyalists in Revolutionary America
  Timothy Compeau

The American Liberty Pole: Popular Politics and the Struggle for Democracy in the Early Republic
  Shira Lurie

European Friends of the American Revolution
  Andrew J. O'Shaughnessy, John A. Ragosta, and Marie-Jeanne Rossignol, editors

The Tory's Wife: A Woman and Her Family in Revolutionary America
  Cynthia A. Kierner

Writing Early America: From Empire to Revolution
  Trevor Burnard

Spain and the American Revolution: New Approaches and Perspectives
  Gabriel Paquette and Gonzalo M. Quintero Saravia, editors

The American Revolution and the Habsburg Monarchy
  Jonathan Singerton

Navigating Neutrality: Early American Governance in the Turbulent Atlantic
  Sandra Moats

Ireland and America: Empire, Revolution, and Sovereignty
  Patrick Griffin and Francis D. Cogliano, editors

www.ingramcontent.com/pod-product-compliance
Lightning Source LLC
Chambersburg PA
CBHW020935230426
43666CB00008B/1684